FLL

Mastering
The Language of Literature

Palgrave Master Series

Accounting
Accounting Skills
Advanced English Language
Advanced English Literature
Advanced Pure Mathematics
Arabic
Basic Management
Biology
British Politics
Business Communication
Business Environment
C Programming
C++ Programming
Chemistry
COBOL Programming
Communication
Computing
Counselling Skills
Counselling Theory
Customer Relations
Database Design
Delphi Programming
Desktop Publishing
e-Business
Economic and Social History
Economics
Electrical Engineering
Electronics
Employee Development
English Grammar
English Language
English Literature
Fashion Buying and Merchandising
   Management
Fashion Styling
Financial Management
French
Geography
German
Global Information Systems

Globalization of Business
Human Resource Management
Information Technology
International Trade
Internet
Italian
Java
Language of Literature
Management Skills
Marketing Management
Mathematics
Microsoft Office
Microsoft Windows, Novell
   NetWare and UNIX
Modern British History
Modern European History
Modern United States History
Modern World History
Networks
Novels of Jane Austen
Organisational Behaviour
Pascal and Delphi Programming
Philosophy
Physics
Practical Criticism
Psychology
Public Relations
Shakespeare
Social Welfare
Sociology
Spanish
Statistics
Strategic Management
Systems Analysis and Design
Team Leadership
Theology
Twentieth-Century Russian History
Visual Basic
World Religions

www.palgravemasterseries.com

Palgrave Master Series

Series Standing Order ISBN 0–333–69343–4
(outside North America only)

You can receive future titles in this series as they are published by placing a standing order. Please contact your bookseller or, in case of difficulty, write to us at the address below with your name and address, the title of the series and the ISBN quoted above.

Customer Services Department, Macmillan Distribution Ltd,
Houndmills, Basingstoke, Hampshire RG21 6XS, England

Mastering
The Language of Literature

Malcolm Hebron

palgrave
macmillan

First published 2004 by
PALGRAVE MACMILLAN
Houndmills, Basingstoke, Hampshire RG21 6XS and
175 Fifth Avenue, New York, N. Y. 10010
Companies and representatives throughout the world

PALGRAVE MACMILLAN is the global academic imprint of the Palgrave
Macmillan division of St. Martin's Press, LLC and of Palgrave Macmillan Ltd.
Macmillan® is a registered trademark in the United States, United Kingdom
and other countries. Palgrave is a registered trademark in the European
Union and other countries.

ISBN 1–4039–0077–9

This book is printed on paper suitable for recycling and
made from fully managed and sustained forest sources.

A catalogue record for this book is available from the British Library.

Library of Congress Cataloging-in-Publication Data
Hebron, Malcolm, 1966–
    Mastering the language of literature / Malcolm Hebron.
        p. cm. – (Palgrave master series)
    Includes bibliogaphical references (p.) and index.
    ISBN 1–4039–0077–9
    1. English language–Style. 2. English literature–History and
    criticism. 3. Style, Literary. I. Title. II. Series.

PE1421.H39 2003
820.9–dc22   2003055879

Typeset in Great Britain by
Aarontype Ltd, Easton, Bristol

10   9   8   7   6   5   4   3   2   1
13   12   11   10   09   08   07   06   05   04

Printed and bound in Great Britain by
Creative Print & Design (Wales), Ebbw Vale

Contents

Acknowledgements

I am grateful to my editor, Suzannah Burywood, for her help at every stage, and to the various anonymous readers who commented on earlier drafts. I am also indebted to my pupils and colleagues for making Winchester a stimulating place in which to try out some of the approaches to criticism explored here, and to my wife Victòria for her encouragement and linguistic expertise. All errors are mine alone.

Note on Pronunciation
In several passages from Old and Middle English I have retained the characters ash (æ), thorn (þ), and eth (ð). The first of these is pronounced (roughly) *a* as in *cat*, the second two as *th* (þ is usually voiced *although*; ð is unvoiced *think*).

⊻ ❙ Introduction

What this book is about

In 1831 a young man wrote to William Wordsworth to ask for his advice on becoming a poet. Having read some of his correspondent's compositions, the great man wrote back, saying tactfully that 'the composition of verse is infinitely more of an art than men are prepared to believe; and absolute success in it depends upon innumerable minutiae' (22 November 1831).

This book is about some of those innumerable minutiae – the arrangements of sound and sentences, the painstaking choice of the right word – which make up the literary art. No doubt this art is also the product of unconscious decisions and an intuitive feel for what works: the decisions of authors, like our own decisions in everyday life, are presumably the result of a mixture of deliberate calculation and instinct, which is why it feels odd, when we analyse a piece of writing, to imply that every effect we find was specifically intended by the writer. But it is interesting that even a Romantic poet like Wordsworth should speak of verse as first and foremost a craft, not as the result of sudden inspiring visitations by the muse. And he is not alone in this: poets and prose writers of different ages have written of the importance of taking infinite pains over tiny details, and in the chapters of this book we shall be looking at the language of texts at this detailed level, in an attempt to understand how the handling of minutiae can generate subtle meanings and express infinite shades of emotion. If the composition of verse is an art, then so is the scrupulous reading of it and of any other kind of literary composition; and both arts, the art of writing and the art of reading, require the patience and the discipline to take time pondering the way in which language works.

There is nothing new in looking closely at the details of texts. Practical Criticism, which trains us to look carefully at many aspects of the form and imagery of texts, has long been established as a foundation of literary study. This book inevitably overlaps with most guides to Practical Criticism at certain points, for example in looking at verse metre and the function of metaphor. But it also, perhaps, adds something new to what students of literature will be used to, by going into a little more detail than is customary in its treatment of such linguistic topics as phonetics and grammar. It is intended as an extension of Practical Criticism, not as an alternative to it. I hope that students of literature who have had little grounding in language study might also find it useful as an introduction to the ways in which the two subjects of language and literature can come together.

As well as providing an introduction to the analysis of the language of literary texts, this book also has another, closely related aim, and that is to show the importance and interest of looking at language as something which changes over time – that is, as something with a history. At a time when there seems to be more and more of an emphasis on modern literature in education, it is valuable to remember that the literature of previous periods was written when English was in quite a different state from the language we use today. If we are to respond to the intricacies of Chaucer and Shakespeare and a host of other writers, we need to know something about the way English worked when they were writing. No amount of reading of contemporary literature or theory, for example, can teach us the difference for Shakespeare between *thou* and *you* or *will* and *shall*. These are topics in the history of language which open up whole dimensions of earlier texts.

Consequently, you will find in this book that points are often illustrated by texts from the periods referred to as Old English (c.449–1066), Middle English (1066–1476) and Early Modern English (1476–1700). I also refer to Renaissance literature, by which I mean very roughly literature written in the century 1520–1620. Writings of all these periods together I refer to as Early English. A little more explanation of the significance of these dates is given in the introduction to Chapter 4 on Lexis, but there is nothing hard and fast about any of them. The division of language into periods, and the definition of 'Early English', are subjects of ongoing debate. My aim is not to contribute an argument to that debate, but merely to suggest some profitable ways in which writings from earlier periods may be read and investigated.

In choosing passages to illustrate points, to comment on and to set for exercises, I have also tended to avoid popular set texts, so that you can come to them without preconceptions -- though some of the lines from Shakespeare are, inevitably, likely to be familiar. No prior knowledge of any of the texts cited is required, and dates are given so that you can place them on a mental timesheet. Above all, the discussions are not intended to provide guidance on particular works, but to help you build up a method which you can then apply to any books, early or modern, which you are studying or reading for pleasure.

What this book is *not* about

A book with the title *The Language of Literature* can give rise to many expectations, and it is important to say at the outset what this one does not propose to deal with. To begin with, it is designed as a practical work, to be used as an aid in developing methods of critical appreciation. It is not a work of theory, and so does not deal explicitly with the interesting question of what 'the language of literature' actually is, or of whether such a concept has any validity at all. However, the topics we concentrate on do owe something to the ideas of theorists, most particularly Roman Jakobson (1896–1982), so it is worth sketching very briefly what principles underlie the arrangement of the present work.

Whether there is a distinct 'language of literature', as there is a recognisable language of, say, religion or sports commentary, is a question which has exercised many thinkers. Efforts have been made in the past to see literature as having a special kind of content – dealing with high and moral matters, for example – but this does not seem a satisfactory definition, since literary works often deal with the mundane and the everyday. The emphasis of Jakobson and other modern linguists has thus been not on content but on form – the way that words are put together into statements. For Jakobson, literary utterances are very often memorable for their structure as well as for what they say. Sometimes this structure is part of a literary convention: a statement like *To be or not to be, that is the question*, for example, is highly ordered by the pattern of metre. In addition to such formal devices as metre, in literary writing we often meet statements with parallel structures: words, clause shapes and sounds are repeated to create patterns. These arrangements can add to the meaning and expressive effect of the works. Take the first two lines of Thomas Gray's *Elegy in a Country Churchyard* (1750):

> The curfew tolls the knell of parting day,
> The lowing herd wind slowly o'er the lea.

Here we notice not only the repeated verse line, but also other kinds of parallelism: for example, there is grammatical parallelism, as both lines are a single statement, starting with the subject (*The curfew*, *The lowing herd*), and going on to the verb. The similarity in structure makes us perceive a similarity in meaning, as if they are two different ways of saying the same thing – the day is ending. We notice, too, repetitions of sound like the persistent *l*, and the chime of *lowing* and *slowly*. The long vowels seem to drag the lines out, as if evoking the slow passing of the day. The more we look at, and listen to these lines, the more our attention is held not only by what the poet says, but the way he says it.

It is formal qualities like these which, for Jakobson and others, mark this writing out as literary, as art. It leaves behind a memory of its form as well as its content. Writers combine words in elaborate ways, set up patterns and depart, or deviate, from them, and all these structural matters affect the way we interpret meaning. On top of that, there are the structures actually built into the language at any one time – for example, the fact that in English the subject generally precedes the verb. These are things we need to be aware of if we are to notice how writers are exploiting the resources of the language as they find it. In this book, therefore, the emphasis is very much on the formal structures of language, and the way writers use these shapes and forms to create meaning and effect.

Another topic which this book does not cover is the geographical varieties of English. The authors which we cite are all from what may be called a central canon of English (though some, although canonical, are perhaps not much read in English courses these days). There is no space given to the great literature in Scots, for example, or to writings in English regional dialects by poets such as John Clare, or to the Afro-American varieties of English, and the many different forms of the language which have arisen in some former colonies. The fact that these other kinds of English are not described here is not meant to imply that they are in any way less worthy of attention than Standard English. There is simply insufficient space to do them justice. My feeling is it would be better to attempt a full study of the grammatical structures of Scots texts, for example, than to present this topic in a page or two as a secondary variation of English. Meanwhile, the great literature of the mainstream English tradition is nothing to be ashamed of, and a study of English literary language is plenty to be going on with.

Finally, this book is not a textbook on Stylistics, the application of modern linguistic concepts and techniques to literary study. To a linguist, the topics will seem traditional, even old-fashioned. But a confidence in describing some basic features of sound and grammar is of special use to the literary critic who wishes to observe and describe the inner workings of texts, and we should beware of treating *traditional* as a dirty word. A course in the techniques offered by Stylistics, such as the study of how people communicate through unspoken understandings (Pragmatics), would be a natural next step. In any case, several excellent textbooks on Stylistics exist, and these are listed in Suggestions for Further Reading at the end of Chapter 5. The emphasis in the present work is to reaffirm the value of established categories of language study for an appreciation of literature, without presenting these as being in competition with the procedures of modern linguistics.

How this book is organised

This book falls into three main sections: Sound, Grammar and Lexis. Each chapter falls into various sections, which end with an exercise or exercises for further practice. The book moves fairly swiftly over a number of topics, and it may be a good idea to take it a section at a time, applying each topic to the texts you are studying before moving on: unless you are already familiar with much of the linguistic material covered, this is probably not a book to take in at one go. At the beginning of Chapter 2 on Sound, I explain why I think this is a suitable place to begin, but you may not agree with that: the chapters are independent of each other, so please take them in the order which suits you best. In general no knowledge of language terminology is assumed, and key terms are defined in the Glossary at the end of the book. If you have doubts about the meaning of any of these terms, a number of helpful books are suggested in the Suggestions for Further Reading lists.

Each chapter concludes with some examples of commentaries on texts, using the techniques just described. Here, too, you may find yourself in disagreement: there is a strong subjective element in critical analysis, and I hope that these commentaries will stimulate debate as well as suggest some lines of enquiry which you can adopt in your own reading. At the end of Chapters 2–5 you will find some Suggestions for Further Reading, and in Chapter 5 (Conclusion) you are invited to build your own commentary on a text, based on the contents of the book as a whole. There are, of course, many aspects of literary language which are not covered in this book, but I hope you will find the subjects which we do concentrate on interesting. After all, the minutiae are, as Wordsworth says, innumerable.

▼ 2 Sound: Music and Meaning

Writing and speaking

We shall start our study of literary language by *listening* to it. Today we associate literature with words on the page, whether we are reading books or writing essays. Most of the work of studying literature is done in silence. But it is important to remember that language is primarily a spoken phenomenon. The written word is simply a means of representing speech on the page, so that we can address people who cannot hear us. Literary expression had a rich life in songs, spells and epic recitations long before it was ever written down. As a first entry into the language of a text, then, we shall try to turn it back into speech – by listening to it in our inner ear, or by reading aloud. It is only then that we can recover the voice, or voices, of a text, with all the range of tones – sarcastic or loving, angry or melancholic – that bring it to life and make reading it a truly human experience.

Terminology

When we have listened closely to a text, we can then *describe* what we hear: this involves a certain amount of technical language, and if the subject of the sounds of language is new to you then you may like to read this chapter slowly, taking a section at a time, and applying it to your own reading for a while before moving on. The technical terms, though, are only words for sounds you can already hear. And, as with other areas of life, technical terms can make us better observers: once we know the name for a thing we are more likely to notice the thing itself.

How this chapter is organised

The chapter is organised in four sections. Section 2.1 is on the patterns created by rhythm – the discussion of metre will probably be familiar to you if you have studied Practical Criticism, though the subject of rhythm in prose is less often treated in textbooks. In section 2.2, we move on to other kinds of patterning in sound – the musical texture created by repetition, in rhyme and in other devices. Then in section 2.3 we consider the use of some phonetic terms, which help us to describe the sounds of language accurately. Over time, the sounds of our speech change, and section 2.4 is an introduction to some of the most important of these changes, and their implications for our reading of older texts, particularly those from the medieval and Renaissance periods. Each section concludes with some exercises, to help you build up a critical method. Suggestions for Further Reading (and listening) come at the end of the chapter.

2.1   Patterns of sound I: stress and rhythm

Stress

Stress is not a literary device, but a feature of English which occurs naturally whenever we speak. In the following examples the stressed syllables are marked in bold:

To**day** I **went** to **town** and **bought** some **or**anges.

This sentence, spoken as marked, illustrates some characteristic features of English stress:

- The words which are stressed are those which carry the important meaning: they are the **lexical**, meaning-bearing words *today* (adverb), *went* (verb), *town* (noun), *bought* (verb) and *oranges* (noun). The unstressed words tend to be the **grammatical words** like *to* and *and*, which do not carry meaning on their own but allow the lexical words to form meaningful patterns. Very often, grammatical words are so unstressed that we slur them or barely say them at all.
- Stressed syllables are usually spaced out, not clumped together. It is relatively unusual to find stressed syllables next to each other. Thus when they are bunched up, our attention is drawn to them.
- Stress normally involves going up in **pitch**, and can also lengthen the syllable slightly. Try saying *I'm going to tell the police!* in an agitated way – you will hear your voice go higher, and the last syllable of *police* will be dragged out. Stress, therefore, does more than just beat out certain syllables. It also helps to establish the melody and rhythm of a phrase.

Stress, or **accent**, therefore involves both meaning and sound: it points out the meaning of a statement by accenting the words carrying the important information; and it also determines a good deal of the sound-shape of an utterance through the distribution of accent, which affects pitch and volume.

The example with which we started – *Today I went to town to buy some oranges* – is also rhythmic, since the stresses are evenly distributed. **Rhythm** is established by a pattern of regular stress.

Regular stress

Regular stress is the 'beat' we feel repeated in a succession of phrases. We usually first encounter it in nursery rhymes, almost always as a four-beat pattern.

•	•	•	•
Old King	**Cole** was a	**merry** old	**soul**
And a	**Merry** old	**soul** was	**he** [rest]
He	**called** for his **hat**, and he	**called** for his **pipe**	
And he	**called** for his **fiddlers**	**three**	[rest]

When we speak these lines, our instinctive need is to establish the basic beat, or pulse. Between each stress there are a number of unstressed syllables. We pace the reading of these to make them fit the rhythm: when there are several, as in *And a merry old*, we say them quickly; if there is only one, like *he* at the end of the second line, we make it last longer. What we are trying to do is to make each 'unit', consisting of stressed syllable and surrounding unstressed syllables, last for the same length of time. The term for this division of rhythm into units of equal duration is **isochrony**, derived from Greek words meaning 'equal time'.

Stress in verse

The rhythm of verse is therefore not primarily to do with counting syllables, for the number of syllables in a line does not of itself tell us anything about its rhythm. Rhythm is based on the establishment of a regular beat of stressed syllables and rests occupying the same time value. These regular measures produce a pattern. There are several such patterns, but the four-beat version which we have looked at is natural to English speech. It is the basic staple of Old English poetry. The first line of an Old English poem, *The Wanderer* (c.950), has much the same rhythm as *Little Miss Muffet*:

•	•	•	•
Little Miss	**Muffet**	**sat** on a	**tuff**et

Oft him an- **haga** **are** ge- **bideð**
(Literally 'Often him the solitary one grace experiences', i.e. 'Often the solitary one experiences grace')

We hear these four beats again in these lines from the poet William Langland, at the start of his great visionary poem *Piers Plowman* (c.1360–86):

> In a **so**mur **se**soun whan **so**fte was þe **so**nne   [þ = th]
> Y **sh**ope me into **sh**roudes as y a **sh**ep **we**re;
> In **a**bite as an **he**remite, vn**ho**ly of **we**rkes,
> **We**nte **fo**rth in þe **wo**rld **wo**ndres to **he**re ...
>   (lines 1–4)

(In a summer season when soft was the sun, I dressed myself in garments as if I were a sheep (or shepherd); in habit like a hermit unholy of works, went forth in the world wonders to hear)

In later writing, we can still hear poets returning to this native rhythm:

> When the **hounds** of **spring** are on **win**ter's **traces**,
>   The **mo**ther of **months** in **mea**dow or plain
> **Fills** the **sha**dows and **win**dy **places** ...
> (A.C. Swinburne (1837–1909), Chorus from *Atalanta in Calydon* (1865))

Both in literary writings, and in examples of everyday English such as advertising jingles and sports commentaries, we often hear phrases organised over four main beats.

The caesura

In many four-beat lines, a pause, called a **caesura**, will naturally fall in the middle. We will hear four beats as two groups of two. A good example is *Líttle Miss Múffet* (,) *sát on a túffet* where, even without punctuation, we pause briefly between *Múffet* and *sát*. This pause occurs in the lines just quoted from Langland, too: *In a somur season* (,) *whan softe was þe sonne*. A caesura gives us space to breathe, making sure that the second half of the line does not die away. This organisation of lines into rhythmic phrases becomes part of the way we receive and understand a work. For conveying thoughts, rhythmic division can be just as important as a grammatical sentence, and sometimes perhaps even more important.

Stress and syllable: metre

So far, we have considered stress in terms of one accented syllable with a varying number of unaccented ones. This gives us the four-beat pulse which runs through English verse from the earliest times.

Much English verse, however, uses stricter metres, in which the unstressed syllables are exactly counted, as well as the stressed ones. Thus a further degree of ordering and discipline occurs, and the 'units' become identical. Here are the main types:

(a) When **I** ¦ consi ¦ der **how** ¦ my **light** ¦ is **spent**   unstressed–stressed
                                                                            (u-s)
(b) **Have** you ¦ **seen** the ¦ apples, ¦ **dar**ling?   s-u
(c) **Isn't it** ¦ **won**derful ¦ **how** they've been ¦ **bloss**oming?   s-u-u
(d) Have you **done** ¦ all the **things** ¦ that I **told** ¦ you to **do**?   u-u-s

These groups are often referred to by their Greek names:

(a) is an **iamb** (single word example *arrest*)
(b) is a **trochee** (*loving*)
(c) is a **dactyl** (*oranges*; it may help to remember that *dactyl* is Greek for finger, which has one long bone followed by two short ones)
(d) is an **anapaest** (*interrupt*).

Each individual unit is called a **foot**. Of these feet, the iamb is the most common in English verse.

Native stress and foreign metre

How did this use of stricter metres occur? Mainly it was due to the influence of foreign tongues. Metres in which syllable-count is important were imported from foreign languages, especially after the Norman invasion of 1066. Syllable-count metres barely occur in Old English, but they appear increasingly from the thirteenth century. Chaucer (c.1343–1400) drew on French and Italian verse models. These languages enjoyed a tradition of poetry which had not, like English, been interrupted by invasion, and they also had a higher status: French was associated with courtly and refined speech, while Italian had been used to sublime effect by Dante and Petrarch. By imitating these patterns, and exploiting the poetic resources of his native language, Chaucer placed English poetry within a larger European tradition.

The result of this import of foreign models is a curious marriage: in early and popular English, as we have seen, stress is more important than syllable-count: we can sing 'Old King Cole', speeding up and slowing down to make the groups of syllables fall under the regular beat marked by the stresses. But in French and Italian, stress is somewhat less pronounced than in English, and verse lines are defined by numbers of syllables rather than stresses: the most usual lines are **octosyllabic** (8), **decasyllabic** (10), **hendecasyllabic** (11) and **alexandrine** (12). In the work of Chaucer, we see these strict syllable-counts being grafted onto the English stress-based verse.

The most convenient marriage occurs in the octosyllabic line, which suits the four-beat pattern discussed above:

> I **have** gret **won**der, **be** this **lyght**,
> **How** that I **lyve**, for **day** ne **nyght**
> I **may** nat sle**pe wel** nygh **noght** ...
> (Chaucer, *The Book of the Duchess* (c.1370), lines 1–3)

Here the stress falls normally on the even syllables, giving us an iambic (the basic foot) **tetrameter** (four beats). On top of this, there is the further pattern of repeated end-sounds, or **rhyme**. The caesura is clear in the first two lines (though we should remember that the commas are put there by a modern editor). The second half of the second line and the third read continuously, depicting perhaps the speaker's sleepless state. This jaunty line manages therefore to combine the native rhythm with the demand for strict syllable-count in the continental European manner. We can see the brilliance with which Chaucer makes it all sound natural, with the little deviation from the basic metre at the start of the second line giving flexibility to the voice. Compare the feel of wonder in *How that I lyve* with a wooden substitute like *that I do lyve*. It is these departures from the basic metrical template which help regular verse to breathe.

Perhaps to achieve a graver sound, Chaucer turned to a line of five stresses and, usually, ten syllables – that is, the iambic **pentameter**:

> Whil**om**, as **oldė** stories **tell**en **us**,   [*Whilom*: once upon a time
> Ther **was** a **duc** that **high**tė **The**seus;   [*hightė*: was called
> Of **Atth**enes **he** was **lord** and **gov**ernour ...
>   (*The Knight's Tale* (c.1386), lines 1–3)

The longer line carries more weight: it is a lorry as opposed to a car. And, like a lorry, it is also asymmetrical: there is no longer a natural central caesura, and so pauses can occur at different moments in the line. Where these pauses come may vary among performances. In the first line, we would probably pause after

Whilom; in the second we might pause after *duc*, or, to add some suspense, before *Theseus*. The varied placement of the caesura allows the poet to create all sorts of different groupings within a line and makes possible these different readings. Even when the basic metre is maintained, the pace of the lines can vary dramatically.

Metrical terms

From this use of Italian and French verse models stems the descriptive language of prosody – the study of poetic metres (*metrics* is also sometimes used). Much of this language comes from Greek and Latin (as in the names for the feet), and some from French (**enjambment**). Add to this the French and Italian terms for poetic forms (stanza, sonnet, ballad) and it becomes clear how much English poetry has been formed by contact with foreign models. Sometimes in English poetry we seem to hear the native stress-pattern in tension with the imported form. Here is Hamlet's famous speech set out as iambs:

> To **be** ¦ or **not** ¦ to **be**, ¦ that **is** ¦ the **ques** tion.
> Wheth**er** ¦ 'tis **no** ¦ bler **in** ¦ the **mind** ¦ to **suffer**
> The **slings** ¦ and **arr** ¦ ows **of** ¦ outra ¦ geous **for** ¦ tune ...

This clearly produces nonsense, with stresses falling on syllables that are not naturally stressed, and grammatical words getting more stress than lexical ones. We may regard the stresses we hear as an irregular variation on the basic iambic pentameter underneath. But we can surely also hear the native four-stress line asserting itself:

> To **be** or **not** to be, **that** is the **ques**tion
> **Whe**ther 'tis **no**bler in the **mind** to **suf**fer
> The **slings** and **arr**ows of out**rage**ous **for**tune
> **Or** to take **arms** against a **sea** of **trou**bles ...

For many years, English verse was described in terms derived from classical and other European languages; and certainly many poets have worked according to these ideas of metre. It is useful to learn some of the traditional metrical terms in order to appreciate the habits of mind of poets of the past, and also to understand critical writings on them. More recent writers on poetic rhythm have doubted whether such terms accurately describe the sound patterns of English, and have drawn on linguistics for a more precise way of describing the movement of a verse line.

Whatever terminology one uses, however, there is no substitute for the experience of hearing and reading aloud. Often, the mind and ear will lead us into the tensions, quickenings, patterns and variations of a text without recourse to analytical language: this language is useful for helping us to describe what we have already heard, and for encouraging us to listen more intently. But it cannot be a substitute for listening with an attentive ear and open mind.

Gradations of stress

The account of stress given above is a very simplified one. Syllable
are not either stressed or unstressed, but graded much more sub
linguists identify at least two levels of stress (**primary** and **seconda**
to give an accurate representation of how verse sounds. An example is from John
Donne. An acute accent (*Bátter*) marks a primary stress, a grave accent
(*pèrsoned*) marks a secondary one:

> Bátter my héart, thrée-pèrsoned Gód, for, yòu
> As yet but knocke, breathe, shine, and seeke to mend ...

In the first line, which is wildly irregular if we try to see it as an iambic
pentameter, we naturally place stresses on *Bátter my héart*. This tum-ti-ti-tum
pattern then seems to be repeated in *thrée-personed Gód*, but *personed* is an
important word, and so gets some stress, perhaps rather less than the other
two words.

  But two levels of stress may still be too simple. The climactic word *Gód* could
be spoken with a stronger stress than any of the others so far. And what of *you* at
the end of the first line? It is clearly too important to be slurred over and must
get some stress, but how much? There is a tension between accenting it and
carrying on with the sentence into the next line. Another way of representing
this is with numbers indicating the degree of stress we hear. This time, we shall
use a four-grade system. The more grades there are, the more room there is for
different readings, and you may well hear the line differently. But however one
reads it, stressed syllables will carry varying amounts of stress:

> 4   1 1   4   3   2   4   1
> Batter my heart, three-personed God, for, you ...

Prose rhythm

Prose also has a rhythm, though it is hardly ever so regular as poetic metre.
Often, though, we can hear certain rhythmic measures dominating. The
following part of a sentence by Laurence Sterne (1713–68) has a pronounced
iambic movement:

> The sún looked bríght the mórning áfter, to évery éye in the víllage bút
> Le Féver's and hís afflícted són's; the hánd of déath pressed héavy upón his
> éyelids ...

> (*Tristram Shandy* (1759–65))

In contrast to this steady rhythm, the action described in this sentence is
brought home by the falling trochees and dactyls:

> Séaward the crést of a róller súddenly féll with a thúnderous crásh, and the
> lóng whíte cómber came róaring dówn upón the bóat.

> (Stephen Crane (1871–1900), *The Open Boat* (1897))

otice, too, how the accumulated stresses on *long white comber* draw this image out, helping us to feel the suspense as it gathers before falling on the boat.

Just as much as any poet, great prose writers organise rhythms in such ways to construct a voice which can speak to us. Sometimes we hear a confiding tone, sometimes a conversational one. At other times we are the audience to grand oratory, suited to the pulpit or parliament. In investigating the way sentences come to have this living quality, attention to rhythm is a good place to start.

Cadence

With prose rhythm, it is a good idea to look closely at the ends of phrases and sentences. The cadence is the ending of a phrase: it comes from the Latin for 'to fall' and occurs at moments when the writing seems, briefly or permanently, to come to rest. Often this cadence is built up to, and coincides with an important idea. A well-written sentence usually feels like it knows where it is going, and gives the impression that the place it ends up is its inevitable destination. Cadence is a rhythmic device, and occurs in both prose and poetry.

Classical cadences: numerus

Ideas about cadences in English writing are best understood if we look briefly at the classical tradition behind them. In Latin, certain rhythmic groupings were found to give a statement a satisfying sense of closure. In the speeches of a writer and orator like Cicero (106–43 BC) these patterns come up frequently, showing that in prose as well as in verse there were conventions for rhythm as well as for grammar. This practice in Latin is the **numerus**.

Cursus

In the Latin language, syllables are classed as long or short – these are known as quantities. As the Classical Latin of the Romans changed into medieval Latin (roughly, from the fifth to the tenth centuries AD), these quantities were not so clearly distinguished. To take their place, stress, as in English, became more important. Cadences then came to be defined differently, according to the placement of accent (stress), usually in the last two words. The numerus was now referred to as the **cursus**, an important part of the art of composition in medieval Latin. There were three main types of cursus, here given with English illustrations. Each one is a particular rhythmic pattern:

Cursus planus (/xx/x): ín the begínning, ínto the súnset, sóme day I'll fínd him
   [dactyl and trochee]

Cursus tardus (/xx/xx): Wásn't it wónderful, wándering trávellers
   [two dactyls]

Cursus velox (/xx xx/x) Háppily ever áfter, sómebody who'll belíeve me

It will be seen that these are all literally cadences since they end with a fall from a stressed to an unstressed syllable. These rhythms make their mark on English prose, particularly in the late medieval and Renaissance periods, when Latin models were carefully imitated. However, there is an important difference between Latin and English speech rhythm: in English, we often end with a stressed syllable, not an unstressed one. So the models could be adapted: a phrase like *when will I see you again?* is *cursus tardus* with an extra stress at the end (/xx /xx /); *can you believe this guy?* is the same with *cursus planus* (/xx /x /), and so on. English writers, with an eye on the Latin and an ear for their own language, exploited this tendency to rise rather than fall at the end of a construction, and created variety by mixing **falling** and **rising** patterns. In the sentences below, the falling rhythms of *cursus planus* [CP] and *cursus tardus* [CT] are answered by the heavy stress in the much shorter and bolder sentence which concludes the passage:

> Like as to a castle or fortress sufficeth one ówner or sóvereign [CT], and where any more be of like power and authority seldom cometh the wórk to perféction [CP]; or being already made, where the one diligently overseeth and the óther neglécteth [CP], in that contention all is subverted and cómeth to rúin [CP]. In semblable wise doth a public weal that hath more chief governors than óne.
>
> (Sir Thomas Elyot, *The Book Named the Governor* (1531), Book 1, ch. 2)

The classical cadences occur at points where a speaker would naturally pause. By marking the segments of the sentence out clearly, they help us to keep the various parts of this syntactic organism in our minds. The same rhythmic groups occur elsewhere in the text: *cástle or fórtress, pówer and authórity, ín that conténtion, áll is subvérted*. The last sentence is given impressive force by the clustering of stresses, including three in a row: *móre chíef góvernors than óne*. The rhythm is not that of verse metre, but it is highly fashioned as a means of foregrounding ideas and expounding them effectively. The repeated group creates a solemn feel, almost like a ritual; combined with the marked pauses, it achieves a stately rhythm, balanced and unagitated, and thus suitable for the expression and evocation of reflective thought.

Cursus and religious writing

The Latin *cursus* patterns are especially frequent in English prose in religious writings which seek to achieve a quiet dignity. Many examples of these cadences can be found in *The Book of Common Prayer*, which emerged over the sixteenth century, and in English translations of the Bible:

> And when the town clerk had appeased the people, he said, *Yé men of Éphesus* [CT], what man is there that knoweth not how that the city of the Ephesians is a worshipper of the great *góddess Diána* [CP], and of the image which *féll down from Júpiter*? [CT]
> Seeing that these things cannot be spoken against, ye *óught to be quíet* [CP], and to *dó nothing ráshly*. [CP]

For ye have brought hither these men, which are neither *róbbers of chúrches* [CP], nor yet *blásphemers of your góddess.* [CV]

(*Acts*, XIX.35–37. *King James Bible* (1611))

Of the three types, the *cursus planus* (/xx /x) is particularly heavily used, as it corresponds to a common English rhythmic pattern. The remaining verses of this chapter in *Acts* all conclude with it: *impléad one anóther, láwful assémbly, accóunt of this cóncourse, dismíssed the assémbly* – the same rhythmic group as we found in the passage from Elyot above. Notice that the cadence accompanies an important idea in the passage of thought: the phrases and sentences thus conclude strongly, focusing our attention on the end of the statement. The *cursus planus* is strictly observed, with a final fall onto an unstressed syllable: this might have reminded listeners and readers in the seventeenth century of Latin habits, lending the English scriptures an air of antiquity and authority.

The *Book of Common Prayer* and the *King James Bible* had a great influence on later English prose writers. In this long sentence by the spiritual writer Jeremy Taylor (1613–67), the falling cadences help to give the writing its gravity. We can also hear how the strict Latin patterns are being varied to suit the rhythms of English. This is usually done by adding extra syllables. For example, the *cursus tardus* (/xx/xx) is adapted in *ínstruments of ácting it* (/xxx /xx). In the layout below, the concluding phrases are underlined, and the last stressed syllable is italicised. More important than any technical analysis, though, is an awareness of how falling cadences appear at pauses. Read it aloud, and you will see how heavy stresses make the end of the sentence majestically slow. The passage is about our preparation for death, and in the way it slows down to its grand final cadence we can almost feel death closing in, as the writer describes it:

Thus nature calls us to meditate of death by those things which are the instruments of *act*ing it; and God, by all the variety of His *pro*vidence, makes us see death *ev*erywhere, in all variety of *cir*cumstances, and dressed up for all the *fan*cies, and the expectation of every single *per*son.

(*Holy Dying* (1651), ch. 1)

Rising endings

We mentioned earlier in our discussion of the *cursus* that while it is natural for Latin sentences to end with a short or light syllable, English often adopts a rising rhythm, gathering to a final stress. This can sound more assertive; it creates a greater sense of closure as it enforces a slight pause in the speaking voice before moving on. (This pause also helps us to remember what we have just read or heard.) A little later in the same passage by Taylor discussed immediately above, the rhythm modulates. There are more falling cadences, but then rising endings come to dominate, making the images of mortality more striking. The same idea is being developed – that reminders of death are to be found everywhere, in every season:

Thus death reigns in all the portions of our *tíme*. The autumn with its fruits provides *disórders fór us*, and the winter's cold turns them into *shárp diséases*, and the spring brings flowers to strew our *héarse*, and the summer gives green turf and brambles to bind upon our *gráves*. Calentures and surfeit, cold and agues, are the four quarters of the *year*, and all minister to *death*; and you can go no whither but you tread upon a dead man's *bones*.

The change in closing rhythms in this passage creates an alternation of pitch and tone. Heavy stresses at the end of phrases emphasise key emotive words, and suggest the finality of death. The closing phrase, *dead man's bones*, with its double or even triple stress, provides a tremendous last flourish to the passage. The text is also a good example of how key ideas can be placed at the ends of phrases and sentences to best effect.

In the following biblical passage, also a meditation on death, the alternation of rising and falling cadences creates a wave-like rhythm as the pitch of the voice moves up and down:

Are not my days *few? Cease* then, and let me al*one*, that I may take comfort a *li*ttle,
Before I go whence I shall not re*turn*, even to the land of darkness and the shadow of *death*;
A land of *dark*ness, as darkness it*self*; and of the shadow of *death*, without any *or*der, and where the light is as *dark*ness.

(*Job*, X.20–22, *King James Bible* (1611))

Read this with feeling and it sounds midway between speaking and singing. Just as the subject belongs to grave contemplation, far removed from the trivialities of everyday chatter, so the movement and music of the writing are heightened to take us in our imaginations into a world of unusual depth and intensity. Rhythmic texture, word repetitions, the rise and fall of cadences – everything works together to make the expression of the thoughts vivid and compelling.

Prose rhythm and metre

Like poetry, English prose rhythm has been studied using terms from classical metre. In some older studies, one can find references to weird and wonderful terms like paeons, cretics and amphibrachs. This approach, which involves such a heavy use of terminology, has become unfashionable. Certainly before venturing any further into metrical analysis, it is important to practise reading slowly, as if the text is being read aloud, and to listen for patterns of stress, changes in pace and the expectation and satisfaction provided by a long sentence and the cadences which mark out its various parts.

Rhythm – Exercises

Verse

Below are two seventeenth-century poems. Once you have read them two or three times, answer the questions which follow.

Take, Oh, Take Those Lips Away
Take, oh, take those lips away
That so sweetly were forsworn
And those eyes, like break of day,
Lights that do mislead the morn;
5   But my kisses bring again,
Seals of love, though sealed in vain.
Hide, oh, hide those hills of snow,
Which thy frozen bosom bears,
On whose tops the pinks that grow
10   Are of those that April wears;
But first set my poor heart free,
Bound in those icy chains by thee.
(John Fletcher (1579–1625), published 1639)

Epitaph on Elizabeth, L.H.
Wouldst thou hear what man can say
In a little? Reader, stay.
Underneath this stone doth lie
As much beauty as could die;
5   Which in life did harbor give
To more virtue than doth live.
If at all she had a fault,
Leave it buried in this vault.
One name was Elizabeth;
10   Th'other let it sleep with death:
Fitter, where it died, to tell,
Than had it lived at all. Farewell.
(Ben Jonson (1572–1637), published 1616. It is not known
who L.H. was, but it is likely that *L* stands for *Lady*)

1. Which syllables are stressed? Experiment with alternative readings.
2. What is the regular metrical pattern being used? Why might this be appropriate for the subject? Which lines, if any, deviate from the basic pattern, and what effect does this variation create?
3. Find two lines which have the same basic rhythm but which differ in other ways. For example, one may feel quicker than another, or feel more heavily stressed. How much does the pace vary over the underlying pattern?
4. In which lines do you hear a caesura? In 'Epitaph', try reading line 10 first with a marked caesura after *other*, and then without a pause. How do these two ways of reading affect the meaning? Which other lines allow this kind of choice?
5. Concentrate on a few lines of each poem and use a graded stress system, using first two levels (primary and secondary) and then four. Again, what alternatives are possible?
6. You will now have identified various elements of sound patterning: stress, variation within a pattern, deviation from the pattern, pauses and stress gradation. Now consider the relation of these features to meaning and expression. How do they help to convey the sense and emotion of the poems?

Prose

Below is the Collect for Ash Wednesday from *The Book of Common Prayer*. Enunciate each phrase so that it makes sense as part of the whole; make sure you have enough breath and bring the passage to a satisfying cadence. The Collects are a particularly good exercise for practising getting hold of a long construction, as they all consist of one sentence. When you have read it a few times, answer the questions which follow.

The Collect
Almighty and everlasting God, who hatest nothing that thou hast made, and dost forgive the sins of all them that are penitent: Create and make in us new and cóntrite hearts, that we worthily lamenting our sins, and acknowledging our wretchedness, may obtain of thee, the God of all mercy, perfect remission and forgiveness; through Jesus Christ our Lord. *Amen*

1. Can you find examples of the different kinds of *cursus* – *planus, tardus* and *velox*? Where is a pause required, even though there is no punctuation? Which phrases or 'members' end with a stress (rising) and which end with an unstressed syllable (falling)? Are there repeated rhythmic patterns, or other devices showing rhythmic control? What is the effect of these patterns on the overall rhythm of the Collect?
2. Choose passages from an anthology of prose and compare the way they use rhythms to create different effects.

2.2 Patterns of sound 2: repeated sounds

Rhythm is the repetition of stress patterns. Another kind of structuring is the repetition of individual sounds. The following types are fundamental to English poetic language:

Alliteration

Alliteration is one of the commonest devices for foregrounding the sound of a text. It may be defined as the repetition of a consonant sound, often marked by being placed on a stressed syllable (the repetition of a vowel sound is generally called **assonance**, and is described later in this chapter).

Alliteration in medieval verse

Alliteration is a basic feature of Old English and much medieval verse, particularly that written in the Midlands and the North. It works together with rhythm: the usual combination in medieval alliterative verse is to have four beats in a line, with three of them alliterating on the same sound. This is the line used in *Beowulf* (usually dated between the eighth and tenth centuries). It evidently survived the Norman invasion and the changes to English language and culture which that brought about, for we find it still being employed in the alliterative revival of the fourteenth century. One such poem is the anonymous *The Parlement of the Three Ages*, a dream vision in which personifications of Youth, Middle Age and Age talk together about a variety of topics. It is based on an early fourteenth-century French poem (c.1312), and could have been composed at any time between then and the end of the century. Here are some lines to illustrate the use of alliteration:

> In the *m*onethe of *M*aye when *m*irthes bene fele,
> And the *s*esone of *s*omere when *s*ofte bene the wedres,
> Als I *w*ent to the *w*odde my *w*erdes to dreghe,
> Into þe *sch*awes myselfe a *sch*otte me to gette
> At ane *h*ert or ane *h*ynde ...
>
> (*The Parlement of the Three Ages*, lines 1–5)

(In the month of May when joys (mirths) be many / and the season of summer when soft be the storms, / As I went to the wood my fate to experience, / Into the thickets myself a shot me to get / at a hart or a hind ...)

Alliteration here is doing the job later taken on by rhyme. It creates a pattern of repetition which gives us a feeling of expectation and resolution. Like rhyme, it also tests the poet's skill in meeting the demands of finding a particular sound without distorting the sense.

Sound effect: functional, meaningful or decorative?

When we encounter alliteration in a text, we might ask *why* it is there. What is it being used *for*? In a poem like *Parlement*, it could be purely functional. Just as a modern building may be supported by a steel frame, so a medieval poem like *Beowulf* or *Piers Plowman* is supported by a frame of stressed and alliterating lines. To pursue the analogy, just as lengths of steel can come readymade, so the alliterative poet could find, in the tradition of verse-making, word families, linked by common sounds. These made up formulae, the joists and struts of the work. *Summer*, *season* and *soft* are one such family: all three words are also present in the passage from Langland which we looked at in the previous section: *In a somer seson whan softe was the sonne.*

We may see the alliteration in such a line as meaningful, that is, supporting the subject of the text. Indeed, if we are trained in Practical Criticism, we probably will: the *s* sounds in line 2 above are used, we might feel, because they seem to suggest summer breezes and the rustling of leaves. In a modern text, where the writer can pick and choose alliteration and other devices, this would be a very plausible reading. But in poems where alliteration is part of the basic structure, we need to be wary of reading meaning into it every time it appears. A general principle of linguistics applies: the less choice there is in using a particular linguistic element, the less meaning that element carries. For example, we say *Dear* at the start of a formal letter and *sincerely* at the end, because they are required by the formulae of letter conventions – we don't have any real choice in the matter, and don't necessarily *mean* them. But the words we use in a love letter will be much more carefully chosen to represent our real feelings (though even here, conventions may still apply).

Finally, alliteration, like other sound effects, could be purely decorative. This is when it is not functional – the writer doesn't have to use it – nor related particularly to meaning, but simply creates a pleasing musical texture. In the following lines by Christina Rossetti (1830–94), is the alliteration reinforcing the meaning, or is it working with rhyme to create an elaborate decorative frame? This is a matter of critical judgment where two readers may well arrive at different conclusions:

> *Eve*
> 'While I sit at the door,
> Sick to gaze within,
> Mine eye weepeth sore
> For sorrow and sin:
> As a tree my sin stands
> To darken all lands;
> Death is the fruit it bore.'
> (Lines 1–7; published 1866)

The decline of alliteration

After this brief discussion of the uses of alliteration, let us return to our historical account of this device. From the late Middle Ages, alliteration gave way to rhyme and metre as a principal structuring element of sound in verse. Since this decline, alliteration has remained an important device for writers. As it is now a matter of choice rather than a formal requirement, so it becomes more important as a tool for pointing mood and meaning. The meaningful and decorative uses take over from the functional. Consider this description of Shakespeare's Mark Antony, carousing with Cleopatra:

> His captain's heart,
> Which in the scuffles of great fights hath burst
> The buckles on his breast, reneges all temper,
> And is become the bellows and the fan
> To cool a gypsy's lust.
> (*Antony and Cleopatra*, Act 1, Scene 1, lines 6–10)

We can feel Antony's power, and the power of the scorn of Philo, who is speaking, in the heavy *b* alliteration of *burst / The buckles on his breast ... bellows*. The effect created is immediately noticeable, suitable for dramatic verse. More subtle suggestions are made through alliteration in these lines from Hardy (1840–1928):

> I leant upon a coppice gate
> When Frost was spectre-grey,
> And Winter's dregs made desolate
> The weakening eye of day.
> (Thomas Hardy, 'The Darkling Thrush, 1900')

Here we might feel that the repeated heavy sounds of *g* (*gate* ... *grey* ... *dregs*) and *d* (*dregs* ... *desolate* ... *day*) help to establish the heavy, melancholy mood being painted in the words: all of them are attached to a similar vowel sound, bringing out the monotony of the scene.

Rhyme

Full rhyme is the repetition of the vowel and consonant sounds which conclude a word. It is commonly found as end-rhyme in poetry, that is, occurring at the ends of verse lines:

> My mistress' eyes are nothing like the s*un*,
> Coral is far more red than her lips r*ed*,
> If snow be white, why then her breasts are d*un*,
> If hairs be wires, black wires grow on her h*ead*.
> (Shakespeare, Sonnet 130)

Both sets of rhyme here – *sun* / *dun* and *red* / *head* – involve the last stressed vowel and final consonant. The first sound of the syllable is not repeated: if it were, then the rhyme would simply become word repetition. Each of the four lines above is a separate statement which makes sense on its own: the verse line corresponds to a grammatical sentence. This invites us to pause at the end of each line, and the pause is emphasised by a rhyme word on the last stressed syllable. This combination of pause, syntactical completeness, monosyllabic rhyme sound and stress has a rather 'heavy' effect. Like shelves on a bracket, the lines rest on the rhyme words, which contain key ideas, further heightened by the contrast of *sun* / *dun*. Rhyme in these lines also underlines the decisive tone, established in the opening affirmation (*My mistress' eyes are nothing like* ...) – the lines seem to build confidently towards their climactic rhyme word. The pauses which mark the end of each line also suggest the mental rhythm of the speaker, thinking things through one idea at a time.

The repetition of final vowel and concluding consonant (if there is one) is the most common form of rhyme in English. If the end word concludes with an unstressed syllable, then that too is repeated to form a perfect rhyme:

> O wild West Wind, thou breath of Autumn's b*eing*,
> Thou, from whose unseen presence the leaves dead
> Are driven, like ghosts from an enchanter fl*eeing* ...
> (Shelley, 'Ode to the West Wind' (1819))

Usually no more than this is repeated to make a rhyme: where a rhyme word has three syllables, the effect is usually comical since it seems so contrived. Lord Byron delighted in comic rhymes. The following occurs in *Don Juan* (1819):

> But – oh! Ye lords of ladies *intellectual* ... have they not hen-*peck'd you all*?
> (*Don Juan*, 1.22)

Advantages and disadvantages of rhyme

Rhyme can have many creative effects, among them the following:

- By repeating a sound regularly, it foregrounds the patterned, musical of a piece of writing, heightening our attention to the general sound texture.
- The anticipation of a rhyme word creates a sense of suspense in the reader or listener, thus adding a psychological drama to the act of reading.
- By meeting the technical demands of rhyme without forcing unlikely words into their writing, poets have a chance to show off their skill. Devices like rhyme and metre can be in tension with natural, colloquial rhythms: they draw our attention to the writing as literary art, while other aspects of style point us to aspects of the language which we recognise from outside literature. For example, in the lines from Shakespeare discussed above, *My mistress' eyes are nothing like the sun* sounds conversational – we could imagine someone saying it in a tavern, perhaps. But the use of regular metre, rhyme and other effects mark the verse as a literary utterance. Thus there is a felt art / life tension in the writing.
- As some poets have testified, searching for a rhyme word can also stimulate the imagination, as it suggests ideas which may otherwise not have occurred to them.
- Like metaphor, rhyme creates a link between two words which we might not otherwise think of together – *red* and *head*, or *being* and *fleeing*, for example. It can also point out semantic links like similarity or contrast, as in the *sun* / *dun* rhyme from the lines in the Shakespeare sonnet discussed above.

Despite offering these kinds of experience to reader and writer, rhyme in English also involves certain problems. This is partly because it is an import rather than a native product. Like syllable-count, and the metrical forms which stem from it, rhyme is imported from abroad. Only a tiny portion of Old English verse rhymes, and the medieval writers like Langland who follow the alliterating, four-beat tradition, have no use for it. A poet using rhyme in English has to surmount the following obstacles:

- English contains relatively few rhymes when compared to a language like Italian. There is therefore an increased likelihood of forced rhymes or word order having to be altered to suit a rhyme scheme. Because the range is so small in some cases, stock rhymes come to be familiar: *love* / *dove* / *above*, for example. As rhyme words get used up, it becomes harder to use the device to create a surprise. There is a risk that a great deal of energy can go into satisfying technical demands rather than into saying something which is worth saying.
- A rhyme word coincides with a heavily stressed syllable at the end of a line. This puts a lot of weight on one particular word, and so causes us to give it much more attention than the rest of the line. Sometimes poets will exploit this imbalance; at other times we see them working to create focus elsewhere in the line, away from the rhyme sound.

- When we read rhyming verse, we are so aware the rhyme word is coming that this expectation can dominate our response. Thus we may not pay sufficient attention to the words leading up to the rhyme, especially at the end of a couplet.

For these sorts of reasons, many poets have dispensed with rhyme. This is not only a modern development. Most of Shakespeare's dramatic verse is unrhymed iambic pentameter (blank verse), and Milton dispenses with it in *Paradise Lost* (1667). Milton's note on verse accompanying that poem is an interesting case against the device of rhyme: 'rhyme being no necessary adjunct or true ornament of poem or good verse, in longer works especially, but the invention of a barbarous age, to set off wretched matter and lame metre' (added in the fourth issue, 1668). Succeeding poets of the Augustan age, such as Dryden (1631–1700) and Pope (1688–1744), nonetheless used rhyme, particularly in couplets, extensively. Among the most inventive users of rhyme today are Glyn Maxwell, John Fuller, Anthony Hecht and Clive James.

Dealing with rhyme

We appreciate rhyming English poetry better when we consider how poets deal with the difficulties outlined above. One approach is to break up the line with pauses, so it does not accelerate forward to the end word. In the following lines from Marvell (1621–78), the sinuous syntax means we give words in the middle of lines as much natural emphasis as the rhyme words:

> Had we but World enough, and Time,
> This coyness Lady were no crime.
> We would sit down, and think which way
> To walk, and pass our long Loves Day.
> (*To His Coy Mistress*, published 1681)

In the second couplet, the force of *way* is reduced by the requirement to read straight on into the next line. This effect of enjambment or **run-on**, where the clause does not coincide with the verse line, is frequently used to avoid the monotonous thud of regular metre combined with a rhyme scheme.

Another approach is to reduce the amount of rhyme going on in a stanza. An example is the opening verse of *Adlestrop*, by Edward Thomas (1878–1917). This has rhyme words only on the second and fourth line, creating the pattern *abcb*. The use of conversational rhythms, run-on and a heavy mid-line pause, all serve to spread the stresses across the verse. The rhyme is there, helping to hold the verse together, but it is unassertive. Indeed, on hearing this for the first time, it is possible not even to notice that the poem has a rhyme scheme:

> Yes. I remember Adlestrop –
> The name, because one afternoon
> Of heat the express-train drew up there
> Unwontedly. It was late June.

A question to ask about any rhyming verse is how much attention the rhyme is drawing to itself. If it seems discreet, what is the poet doing to deflect our attention from it? If it is prominent, what is the poet using it for? It might, for example, be stressing an idea, tying up a couplet with a witty surprise, or bringing a stanza to a marked close.

Half-rhyme: consonance

Rhyme becomes less emphatic when, instead of repeating both vowel and consonant (as in *red / head*) we repeat only one of these elements. The general term for this is half-rhyme (also known as **slant rhyme** and pararhyme). In the following lines, only the consonants are repeated, while the vowels are altered:

> It seemed that out of battle I e*scaped*
> Down some profound dull tunnel, long since *scooped*
> Through granites which titanic wars had *groined.*
> Yet also there encumbered sleepers *groaned* ...
> (*Strange Meeting* (1918) by Wilfred Owen (1893–1918))

The repetition of consonants either side of a vowel sound is a particular kind of half-rhyme known as **consonance**. Here, the echoing effect helps to suggest the strange tunnel, with its eerie sounds. There also seems to be something organic and self-generating about this use of consonance, as if words are mutating into each other – an appropriate accompaniment for Owen's dream vision.

Half-rhyme: assonance

The second kind of half-rhyme is the repetition of vowels. This produces **assonance** (or vocalic rhyme). Owen uses this technique in the lines above, too, not in the rhyme position, but within the lines: *out ... down ... profound, dull tunnel, seemed ... sleepers.* There is also a sort of near-full rhyme in *granites ... titanic.* As well as these effects of half-rhyme, where assonance creates an internal half-rhyme, we can also see alliteration (**granites ... groined ... groaned**). The total effect is to create a rich musical texture in which numerous sounds become foregrounded, an appropriately unusual echoing aural world for this ghostly strange meeting to take place in. In the English tradition, Spenser, Tennyson and Owen create musical verbal fabrics so elaborate that it is a common experience for the ear to take over from the mind. After a few lines we realise we have been listening to the sound but not closely following the sense.

Effects of sound repetition in prose

Like rhythm, the effects described above are also a feature of literary prose, as we can see in the following passage on spiritual comfort (in these lines, *comforted* means 'strengthened' and *hopeless* means 'desperate'):

> I will in my poor mind assign for the first comfort the desire and longing to be
> by God comforted, and not without some reason call I this the first cause of

comfort. For like as the cure of that person is in a manner desperate that hath no will to be cured, so is the discomfort of that person desperate that desireth not his own comfort.

(Thomas More (?1477–1535), *A Dialogue of Comfort against Tribulation* (1534))

Rhythm

This is clearly carefully arranged, with its grouping of stresses in twos: ... *for the first cómfort / the desíre and lónging /to be by Gód cómforted*. This gives the prose a stately forward movement, suitable for reading aloud or for medita-tion – More wrote this when in prison awaiting execution. The two-beat rhythm also lends weight to the **end-focus** which occurs just before each comma and full stop. The need to sustain this rhythmic pattern also explains the **doublet** *desire and longing* which is not strictly necessary for the meaning. Such elaborate touches may seem an unlikely luxury in a writer awaiting trial and death, but More was saturated in a rhetorical tradition which would have made such an approach to composition instinctive in him; furthermore, it is surely not implausible that in approaching a theme of such high seriousness – how man prepares for his end – a writer will also take seriously the artistic manner in which this matter is delivered.

Sound effects

There is some elaborate alliteration, from the simple *cause of comfort* to the group *discomfort ... desperate ... desireth*, where the whole *dis-* element is repeated, with very slight variation. Alliteration ties words together even further in the last sentence, marking the intensity of the concluding thought with a close weave of sound: *c* in *cure ... cured ... discomfort ... comfort*, *p* in *person ... desperate*. Assonance helps to bind the construction together even further: the *I* sound (which would probably have sounded differently to More) in *I ... mind assign ... desire ... I ... like ... desireth*.

More is writing what we may call 'art prose', prose which is comparable to poetic language: the sound effects, together with other devices, foreground the exact form of language employed, and make us aware of the way the words are put together as well as of what they are saying. The tradition of art prose continued for many centuries, particularly in shorter, more intense genres like sermons and public speeches. But highly ornate sound patterning does not always suit the longer literary forms. Reading a novel, we do not necessarily want the language to be constantly impressing itself on us, and as a result such stylistic effects in narrative prose and plays are often deployed with restraint. One of the exciting challenges of reading modernist writers like Joyce, Faulkner or Gertrude Stein is that the formal construction of their experimental prose is as noticeable as the story or subject – and sometimes more noticeable. As with More, their carefully patterned writing can be a way of expressing certain psychological states.

Repeated sounds – Exercise

How many sound patterns can you find in the following texts? How do they enhance the meaning, expressiveness and musical variety of the piece? Comment on the poet's handling of rhyme.

(a)
       Happy ye leaues when as those lilly hands,
          which hold my life in their dead doing might,
          shall handle you and hold in loues soft bands,
          lyke captiues trembling at the victors sight.   4
       And happy lines, on which with starry light,
          those lamping eyes will deigne sometimes to look
          and reade the sorrowes of my dying spright,
          written with teares in harts close bleeding book.   8
       And happy rymes bath'd in the sacred brooke,
          of *Helicon* whence she deriued is,
          when ye behold that Angels blessed looke,
          my soules long lacked foode, my heauens blis.   12
       Leaues, lines, and rymes, seeke her to please alone,
          whom if ye please, I care for other none.
              (Edmund Spenser (c.1552–99). This is the first sonnet in the
                     sequence entitled *Amoretti* (1595))

(b) Poetry is the record of the best and happiest moments of the happiest and best minds. We are aware of evanescent visitations of thought and feeling sometimes associated with place or person, sometimes regarding our own mind alone, and always arising unforeseen and departing unbidden, but elevating and delightful beyond all expression: so that even in the desire and the regret they leave, there cannot but be pleasure, participating as it does in the nature of its object. It is as it were the interpenetration of a diviner nature through our own; but its footsteps are like those of a wind over a sea, where the coming calm erases, and whose traces remain only as on the wrinkled sand which paves it.
            (Percy Bysshe Shelley (1792–1822), from *A Defence of Poetry*,
                     written 1821, published 1840)

2.3 Types of sound: phonetics

When we describe the sounds of a poem, we often use words like 'soft', 'harsh' or 'smooth'. These sorts of words certainly communicate a general impression, but they do not describe precisely the sounds of a text. If we are prepared to learn a few technical terms, we can turn to the linguistic science of phonetics, which is concerned with describing speech sounds exactly and studying the ways in which they are produced. Though there is little need for the student of literature to study phonetics into its higher regions, some elementary knowledge gives us a much more exact vocabulary for describing sounds, and might help us to notice sound patterns in the first place.

The phonetic analysis of a sound considers whether it is made by vibrating the vocal cords (**voiced** if it is, **unvoiced** if it isn't), the part of the mouth in which the sound is produced (**place of articulation**), and the way in which air is blocked and channelled to produce it (**manner of articulation**). For example, the sound *v* as in *very* is a *voiced labiodental fricative*:

- *Voiced* because we vibrate the vocal cords when we pronounce it, as you will find if you place your fingers lightly on the throat while saying it.
- *Labiodental*, because to say *v* we bring our lower lip (Latin *labium*) and teeth (dental) together. This is the *place of articulation.*
- *Fricative*, because the air is forced through the obstruction of lip and teeth, creating friction. This is the *manner of articulation.*

Learning about the way the mouth forms sounds can make us more aware of texts as physical experiences when we say them aloud: an important part of the pleasure of poetry is the purely sensual one of getting your mouth round the words. The sensation is often one of having to use your mouth muscles and control your breathing more than usual – physical evidence that the language is being used to do things it does not normally do.

Here are the main sounds of English, as phonetics describes them, starting with consonants. In phonetics, sounds are represented with a special set of symbols, known as the International Phonetic Alphabet (IPA). This is because in the usual alphabet, letters can stand for a number of sounds, such as *g* in *goat* and *gyrate*; equally the same sound can be spelled with different letters, as in *cat* and *king*. In the IPA one symbol stands for one sound, so there can be no confusion.

In the discussion below, we do not use the IPA, which would take some space to introduce. For literary critical purposes, one can go some way without it. It is important to remember, though, that we are discussing sounds rather than letters. It should be clear at any point which sound is being referred to.

Consonants

Plosives

b, *p* – made with the lips

d, *t* – made by pressing the tip of the tongue against the front roof of the mouth

g (as in **goat**), *k* (as in **cat**, **king**) – made by pressing the back of the tongue against the back roof of the mouth

All these sounds are made by pressing things together – lips, tongue and palate – and then suddenly releasing them. Hence the name *plosives*. They are literally little explosions of air: like other explosions, they are made once, and cannot be sustained. With plosives we trap the air coming up from the lungs, and then release it. In the list above, the first in each pair is unvoiced (made without vibrating the vocal cords) and the second is voiced. Here is an example of some of these plosive sounds put to use in a piece of verse:

> *B*ut on his *b*rest a *b*loudie *C*rosse he *b*ore,
> The *d*eare remembrance of his *d*ying Lord,
> For whose sweete sake that *g*lorious *b*adge he wore,
> And *d*ead as liuing euer him a*d*or'd.
> (Edmund Spenser (c.1552–99), *The Faerie Queene*, Book One,
> Canto 1, verse 2 (published 1590))

These lines describe a knight as he rides out in quest of adventures. The passage is marked by a cluster of alliterated voiced plosives, mainly *b* and *d*, but there is also an effective instance of *g* in *glorious*. Often Spenser seems to weave sound patterns for the sheer pleasure of doing so, but here there is a possible link with meaning, as the percussive sounds make the Knight's piety seem energetic and heroic, an extension of his martial valour.

A rather quieter texture is produced by unvoiced plosives. In these lines by Pope (1688–1744), they perhaps suit the clipped nature of the couplet, and the secret, inward distress described:

> But anxious *c*ares the *p*ensive nymph o*pp*resse*d*,
> And secre*t* *p*assions labored in her breas*t*.
> (*The Rape of the Lock* (1714 edition), Canto 4, lines 1–2)

Note that *oppressed* ends in a *t* sound – a reminder that letters are a misleading guide to sounds.

The other consonant sounds are as follows.

Affricates

The sounds of **ju*dg*e** (voiced) and **chur*ch*** (unvoiced). These are the 'hardest' sounds after the plosives.

Fricatives

f, v, th as in **thick, this**; *s, z*; **ship, measure**. Other fricatives have particular names: the hissing *s* sound is often referred to as a **sibilant**, and the *h* as in *heart* as an **aspirate**.

Nasals

m, n, sing. The passage of air through the mouth is blocked, so that air is mostly released through the nose.

Lateral / Liquid

l (air comes down the sides of the tongue).

Approximants (semi-vowels)

r, w, year.

Unvoiced fricatives, nasals, the liquid *l* and the approximants are all drawn-out, mellifluous sounds. They can suggest a soft, sensuous atmosphere, in contrast to the harder effects of the plosives and affricates. One English poem which makes full use of these qualities of sound is Tennyson's 'The Lotos-Eaters'

(1832, revised 1842), in which sailors, drugged by the lotos plant, celebrate the comforts of an exotic island. In these lines, the voiced plosives are drowned out by the drawn-out consonants of the lazy mariners' song:

But, propt on beds of amaranth and moly,	[nasal]
How sweet (while warm airs lull us, blowing lowly)	[liquid]
With half-dropt eyelid still,	[sibilant]
Beneath a heaven dark and holy,	[aspirate]
To watch the river drawing slowly	[approximants]
His waters from the purple hill … (133–38)	[approximant]

The effects of the sounds are enhanced by the hypnotic insistent rhyme on oly, which ensures that lines die away onto an unstressed syllable. The position of still and hill at the end of lines makes us give the l sound its full value.

Example

We can discuss the effect of various sounds in the first stanza of 'Ode to Autumn' (written 1819, published 1820), by the famously musical poet John Keats (1795–1821):

Season of mists and mellow fruitfulness,
Close bosom-friend of the maturing sun;
Conspiring with him how to load and bless
With fruit the vines that round the thatch-eaves run;   4
To bend with apples the mossed cottage-trees,
And fill all fruit with ripeness to the core;
To swell the gourd, and plump the hazel shells
With a sweet kernel; to set budding more,   8
And still more, later flowers for the bees,
Until they think warm days will never cease,
For Summer has o'er-brimmed their clammy cells.

Commentary

Line 1
Season of mists and mellow fruitfulness
There are no plosives. The nasal *m*, fricatives *s* and *f* all induce a quiet, long-drawn-out sound. The line does not sound heavily-stressed: it oozes out of the mouth, which is already heavy with sounds as the trees are with fruit.

Line 2
Close bosom-friend of the maturing sun
There is a pleasing pattern as the sequence *season … mists … fruitfulness* is repeated backwards: *friend … maturing sun*.

Lines 3 and 4
Conspiring with him how to load and bless
With fruit the vines that round the thatch-eaves run

The sound suits the action described: in *load and bless*, the initial consonants bring out the full value of vowels which follow, which are lengthened by stress. This richness of sound helps us to imagine the luscious, ripe fruit. Line 4, with its sequence of affricates, runs easily and softly, like the fecund vines spreading around the house.

Line 5
To bend with apples the mossed cottage-trees
The heaviness of the trees is suggested by the voiced plosive in *bend*. Again, the vowel is lengthened by being in a stressed position. Physical heaviness is also suggested by the accumulation of stresses in *móssed cóttage-trées*. Patterns of consonance and assonance are developing across lines: *bosom ... bless ... bend, mists ... mossed.*

Lines 6 and 7
And fill all fruit with ripeness to the core;
To swell the gourd, and plump the hazel shells
The sensuous suggestions of liquid *l* are illustrated, particularly at or near the ends of words: *fill ... swell ... shells*. Keats exploits the qualities of *swell* and *plump*, with their rich vowels enclosed within soft consonants irresistibly suggestive of the fruit itself.

Lines 8–end
With a sweet kernel; to set budding more,
And still more, later flowers for the bees,
Until they think warm days will never cease,
For Summer has o'er-brimmed their clammy cells.
The *b* pattern continues in *budding ... bees ... brimmed*. As well as this alliteration, the lines are also linked by assonance in *more ... warm ... o'er*. The final lines suggest a drift of wind in the sibilances of *cease ... Summer ... cells.*

You may disagree with some of the commentary I have offered, or feel that it is reading too much in. It is certainly impossible to prove that Keats deliberately decided to use these sounds for these reasons. Presumably his creative process would have involved a mixture of conscious decision and instinct which we cannot now hope to unravel. Nevertheless, it is always the effects of literary language we discuss, not the supposed cause of this or that effect. Whether you agree with all of my readings or not, I hope that the commentary makes clear that using phonetic terms can help us to find our way into the sound world of a text, and to describe accurately what we hear there.

Vowels

Vowels, which are always voiced, are divided into **pure vowels** and **diphthongs**. Pure vowels are single sounds, which can be short or long.

Pure vowels

Short	Long
Bit	bead
Bet	bird, fern
Bat	bark, farm, calm
Bot	bore, hoard, store
But	boot
Put, soot	soon
The, pit*er* pat*er*	(cannot be lengthened)

The last, colourless sound is called **schwa**. In *If you want to be **a** writer*, here's **a** *leaflet on the matter*, every syllable in bold is schwa (in a received pronunciation (RP) accent, and in many dialect accents). This gives some idea how frequent this sound is.

Diphthongs

Diphthongs are combinations of two vowel sounds in one syllable. Say the words below slowly and you will feel your mouth changing position as you pronounce the vowel element:

bide	mate	joy	Joe
mouse	jewel	clear	rare

Vowel sounds in literature

Here are some more lines from Tennyson's 'The Lotos-Eaters'. They give a good example of how a poet can have certain sound colours dominating the aural canvas:

> The Lotos blooms below the barren peak,
> The Lotos blows by every winding creek;
> All day the wind breathes low with mellower tone;
> Through every hollow cave and alley lone
> Round and round the spicy downs the yellow Lotos-dust is blown. (145–9)

These lines are dominated by a few long vowels and diphthongs. From these, various patterns emerge:

- Half-rhyme (*blooms / below / blow, hollow / yellow*)
- Internal rhyme (*mellower / yellow*)
- Alliteration (especially of plosive *b*, softened by a succeeding liquid or approximant in *bl* and *br* clusters, and by liquid *l* in various positions)

In practice, it is not easy and perhaps not even worthwhile to distinguish one device from another: alliteration, assonance and consonance all interweave. The sound effects work together with rhythm. In the lines above we find metrical variation (the double stress on *Áll dáy*) and changing line length: the final line slows everything down to a standstill. We do not need to try to assign a 'meaning' to each of these effects. Together they make up a sumptuous composition of sound, something like a chant or a drone, which conveys the languid, easy life of the Lotos-eaters and the timeless atmosphere of the island. The sonorous vocal music saps the energy of the lines until they resemble the drawn-out sound of a yawn.

Often it is the balance or contrast between long and short vowel sounds which creates an effect. The following is a complete poem by Edward Thomas (1878–1917):

> In Memoriam [Easter 1915]
> The flowers left thick at nightfall in the wood
> This Eastertide call into mind the men,
> Now far from home, who, with their sweethearts, should
> Have gathered them and will do never again.

The single sentence is beautifully modulated in pitch and rhythm over its four lines. The rhythm and sounds follow the contours of the thought which is being expressed. First, there is the image of flowers, assisted by the rustling sounds and clustered stresses of *flowers left thick*. The first two lines are slow and uninterrupted, suiting the haunting picture of flowers in the wood at night. Then, in the third line, the regular tread is disrupted by the punctuation and the complicated syntax. A strong caesura lends weight to the idea of *far from home*. The last line is distinctly quicker. It moves decisively to its concluding devastating statement, and this is somehow made more final by the short, abrupt vowels. In context, the *g* plosive of the last line represents a subdued, violent intrusion into pastoral calm.

Intonation

When we speak, we not only produce vowels and consonants and stress particular syllables. We also introduce changes in volume and pitch to convey more fully our meaning and feeling. In every language, certain patterns become habitual. In English, there are often marked contours of rising and falling:

Rising
Is there someone at the door? I don't know (focus on *know*). *Would you mind checking? Are you listening? This is amazing!*

Falling
That's the end of the matter. What a pity!

Of course, these sentences could be said in different ways depending on the context. Longer sentences will contain rising and falling phrases, build up to a climax or die away. They may sound conclusive, or hesitant and incomplete. The term for this phenomenon of rising and falling is *intonation*.

Intonation enables us to add another dimension of meaning when we speak: beyond the meaning of the words (lexical meaning), there is a meaning conveyed purely by the shape of pitch (sentence meaning), which depends on the context of the situation. For example, with the simple sentence *Will you shut the door, please* we could convey meanings like *I am angry* or *I'm impatient with you, I'm in charge* or *I'm a polite person* through the pitch and volume we give to the words.

An interesting example of how the voice can add meaning through shifts in pitch, volume and tone is given by Roman Jakobson. Jakobson once met an actor from the company of the famous Russian director Stanislavsky. At his audition Stanislavsky had asked the actor to take the Russian phrase for 'this evening' and say it in no fewer than forty different ways, each time conveying a different meaning. Jakobson asked the actor to repeat the experiment. This time he delivered the phrase fifty times and his performance was recorded. He kept a note of the precise meaning he had in mind with each delivery of the phrase. Simply by listening to his voice, without even the help of facial expression and gesture, Russian speakers listening to the recording were able to guess the meaning in almost every case.

Performances, broadcasts and recordings of both dramatic and non-dramatic texts give us an opportunity to consider how intonation adds to the total meaning of a statement. When we listen to recordings of, for example, Shakespeare, made decades apart, we can also hear changes in style and accent taking place over the twentieth century. Older performances often involve a declamatory style which sounds over-the-top to us, while more recent ones come closer to natural conversational rhythms – at the risk of disguising the metre. Even in this more naturalistic mode, however, intonation is often heightened and emphasised to a degree we rarely experience in real life. Turn on Radio 4, and you can tell within a few seconds whether the broadcast is drama or a real-life discussion, simply by the intonation of the speakers.

The intonations of English at the time most of our literature was written are lost to us. We can only guess at the melodic patterns spoken by Chaucer, Shakespeare or Milton. To some extent they can be guessed from verse, in which pauses and distribution of sounds seem to make some patterns more plausible than others, and of course the basic sense of what is being said will determine many of the basic curves of expression. Within these, though, one can always discover possibilities of meaning by experimenting with different ways of stressing and intoning the texts of the past.

Body language

Body language is not, of course, a feature of sound, but in everyday use of language the two are often inseparable. Speech in real life is a performance: besides the words themselves, it involves features such as noises and gestures, facial expressions and body movements. In the appreciation of theatrical and film performances, it is important to pay as much attention to expressions and movements as it is to the words: the 'meaning' of a speech by Shakespeare lies as much in the physical performance of the actor before us as it does in the words on the page. Even in non-dramatic literature, it can be helpful to imagine the speaker or narrator before us, gesturing, smiling, frowning, winking. A famous picture shows Chaucer reading to a court audience; we know that Jane Austen read her novels to her sister Cassandra amid fits of laughter; and Dickens performed passages from his works at one-man shows. Many writers must have written with the spoken voice in mind, just as contemporary writers may be influenced by thoughts of film.

These performances, which gave extra life to texts, can now only be reconstructed in the imagination of the reader: doubtless they contained elements of mimicry which we would be unlikely even to guess at today. Traditions of live storytelling, of acting, preaching and pleading in court, have all fed into the literary tradition. By imagining, or even better enacting, such recitations, we can enter more fully into the experience which literature offers, and become aware of how the meaning of a text, and the relation between writer and reader, spread well beyond the words on the page.

Today, we can communicate frequently without seeing each other (mobile phones) and without either seeing or hearing (text messaging, e-mail). All this runs the risk of unwittingly giving offence because we are unable to add the extra dimension which comes from vocal tone, face and the body, or even from the human touch of handwriting. An increase in voiceless and bodiless communication is presumably having an effect not just on the language, but on the ways in which we relate to each other more generally.

Phonetics – Exercise

Describe as exactly as you can the sounds of the following poem. Concentrate on sounds which seem to be used to poetic effect, and say how sound contributes to meaning and expression.

> Silent Noon
> Your hands lie open in the long fresh grass –
>   The finger-points look through like rosy blooms;
>   Your eyes smile peace. The pasture gleams and glooms
> 'Neath billowing skies that scatter and amass.   4
> All round our nest, far as the eye can pass,
>   Are golden kingcup-fields with silver edge
>   Where the cow-parsley skirts the hawthorn hedge.
> 'Tis visible silence, still as the hourglass.   8
>
> Deep in the sun-searched growths the dragonfly
> Hangs like a blue thread loosened from the sky –
>   So this winged hour is dropped to us from above.
> Oh! clasp we to our hearts, for deathless dower,   12
> This close-companioned inarticulate hour
>   When twofold silence was the song of love.
> (Dante Gabriel Rossetti (1828–82), from *The House of Life* (1870))

2.4 Variation in sound

Variation exists in time and space. **Historical phonology** studies the changes in pronunciation over time, while dialect studies describe differences within a speech community at any one time. Neither of these fields is strictly literary, but they can teach the critic useful things – about the language as it existed for writers of the past, and about the speech patterns being represented on the page.

Historical phonology

As readers of literature, we see evidence of sound change most clearly in rhyme words which no longer rhyme: *prove / love, past / waste, there / deer*, for example. These are sometimes called eye- or printer-rhymes, that is words which only look as though they rhyme, and which writers had poetic licence to present as rhymes. But the examples above would all have been full rhymes at the time of Shakespeare.

How can we know how people of previous ages spoke? There are various kinds of evidence: alterations in spelling which indicate changes in sound; texts written by semi-educated writers who spelled words more as they sounded; metre and rhyme; the comments by grammarians who tried to represent in writing the sounds they heard. None of these sources of evidence is without its problems but, by drawing on all of them, scholars have been able to take us beyond mere guesswork in reconstructing how English used to sound.

The subject of historical phonology is a very technical one, conventionally presented in the language and symbols of phonetics. As a linguistic science, it is central to the study of the history of the English language, but it is of less obvious benefit to the student of literature. Nevertheless, some familiarity with the outlines of the subject can be useful for the following reasons:

- It allows us to form an idea of the general texture of sound in writings from the past, and so 'hear' it better. This can help us to appreciate the artistry of writers and avoid the mistake of thinking that where problems arise there must be something wrong with the writing. Dryden, for example, thought that Chaucer was 'a rough diamond, and must first be polished ere he shines,' because to him Chaucer's metre sounded faulty. Now that we know more about the sounds of Chaucer's English, we can see how Chaucer was in reality much more regular metrically than Dryden thought.
- We live in an age where, in linguistic matters as in others, standardisation and central intervention are common. The regularising of pronunciation started in the later eighteenth century. We are now used to hearing one accent as 'correct', and others as corrupt or uneducated or even comic. These concepts mislead us if we apply them to writings before such standardisation occurred. In Shakespeare's time, for example, there were often different pronunciations available, which did not carry the same associations that they have for us. Learning to 'hear' literature in a non-RP (received pronunciation) sound is a lesson in not making literature fit into modern values and assumptions.
- We can avoid basing critical interpretations on such things as exact vowel sounds when we know that vowels have altered a great deal over the centuries.

- It is essential to know something about changes in sound if we are to understand the spelling of English. This in turn can help us to identify when a writer may be using a particular spelling to create meaning.
- Sometimes, the meaning of a word or phrase becomes much clearer when we know how it might have sounded. This is particularly the case with puns.

In a few pages, it is not possible to attempt any systematic account of the historical phonology of English. We shall instead attempt only a few 'snapshots' from medieval and Renaissance texts, and consider some issues concerning their pronunciation.

Reading medieval poetry aloud

The best way to appreciate the sounds of Old and Middle English is to listen to the audio recordings which are available. Ideally, listen to more than one version, to discover some of the differences of opinion among scholars and the varied effects which are created by different voices. Details are given at the end of the chapter.

An important point to bear in mind when reading medieval poets aloud is to pronounce the words as they are written, not as they sound today. Medieval scribes after the Old English period did not have a regular spelling system, and tended to write words more as they sounded in their own dialect. English spelling has never corresponded exactly to its sound system, but in pre-Renaissance texts sound and spelling were generally closer than they are today.

English spelling began to be standardised in the fifteenth century, in particular as a result of the introduction of printing: Caxton started publishing books in Westminster in 1477. This standardisation did not, though, necessarily mean spelling words as people spoke them at that time. Printers tended to copy the spellings of manuscripts, even though the actual sounds of English had moved on since the time these manuscripts were written. The result is that even early printed books do not spell English as it sounded then, and subsequent changes have made the shape of the written word even more distant from the sound of the spoken one. English spelling preserves, like a fossil, pronunciations which have long since vanished: we still write *knight* many centuries after the *k* and *gh* sounds vanished in speech.

To illustrate some of the most significant changes, here is the opening to Chaucer's *Canterbury Tales* (c.1387):

> *The General Prologue to The Canterbury Tales*
> Whan that Aprill with his shoures soote
> The droghte of March hath perced to the roote
> And bathed every veyne in swich licour
> Of which vertu engendred is the flour;
> Whan Zephirus eek with his sweete breeth   5
> Inspired hath in every holt and heeth
> The tendre croppes, and the yonge sonne
> Hath in the Ram his half cours yronne,
> And smale foweles maken melodye,

That slepen al the nyght with open ye   10
(So Priketh hem Nature in hir corages),
Thanne longen folk to goon on pilgrimages,
And palmeres for to seken straunge strondes,
To ferne halwes, kowthe in sondry londes;
And specially from every shires ende   15
Of Engelond to Caunterbury they wende,
The hooly blisful martir for to seke,
That hem hath holpen whan that they were seke.

The sounds of Chaucer's English have undergone change in stress pattern, in the division into syllables and in the qualities of both consonants and vowels.

Stress

Chaucer's metre sounds smoother when we bear in mind that several of the words here have changed their stressed syllable. In English, the tendency is to stress the first syllable of a word, unless it is a **prefix** (*entrápment, bedázzled*). Thus we have normal English stress in *To férne hálwes, kówthe in sóndry lóndes*. In French, the tendency is for the accent to come at the end of the word. This is where it falls here in French-derived words, which have since been changed to the English pattern: *licóur, vertú, melodýe, Natúre, coráges*. This does not mean that these words 'sounded French' to Chaucer's audience: by that time they may have been assimilated into normal vocabulary and have lost any foreign shades.

Sometimes in Chaucer the stress is inconsistent: this could indicate a flexibility over such matters in verse. It also suggests that some words were in a state of transition as the stressed syllable moved gradually from the back to the front. An example, not from these lines, is *When that hym list, upon his creatures, / In dívers art and in divérse figures* (*Friar's Tale*, lines 1486 and 1487; note the final stress on the French-derived rhyme words).

Syllables

-ed

Some words have more syllables in Chaucer than they do today. The *-ed* ending is normally sounded as a separate syllable: hence, in reading these lines, we should say *perc-ed, bath-ed, engendr-ed, inspir-ed*. This *-ed* ending is sometimes used in Shakespeare and later poets as a licence to satisfy metre. As a consequence we tend to associate it with 'poetic' effects such as rhyme. In medieval verse, though, pronounced *-ed* is not a heightening poetic device: it is how the words normally sounded.

Final -e

The final *-e* in many words is pronounced, as a schwa, like the last syllables of *matter* or *later*. This is a remnant of Old English, when words had a series of **inflections** to denote their function. In Chaucer's time, it is thought that some speakers would still have pronounced these schwa sounds and others not. Poetry might have tended to preserve the more formal and conservative style. Thus, for the metre of line 5 to work, the last -e of *sweetė* must be sounded. In line fourteen we have *fernė*, but the -e of *kowthe* in *kówthe in sóndry* is elided, that is to say it is swallowed up by the vowel which comes next. When -ė occurs at the end of a line, it gives those lines an unstressed last syllable called a weak ending: hence we have rhymes like *sootė / rootė, sonnė / yronnė*. Observing this brings out a gentle texture in the verse: the lines 'die away' into these schwa sounds, and even strong stressed final syllables are softened by unvoiced consonants: *breeth / heeth*.

Consonants

Chaucer's consonant sounds were probably much the same as ours: the one lost sound here is represented by the *gh* in *droghte* and *nyght*: this would have been an **aspirate**, something like the slight rasp in Scottish *loch*, or the emphasised *h* in modern *hue* or *hurry*.

Since Chaucer's time, we have stopped enunciating many of the consonants which used to be pronounced. As a general rule, when reading Chaucer aloud, pronounce all the consonants. Here are some of the most important:

-r

Both Chaucer and Shakespeare would have spoken English in a **rhotic** accent. This means they pronounced *r* even in the middle of words like *hard*. That is why the *r* is there in the spelling, though exactly what the nature of the *r* sound was is harder to establish.

American English and West Country English are familiar rhotic accents today, and we might use these as models for pronouncing the sound in Chaucer. Even when we do pronounce *r* in standard UK English, we draw the tongue to the back of the mouth to say words like *right* or *correct*. Try moving the tongue forward to the palate just above the teeth and trilling it as in *tralala*: brrrrilliant! If we remember this when going back to Chaucer, we can hear the beautiful recurrence of *r* over the first two lines:

> Whan that Aprill with his shoures soote
> The droghte of March hath perced to the roote ...

-ng

It is likely that in Chaucer this represented the two sounds we get in some two-syllable words like *finger* and *England*: thus we have *yonge, longen, Engelond*.

-h

It is unclear when *h* was sounded: nobody before the eighteenth century seemed to worry much about whether it was pronounced or not. Chaucer may well have said *that hem hath holpen* without sounding any of the initial *h*s, and this would not have sounded vulgar or incorrect to anyone. When sounded *h* is optional, then of course its use can carry meaning – it becomes a matter of choice rather than a rule. It is conceivable that if the *h* was sounded in the line which describes how Zephirus *Inspired hath in every holt and heeth* then that might suggest the blowing or 'inspiration' of the wind, but this is only a cautious speculation.

Vowels

As a rule, stresses and consonants change least with time, vowels most. Consonants have been compared to the bones, and vowels to the flesh – softer, more vulnerable to change. Certainly Chaucer's vowel system would have been radically different from the English we hear today, just as many of the sounds of *Beowulf* would have sounded strange to Chaucer. A written account of his vowel system would take too long to cover here: again, listening to recordings based on the findings of scholars is the best way to familiarise oneself with his sound world. As a general principle, stay closer to the spelling and on no account give words their modern sound: so there is a full *a* as in *I am* in *What that*, a pure *o* as in *hot* in *droghte, yonge, corage* and so on. In long vowels, too, avoid modern diphthongs: *shoures* has a sound like *shoe*, not modern *showers*; **shires** rhymes with *sheer*, not modern *shire*.

The rhythms, melodies and musical values of Chaucer's verse are locked into the sound system of his time. Try saying in a modern accent *When that April with his showers sweet, The drought of March hath pierced to the root*, and it becomes clear how extensive the change has been. In modern pronunciation, there is no metre, no rhyme, the lines are of unequal length, and there is really no musical value to the lines at all. So in a general sense, we need to get to the sounds, as far as we can, to get to the poetry.

One of the pleasures of studying Chaucer's pronunciation is the recovery of lost sounds: vowels which have since been diminished to schwa sound clear and bright, the trilled *r* sounds again, we have the 'softer' falling sound of *sootè* in place of monosyllabic modern *sweet*. This does not mean his pronunciation is 'better' than ours, but it does open our ears to a wider and different range of vocal colour than we are accustomed to.

Shakespeare

While Chaucer is hard to enjoy unless we have some knowledge of his pronunciation, Shakespeare is spoken melodically and widely understood in contemporary English speech. Clearly, we do not have to study Elizabethan pronunciation in order to make sense of his writing. Nevertheless, it is worth spending some time on the topic, if only to satisfy natural curiosity and to understand the fairly frequent occurrence of rhymes which no longer rhyme. We shall start with some general reflections on speech and accent in Shakespeare's time, and then consider some more detailed points concerning individual sounds.

The sound an English speaker makes sends signals suggesting region, class and social background: these in turn may be associated in the culture with certain values and stereotypes. Today we often hear Shakespeare in received pronunciation (RP). This often sounds refined and correct, and for some it carries connotations of privilege and snobbery. When hearing, or even reading, Shakespeare, we have to choose accents, and those choices are acts of interpretation. We let these 'meanings', which are carried in sound, influence our understanding of a text: an actor with a 'posh' voice can seem appropriate for a king, while a rustic voice may have a comic value for a clown or peasant. Thus we let the codes of the modern speech community become part of our reception of the literature of distant periods.

On Shakespeare's stage, however, it is quite possible that king and clown would have sounded more similar than they do today. Accepted variety is an important feature of the spoken English of Shakespeare's time. There was really no such thing as a standard Elizabethan pronunciation. In Shakespeare's London, as in Chaucer's, people spoke a variety of provincial accents: Kentish, South Eastern and the Southern Midlands would have predominated, alongside speakers from farther afield. As well as this regional variety, English prounciation was also changing dramatically over Shakespeare's lifetime: some speakers would have sounded rather archaic, while other sounds would have been fashionable. On the stage, we may speculate that the English spoken must have avoided extremes so that everyone could understand it; within that range, however, several kinds of pronunciation were possible. Shakespeare's lines could be spoken in numerous accents, and in the course of a play an audience might have heard several.

Shakespeare therefore did not have at his disposal the idea of a correct manner of speech and marked dialectal departures from it. Occasionally speech sound seems to be important for character, as in Fluellen and other non-English speakers in *Henry V*: what is notable here is the heavily marked spelling to make sure actors exaggerate it sufficiently for the audience to see (or rather hear) the point. In *King Lear* the nobleman Kent disguises himself as a serving-man and borrows 'other accents' (4.1.1), which is generally taken in performance to imply a kind of working-class voice. However, there is no indication of this in the writing or spelling, and it may simply refer to him putting on a different voice or slipping into the language of prose rather than verse.

Still, a stage 'worker's' speech may have been available to the actor playing Kent. Class-based prejudice undoubtedly existed: the Tudor writer George Puttenham recommends speaking 'the usuall speech of the Court, and that of London and the shires lying about London within 60 miles, and not much above' (*The Art of English Poesie*, 1589). Sir Walter Raleigh's Devonshire accent identified him as outside this charmed circle. This marks the early stage of a process of standardisation that has become such a feature of modern English. But we do not know how much attention Shakespeare or his actors paid to these views, and they certainly did not speak RP. It is safe to say that in Shakespeare's plays, while the social rank of characters is obviously important, it is not usually indicated by accent.

Wordplay

Shakespeare's plays, in common with much of the writing of the time, have a relish for the shape and noise of words. Nowhere is this clearer than in the wordplay, much of which depends on **homophones** – words which sound the same – and is thus incomprehensible as soon as the sounds of the words change. Through studying sounds, we can start to enjoy the sophistication and vitality of Shakespeare's puns, and perhaps from there get a picture of some of the sound patterns that may have been going on, but which are now inaudible.

Examples

The following are some of the more notable aspects of Shakespeare's pronunciation. They include both puns and sounds where wordplay is probably not involved. Examples will be considered under separate headings, but other aspects of their sound will be discussed in passing.

Stress

RICHARD My manors, rents, *reuénues*, I forgoe (*Richard II*, 4.1.202)

The stress is on the second syllable of *reuénues*. This may be to fit the metre, though other examples suggest the stress has not yet settled at the front of the word. Note that Shakespeare's accent was still rhotic: all the four *r* in this line would have sounded, giving an alliterative thread diminished in modern English.

HENRY Disguise faire *Náture* with hard-fauour'd Rage:
Then lend the Eye a terrible *aspéct*:
Let it pry through the *pórtage* of the Head ... (*Henry V*, 3.1.8–9)

Nature, which we saw with a stress on the second syllable in Chaucer (*So Priketh hem Nature in hir corages*), now has its modern English sound, as does *portage*. There is a stress on the second syllable of *aspéct*, again perhaps for metrical purposes.

Syllables

HENRY ... Swilled with the wild and wasteful *ocean*
(*Henry V*, 3.1.14)

CRESSIDA Why tell you me of *moderation*?
(*Troilus and Cressida*, 4.5.2)

CANTERBURY Therefore doth *heaven* divide
The state of man in dívers *functions* ... (*Henry V*, 1.2.184–5)

Ocean and *functions* must have three syllables, and *moderation* five (making it a more weighty contrast to the short words preceding it). The *sh* and *ch* sounds we get in modern *function* and *Christian* were not yet the norm in Shakespeare's time. The sound of these words was thus probably something like *mo-der-a-ci-oun* and *o-see-an*. *Heaven* is shortened to one syllable. In the line from *Henry V*, as well as the *w* alliteration, there may have been a much closer similarity in the vowels of '*Swilled* with the *wild*', giving not just consonance but a fuller internal rhyme, since lost.

> HAMLET   Nor *customary* suits of solemn black
>   Nor windy *suspiration* of forced breath   (*Hamlet*, 1.2.78–9)

Customary is given its full value of four syllables, with a secondary stress on the *a*, a pronunciation that is still common in North America. This highlights its chime with *suspiration*, which also has four syllables, in contrast to the -*tion* words discussed above: as both four or five syllables, it could have sounded normal to Shakespeare's audience. The italicised words might also have been drawn together by a more marked *cus / sus* as the vowel would have had a longer *oo* sound (taken up in the lines by *suit*), and not the short sound we get in modern *custom*. Note that *forced* is one syllable; elsewhere we often find -*ed* endings treated as a full syllable, where the metre requires it.

Short vowels

Short vowels have changed in a rather haphazard way since Shakespeare's time. Though not as mutable as long vowels, they still have a tendency to move around. We might hear *Mummy* pronounced as *mommy*, *mammy* or *memmy* by different English speakers (for an example of the last, see a film like *Brief Encounter* (1945)). The following are all examples of this kind of instability in the short syllables in Shakespeare's time.

1. HAMLET   O that this too too *solid* flesh would melt   (1.2.129)

Here, *solid* hints at *sullied*. The *o* vowel of *solid* was probably somewhere between the modern sound, as in *body*, and the *u* of *put*. The *u* sound we get in *hut* did not exist, and so both *solid* and *sullied* would have been something like *soolid*. For the same reason, *solemn* in *customary suits of solemn black* was close in both sound and meaning to *sullen*, which is a variant form of the same word: when King Henry in *Richard II* talks of putting on *sullen black* (5.6.48) he refers to the same funeral garments as Hamlet. In modern English, the *o* sounds in *O*, *too* and *solid* are very distinct: closer resemblance in Shakespeare's time would have given the line a further sonority.

2. HAMLET   A little more than *kin*, and less than *kind*.   (1.2.65)

Here, *kind* may have had the sound of *keened* – that is, the *i* of *kin* but lengthened. The line also accentuates the link in meaning between the words: *kin* is a natural relation, and *kind* could describe both this relationship and the natural feeling appropriate to it. *Kind* might also be a noun here meaning family: since Hamlet is talking about his uncle's marriage with his mother, one interpretation is 'closer than a natural family relation, and so not really a family'. Several other readings are possible, but it is the foregrounded element of sound which makes us look for them. Sound and sense work together to charge the line with possibilities.

3. POLONIUS   I was killed i'th'*Capitol*. Brutus killed me.
   HAMLET   It was a brute part of him to kill so *capital* a calf there.
                                                        (*Hamlet*, 3.2.100–2)

In production, this can provide one of those awkward moments when the actors all roar with laughter and the modern audience look on, stony-faced. This is partly because we need to know that *calf* means idiot. The key words, which we pronounce with a final schwa today, would have been sounded with a vowel at the end, somewhere between modern *o* and *a*, possibly a sound like the *o* in American *hot*. The same homophony is played on in the same scene in a less obviously punning line, when Hamlet says *The Mousetrap. Marry, how? Tropically* (3.2.226). The *o / a* case has left its traces much later: the exclamation *drat* derives from *God rot*, and a barber's *strop* is the only kind of strop which never became a *strap*.

4. BOTTOM   Now die, die, die, die, die.
   DEMETRIUS   No die, but an *ace* for him; for he is but one.
   LYSANDER   Less than an *ace*, man; for he is dead; he is nothing.
   THESEUS   With the help of a surgeon he might yet recover and prove
               an *ass*.   (*A Midsummer Night's Dream*, 5.1.301–6)

Ass sounded as it does today with a short vowel, while the *a* of *ace* was on the move from the same short sound to the diphthong we use now.

Long vowels

Over the fifteenth and sixteenth centuries, a process known as the **great vowel shift** radically altered the long vowel sounds of many English words. Since by then the spelling had already become more or less fixed, the result was that spelling became a less and less reliable guide to pronunciation. Long vowels continue to be unstable: as with *Mummy* above, we can experiment with the number of ways English speakers might pronounce *I'll see you*. The great vowel shift leaves its mark in Shakespearean puns like the following:

1. POINS   Come, your *reason*, Jack, your reason.
   SIR JOHN   ... Give you a reason on compulsion? If reasons were as
              plentiful as blackberries, I would give no man a reason upon
              compulsion, I.   (*Henry IV*, 1, 2.5.239–44)

This is rather meaningless unless we recognise that *reason* sounded like *raisin* – hence their comparison to blackberries. The same two sounds seem to me to form a wordplay in these lines:

2. POLONIUS   My lord, I will take my *leave* of you.
   HAMLET   You cannot, sir, take from me anything that I will more
              willingly part withal – except my *life*, my life, my life.
                                                     (*Hamlet*, 2.2.215–19)

Just as *reason* could rhyme with *raisin*, so both *leave* and *life* could have had a similar sound, like the diphthong in *pain*. The repeated *life* is usually played as a moment of introspective glumness, which certainly makes sense. But is it possible that Hamlet is also mimicking something in the older man's pronunciation?

3. CASSIUS Now is it *Rome* indeed, and *room* enough
       When there is in it but one only man.
                 (*Julius Caesar*, 1.2.157–8)

The two italicised words probably sounded identical: there is a *Rome* / *doom* rhyme in *The Rape of Lucrece* (lines 1849–51). The movement of *o* sounds since Shakespeare's day is clear from the sonnets where we find rhymes such as *loan* / *one* (Sonnet 6), *noon* / *son* (7) and *love* / *prove* (10). The *oo* rhymes, as in *brood* / *blood* (19), might have rhymed on the long sound of modern *mood* or the short one of *good*. To return to the example, the words making the phrase *one only* might have sounded like *awn awnly*, giving a repetition which would lend itself to an embitterred, sarcastic delivery.

These are only some of the sound changes going on in Shakespeare's plays. For some reason, while there has been a vigorous movement in authentic music, combining scholarship and performance, there has been no comparable attempt to reconstruct, perform and record what Elizabethan English might have sounded like. Yet the consideration of older sounds makes us realise that there are possible meanings which depend on earlier sounds and become lost in modern pronunciation.

Changes since Shakespeare

Sound change in English slowed down after Shakespeare's time, but it has never stopped. For Pope, in the eighteenth century, the following were full rhymes:

> Some thought it mounted to the Lunar sphere,
> Since all things lost on earth are treasur'd there.
> There Hero's wits are kept in pond'rous vases,
> And Beau's in snuff-boxes and tweezer-cases.
>   (*The Rape of the Lock* (1714), lines 113–16)

In both cases, the rhyme would have been on the sound of the second of the pair, pronounced as today. Elsewhere, Pope rhymes *join* / *line* and *besieged* / *obliged* (pronounced *obleeged*), while the early eighteenth-century writer Gay, among others, rhymes *traitors* with *creatures* (pronounced *craters*).

Occasionally, the choice of sound itself carries a meaning. An example is the battle between the open *ay* sound of *play* and the *ee* sound of *sea*. Shakespeare, or his collaborator Fletcher, uses these as a 'fashionable' rhyme, where the *ay* sound dominates:

> Everything that heard him play,
> Even the billows of the sea.
>   (*Henry VIII*, 3.1.9–10)

The fashionable *ay* sound was the one favoured by Swift (1667–1745), who was much concerned with preserving the 'polite' forms of English. For him, the *ee* sound would have been vulgar, and he is thus making a point in a rhyme like this one:

> But Man we find the only creature
> Who, led by Folly, fights with Nature.
> (*On Poetry: A Rhapsody*, lines 19 and 20).

When Gay in *The Beggar's Opera* (1728) rhymes *appear* with *care* he is also preserving the *ay* sound of the *ea* spelling against the *ee* sound, which of course eventually won. The older sound is preserved in names like *Yeats* and some words like *great*, which for some reason did not go the same way as *meat*.

Dialect

Another kind of variation in the sound of language is dialect. Sometimes we find writers trying to represent a dialect sound in spelling: Dickens's uneducated London characters speak a form of Cockney evidently different from the modern version, though presumably similar to how Keats would have spoken. D.H. Lawrence has some heavy Nottinghamshire dialect speech in *Sons and Lovers* and other writings. At times, too, we hear the accent of writers themselves, as in Wordsworth's rhyme of *water* and *matter*, reminding us that he would have read his poetry in a broad Cumbrian accent. Today, there is a vibrant English literature from former colonies of the British Empire, and works written by authors in Britain with marked accents. Those who have heard Seamus Heaney and other Irish poets read in their own voice, or Derek Walcott read in the intonations of Caribbean English, often feel they have understood the works better.

Exercise

Look again at the Spenser sonnet in the Exercise at the end of section 2.2 (page 25). Which sounds are likely to have been different in Spenser's time? What further patterns and possible wordplay may be brought out by earlier pronunciation?

Commentaries

Commentary I

The first passage we shall look at closely is from the thirteenth century. It is a passage from *Ancrene Wisse* – Anchorites' Guidance, a book of instruction for female hermits. The language is very difficult, and it is worth reading the translation a few times first before tackling the original. In one way, this difficulty can be an advantage, as it makes us read slowly and pay attention to details; with more modern texts, we have to combat a tendency to read fast and assume we understand things. Some brief notes on the background of the text precede a discussion of its sounds. (þ and ð = *th* sound.)

Ancrene Wisse (c.1225)

Al þet ich habbe iseid of flesches pinsunge nis nawt for ow, mine leoue sustren, þe oðerhwile þolieð mare þen ich walde, ah is for sum þet schal rede þis inohreaðe, þe grapeð hire to softe. Noðeles, yunge impen me bigurd wið þornes leste beastes freoten ham hwil ha beoð mearewe. Ye beoð yunge
5   impen iset i Godes orchard. Þornes beoð þe heardschipes þet ich habbe ispeken of, & ow is neoð þet ye beon biset wið hem abuten, þet te beast of helle, hwen he snakereð toward ow forte biten on ow, hurte him o þe scharpschipe & schunche ayeinwardes. Wið alle þeose heardschipes beoð gleade & wel ipaiet yef lutel word is of ow, yef ye beoð unwurðe, for þorn is
10   scharp & unwurð. Wið þeose twa beoð bigurde. Ye ne ahen nawt to unnen þet uuel word beo of ow. Scandle is heaued sunne, þet is, þing swa iseid oðer idon þet me mei rihtliche turnen hit to uuele & sunnegin þrefter þer þurh wið misþoht, wið uuel word on hire, on oþre, & sungin ec wið dede. Ah ye ahen unnen þet na word ne beo of ow ne mare þen of deade, & beon
15   bliðe iheortet yef ye þolieð danger of Sluri, þe cokes cneaue, þe wescheð and wipeð disches i cuchene. Þenne beo ye dunes ihehet toward heouene. For lo, he spekeð þe leafdi i þet swete luue boc: *Venit dilectus meus saliens in montibus, transiliens colles*: mi leof kimeð leapinde, ha seið, o þe dunes, þet is, totret ham, tofuleð ham, þoleð þet me totreode ham, tuki ham al to
20   wundre, schaweð in ham his ahne troden, þet me trudde him in ham ifinden hu he was totreden, as his trode schaweð.

(From Part Six, Penance)

Translation

All that I have said about mortification of the flesh is not intended for you, my dear sisters, who sometimes suffer more than I would have you, but for some who are quite likely to read this and who treat themselves too gently. Nonetheless, young trees are encircled about with thorns for fear animals
5   will feed on them while they are tender. You are young trees planted in God's orchard. The hardships which I have spoken of are the thorns, and it is necessary for you to be encircled with them, so that the beast of hell, when he sneaks towards you, intending to bite you, may be hurt by their sharpness and turn back frightened by all those hardships. Be glad and be
10   well content if there is not much talk about you, and if you are of little account, for a thorn is sharp and unnoticeable. Be encircled, then, by these two things. You ought not, however, to allow any evil reports about yourselves. Giving scandal is a mortal sin, that is, saying or doing something in such a way that a bad interpretation may easily be put upon it, resulting
15   in sins of evil thought or evil speech on the part of those who misinterpret, and on the part of others, and sins also of deed. You should be content that there be no talk of you at all, any more than there is of the dead, and if you

incur disdain from Slurry, the cook's boy, who washes and dries the dishes
in the kitchen, you should be happy in your hearts. Then you will be
20   mountains lifted up towards heaven, for see what is said by the lady in the
sweet Book of Love, *My beloved cometh, leaping upon the mountains,
skipping over the hills.* 'My love comes leaping,' she says, 'upon the mountains, that is he treads them underfoot, making them vile, allows them to be
trodden on, to be outrageously chastised, and shows on them his own
25   footmarks, so that by them people might follow him, and discover how he
was trodden upon, as his traces show.'

      (Trans. M.B. Salu, *Ancrene Riwle* (Exeter: Exeter University Press, 1990))

Background

The *Ancrene Wisse* (also referred to as *Ancrene Riwle*) is a manual written for the
spiritual guidance of English female recluses. We do not know the identity of
either the author or its audience, but it seems to be the work of a cleric, aimed at
women who were well educated and respectable, and who had decided to enter
a life of solitude and penance. The original version of the work is lost, but it
survives in French, Latin and English manuscripts.

Sound

Ancrene Wisse is written in the West Midland dialect of the earlier thirteenth
century (c.1200–40). Later West Midlands writers include Langland and the
Gawain poet. Medieval English from this region is harder for us to understand
than Chaucer's English, since Chaucer's regional dialect, based on the East
Midlands, was the basis for later standard English.

    The nature of the exact sounds of the dialect of *Ancrene Wisse* does not have a
direct bearing on the literary qualities of the piece. It is helpful, however, to
remember that no standard accent existed at this time: everything from popular
songs to the highest flights of theology was spoken in a regional accent, since
there was simply no other way to speak. Scribes customarily 'translated' texts
into their own dialect when copying: there seems to have been no sense that the
particular sounds and spellings of an English text were important enough to be
worth preserving.

    Other aspects of the sound of the text, such as the precise intonation and
stress pattern, are largely a matter for guesswork. We can be sure, though, that it
is written with the speaking voice in mind. We could regard this passage as the
script for a performance in which the rhythms and climaxes of the writing come
alive and dramatise the points being delivered. The rhetorical term for this style
of writing is *sermo*, or speech. The words are intended to reach the mind and
memory through the ear. Not all medieval writings are based on *sermo*: a
different sort of text would be, for example, a logical treatise, which would
appeal directly to the mind. But *Ancrene Wisse*, though it contains argument, is
not simply a work of logic. It is full of emotional appeal, of vivid dramatic images
and suspense. For prose of any period, educated conversation represents a
model, and we can hear elements of conversation in this section in the direct
addresses to the audience – *mine leoue sustren* – and in the call for attention –
For lo.

While we can only partially and approximately reconstruct the rhythms of the writing, we can nevertheless detect some dominant patterns. One is the trochaic scheme (*Háve you réad the pápers látely?*) used in several cadences. A modern equivalent to the pattern we find is *in the early evening* or – with an unstressed syllable at the start – *as if I haven't told you*. If we pronounce most of the final *es* (and admittedly it is hard to know whether original readers would have done this) this is what we hear in several phrases: *míne léoue sústren* / *máre þén ich wálde* / *réde þís inóhreaðe* / *grápeð híre to softe* / *isét i Gódes órchard* / *bisét wið hém abúten*. There certainly seems to be some correspondence between the sound of these phrases, binding the statements together and bringing some clauses to a graceful close. Sometimes the rhythm is so insistent that it brings the prose close to the metrical regularity of verse:

Wið alle þeose heardschipes / beoð gleade & wel ipaiet / yef lutel word is of ow, / yef ye beoð unwurðe, / for þorn is scharp & unwurð.

These repeated patterns give the passage a musical cohesion, and create a feeling of unity even when there is a transition to a new subject. Thus the music continues in the same rhythm, as it were, even when there is a striking alteration of image, rather like a change of key. For example, the repeated little rhythmic pattern in *wescheð and wipeð* / *disches i cuchene* (washeth and wipeth / dishes in kitchen) seems to be echoed in the phrase ending the next sentence: *ihehet toward heouene* (lifted up towards heaven), even though we have moved from the domestic to the heavenly.

Rhythm is not the only kind of repetition. We also find it on the level of individual sounds:

Þornes **b**eoð þe heardschipes þet ich ha**bb**e ispeken of, & ow is neoð þet ye **b**eon **b**iset wið hem a**b**uten, þet te **b**east of helle, hwen he snakereð toward ow forte **b**iten on ow, hurte him o þe **sch**arpschipe & **sch**unche ayeinwardes.

We might read these from the point of view of an actor, looking for something which will give an opportunity to perform. Here the voiced plosive **b** sounds surrounding the beast of hell invite a suitably violent pronunciation; and we can hear the serpent hissing and retreating in the vivid *scharpschipe & schunche*. Elsewhere in the passage, the alliteration has the tang of colloquial language: *cokes cneaue, wescheð and wipeð*.

It is clear that the writer is highly attentive to the sounds of the words from the instance of subtle wordplay which occurs in these lines:

       ... wið uuel **word** on hire, on oþre, & sungin ec wið **dede**
       ... na **word** ne beo of ow ne mare þen of **deade**

The *word* ... *dede* pairing is repeated, with the second word varied on repetition. *Deade* picks up *dede*, giving us a striking similarity of sound while conveying a very different meaning. It also initiates an alliteration on the **d** sound which threads through the following constructions: *deade ... danger ... disches ... dunes ... dilectus*. Together with the other features mentioned, it makes us aware of the writing as a carefully elaborated composition for the voice.

Commentary 2

The second text we shall look at here is from many centuries later. Though the language is very different from *Ancrene Wisse*, and the text is in verse rather than prose, there are some similarities: again, we are led along by a civilised conversational voice, which gives a 'natural' feel to a highly finished and meticulous composition; and patterns of sound in both cases help to make vivid images memorable.

Oliver Goldsmith, *The Deserted Village* (1770)

SWEET AUBURN, loveliest village of the plain,
Where health and plenty cheared the labouring swain,
Where smiling spring its earliest visit paid,
And parting summer's lingering blooms delayed,
5   Dear lovely bowers of innocence and ease,
Seats of my youth, when every sport could please,
How often have I loitered o'er thy green,
Where humble happiness endeared each scene;
How often have I paused on every charm,
10   The sheltered cot, the cultivated farm,
The never failing brook, the busy mill,
The decent church that topped the neighbouring hill,
The hawthorn bush, with seats beneath the shade,
For talking age and whispering lovers made.
15   How often have I blest the coming day,
When toil remitting lent its turn to play,
And all the village train from labour free
Led up their sports beneath the spreading tree,
While many a pastime circled in the shade,
20   The young contending as the old surveyed;
And many a gambol frolicked o'er the ground,
And slights of art and feats of strength went round.
And still as each repeated pleasure tired,
Succeeding sports the mirthful band inspired;
25   The dancing pair that simply sought renown
By holding out to tire each other down,
The swain mistrustless of his smutted face,
While secret laughter tittered round the place,
The bashful virgin's side-long looks of love,
30   The matron's glance that would those looks reprove.
These were thy charms, sweet village; sports like these,
With sweet succession, taught even toil to please;
These round thy bowers their chearful influence shed,
These were thy charms – But all these charms are fled.

Most lines keep to a regular iambic pentameter (x/ x/ x/ x/ x/). This metrical regularity is marked by the high degree of end-stopping – punctuation enforcing a heavy pause at the end of lines. In fact there are only two points (lines 17 and 25) where the syntax creates an enjambment, and even there a pause makes sense. One effect of all this is to make us aware of each line as a metrical unit. We get a sense of discipline, order and conformity, and we associate these qualities with the speaker, who comes over as being in control of his thoughts, even when in a state of emotion. The handling of the couplet rhyme scheme, which we shall consider further below, adds an effect of balance and symmetry. The regular sound patterns of metre and rhyme help to create a measured, reasonable voice, one whose sentiments we are likely to trust.

Because of this emphasis on measure and balance, metrical disruption is rare, and where it does occur it indicates an unusually strong feeling. The opening words, *Swéet Aúburn*, may be read as a double stress, as may the succeeding *Déar lóvely*: this extra weight is suitable for the commencement of an address. The inversion of *Séats of my yóuth* adds a further variation to the pattern. In each case, the metrical irregularity emphasises the speaker's strong feeling. The repeated phrase *How often* seems to demand at least some positive stress on the first syllable, marking out this recurring pattern. In the final lines, the passage build up to a climax, and here metre contributes to the syntax in the emphatic *These* at line-openings. This prevents the iambic rhythm from progressing: in effect, the repeated inversions combined with end-stopping act as a brake. The dramatic final half-line clause then sounds with a satisfying cadence.

Disruption of the metrical scheme is only one kind of deviation from the basic pattern. In Goldsmith's handling of metre, effective variation often occurs at a more subtle level. One such effect is the varying position of the caesura. The first half of the line will often be the first two feet, making four syllables: *Dear lovely bowers, The sheltered cot, The decent church, For talking age* are a few examples. This gives us, in terms of syllables, a 4 / 6 line as a standard, usually corresponding to two and then three beats. Departures from this are then foregrounded:

> The never failing brook, the busy mill (6 / 4)
> How often have I paused ...
> How often have I blessed ...

> And many a gambol frolicked o'er the ground
> With sweet succession, taught even toil to please (5 / 5)

A notable variation occurs in line 4, *And parting summer's lingering blooms delayed*. We may read this without a caesura at all, or perhaps place a slight pause before the verb *delayed*, giving a line which divides into eight and then two syllables. However we read it, the line, with its long vowel sounds, seems to evoke the drawn-out summer it describes.

The couplet rhyme, accompanied by the high degree of end-stopping, causes the rhyme words to be given full stress. The impression of finality at each line-ending is further strengthened by the fact that only strong endings are used: there are no weak extra-metrical syllables to cause a 'tailing off', and there is a kind of robustness about the consequent effect. Couplet rhyme allows the poet to find many different rhyme sounds, but it is notable here how many are repeated. We can see this in the first 8 lines: first the diphthong of *plain* is continued over two couplets (*swain ... paid ... delayed*), and then the long vowel sound in *ease* is repeated over four lines in the same way. We should bear in mind that Goldsmith himself spoke with an Irish accent, and that these inherently unstable long vowel sounds would have sounded differently even among English speakers. Quite possibly in the accents of the time the *ai* and *ee* sounds would have been very similar. Whatever their exact values, though, these vowels do seem to repeat themselves frequently. They form a kind of echo working across the couplets and drawing ideas together. Other rhyme sounds are similarly long vowels, with the exception of *hill / mill*. When the final *fled* appears, the dramatic meaning of the word is emphasised by its sound – a sudden short vowel coming after a sequence of long sounds. In the rhymes we can hear the sense of lingering nostalgia switching into present despair.

Other patternings of sound occur throughout the lines. From the beginning we can find alliteration and half-rhyme forming a cohesion across phrases, as in *plain ... **pl**enty*. The device is used to link separate elements in a list: ***c**ot, **c**ultivated, **br**ook, **b**usy*. Alliterated phrases such as *smiling spring* and *humble happiness* mark these little moments of personification, perhaps making them seem more like artificial idealisations than moments of real observation. Elsewhere we can find alliteration and assonance forming more elaborate patterns, as in the play of *p* and *s* sounds in *spring paid ... parting summer* and the repetition of *l, b, bl* and *oo* over a number of lines in *labouring ... lingering blooms ... lovely bowers ... failing brooks ... busy mills ... blest*. In such phrases we hear the liquid *l* creating a sensual, soft effect: the village sounds, as well as looks, peaceful and gentle. Occasionally a sound effect is foregrounded as in the *sw / sm, s* sounds of *the swain mistrustless of his smutted face*, but for the most part sound patterning is restrained and creates rather the sense of an elegant verbal texture: the effect is one of refinement rather than drama. Again, the patterning is in tune with the measured voice which is speaking to us. Throughout, there is a plenitude of sound, exploiting the sonority of vowels. Beautiful lines like *And parting summer's lingering blooms delayed*, or *The dancing pair that simply sought renown* take us through a melodic sequence of vowels: this aural richness suits the speaking voice, and conveys a sensual pleasure accompanying the passage of rational thought.

Suggestions for Further Reading

Metre and rhythm

Many books cover verse metre. The following are clear and useful:

James Fenton, *An Introduction to English Poetry* (London: Viking, 2002).
Philip Davies Roberts, *How Poetry Works* (London: Penguin, 1986).

For a modern linguistic approach see:

Derek Attridge, *The Rhythms of English Poetry*, The English Language Series, 14 (London: Longman, 1982).

There are far fewer studies of prose rhythm than verse rhythm, and the important studies can probably only be found in a good university library. The following are all informative and stimulating:

M.W. Croll, *Style, Rhetoric, and Rhythm*, ed. J. Max Patrick and others (Princeton, New Jersey: Princeton University Press, 1966).

Ian Robinson, *The Establishment of Modern English Prose in the Reformation and the Enlightenment* (Cambridge: CUP, 1998). Considers rhythm alongside syntax and punctuation. An account of the arrival of the modern grammatical sentence.

N.R. Tempest, *The Rhythm of English Prose* (Cambridge: CUP, 1930).

Repeated sounds

John Lennard, *The Poetry Handbook* (Oxford: OUP, 1996) has an excellent chapter on rhyme and suggestions for more specialised reading.

Seamus Heaney's essays in *Finders Keepers: Selected Prose, 1971–2001* (London: Faber, 2002) contain much stimulating discussion of sound effects in verse.

Peter Sansom, *Writing Poems*, Bloodaxe Poetry Handbooks, 2 (Newcastle upon Tyne: Bloodaxe Books, 1994) is a poet's guide to metre and rhyme as well as other aspects of the craft.

Phonetics

Ronald Carter and others, *Working with Texts: A core book for language analysis*, Intertext (London: Routledge, 1997). Useful chapter on phonetics and its application to literary analysis. Several other aspects of the linguistic analysis of texts are covered in this book.

Philip Davies Roberts, *How Poetry Works* (see above) offers a useful introduction to phonetics in poetry.

For exploring the sounds of verse without getting into technicalities, the guidance of voice coaches is enormously valuable:

Cicely Berry, *Text in Action: A Definitive Guide to Exploring Text in Rehearsal for Actors and Directors* (London: Virgin Books, 2001).

Leslie O'Dell, *Shakespearean Language: A Guide for Actors and Students* (Westport: Greenwood Press, 2001).

Patsy Rodenburg, *Speaking Shakespeare* (London: Methuen, 2002).

Variation in sounds

Recordings

A first step towards exploring variation in sound, over time and space, is to listen to recordings.

Old and Middle English

Trevor Eaton has recorded *Beowulf* and numerous Middle English works on CD with Pavilion Records. Excellent readings of Old English and Middle English are produced by the New Chaucer Studio (website: http://humanities.byu.edu/chaucer/about.htm).

Stephen Pollington, *Aergeweorc: Old English Verse and Prose* (Hockwold-cum-Wilton, Norfolk: Anglo-Saxon Books, 1997). Audio-cassette with booklet of texts. May be used alongside the same author's *First Steps in Old English* (Anglo-Saxon Books, 1997).

The following CDs are currently available in the Cambridge Chaucer series:

Chaucer, *The Merchant's Prologue and Tale*, ed. and read by A.C. Spearing (Cambridge: CUP, 1999).
Chaucer, *The Miller's Prologue and Tale*, ed. James Winny, read by A.C. Spearing (Cambridge: CUP, 1999).
Chaucer, *The Wife of Bath's Prologue and Tale*, ed. James Winny, read by Elizabeth Salter (Cambridge: CUP, 1999).

Later English

Of particular interest to students of literature are recordings of authors reading their own works. Two CDs published by the British Library reveal, among other things, how much pronunciation has changed since the late nineteenth century: *The Spoken Word – Writers* and *The Spoken Word – Poets* (both published in 2003).

Reading

Dennis Freeborn, *From Old English to Standard English* (Basingstoke: Palgrave Macmillan, 2nd edition, 1988). Textbook on the history of English, including changes in sound.
Manfred Görlach, *The Linguistic History of English* (Basingstoke: Palgrave Macmillan, 1997). Advanced study with a chapter on phonology and several reconstructions of earlier English in phonetic transcript.
Daniel Jones, *The Pronunciation of English* (Cambridge: CUP, 4th edition, 1956). Older study, which includes some reconstructions of earlier English in phonetic transcription.
Helge Kökeritz, *A Guide to Chaucer's Pronunciation*, Medieval Academy Reprints for Teaching, 3 (Toronto: University of Toronto Press, 1998).
Roger Lass, 'Shakespeare's Sounds' in Sylvia Adamson and others, *Reading Shakespeare's Language: A Guide* (London: The Arden Shakespeare / Thomson Learning, 2001), 256–68. This contains a helpful bibliographical essay on more specialised works.

Dialect

Norman Page, *Speech in the English Novel*, English Language Series, 8 (London: Longman, 1973). On handling of dialect and other speech forms in fiction.

It is also instructive to see and listen to productions of Shakespeare by companies such as Northern Broadsides, who present them in regional accents.

▼ 3 Grammar

Grammar deals with the form of words (**morphology**), and with the way they are joined together to make meaningful sentences (**syntax** – literally 'tied together'). In this chapter we shall be concerned with the ways in which grammatical structures can be used for literary effects, and in the changes these structures have undergone over time.

Grammar and literary criticism

We might feel disinclined to study the structures of a language we speak and write already; and we may also feel that syntax belongs to linguistic analysis rather than to literary appreciation. It is also true that grammatical changes rarely make a text incomprehensible. With a normal native command of modern English structures, we can enjoy literature written as long ago as the tales of Chaucer. It is possible to enjoy Shakespeare in the theatre, and have a good idea of what is going on, without even reading the words, let alone studying their syntactic arrangement.

Nonetheless, as students of literature we can gain a great deal from studying English grammar, and becoming aware of its history. Indeed, unless we do, many aspects of earlier texts will seem odd, or quaint. Even worse, we might see them as primitive forms which have not 'developed' into modern English. For example, we are probably used to seeing older forms such as *he saith* or *thou dost*, and no doubt we readily understand their basic sense. But these forms belong to a grammatical system of their own: we do not do justice to texts if we see them as being in an 'old-fashioned' language, or think that there is something primitive about forms like *thou dost*. In fact, as we shall see, the *thou* form has meanings built into it which are not immediately obvious to a modern reader. From Old English onwards, English grammar is a highly sophisticated instrument; a medieval text did not sound medieval to its readers, and its structures are not rough attempts at modern English.

The grammar of a text not only allows a writer to convey meaning: it plays a part in shaping that meaning and our response to it. Grammatical details, such as the choice of the pronouns *thou* or *you*, or the ordering of parts of a sentence, have important effects on the significance and expressive power of a piece of writing. If we 'more or less' follow a writer like Chaucer or Shakespeare according to modern English grammatical standards, then we will miss an important part of their meaning. Tenses in other centuries, for example, did not carry exactly the same range of meanings as they do today; and some words, like *shall* and *will*, carried ideas which they have since largely lost.

A modern reader can miss meanings, but also read them in. Things can seem like deviations to us because they deviate from our idea of a standard. When Othello describes Desdemona's *whiter skin of hers than snow*, the word order probably seems much more striking to us than it did to Shakespeare's audience. This is not to deny the beauty of the line, only to warn us not to base our interpretations on the idea that something is deviant before we have measured it against the standard of the language of the time. When *Othello* was written, there was greater freedom to use such phrases than there is today.

Writers in the past, then, could do some things which we cannot do today; and their phrasing and structuring of sentences should be interpreted against the standard of their time, not of ours. There were also things authors could *not* do. For example, the so-called **continuous** verb forms like *I am going* are rare in medieval and Renaissance English. **Simple** forms (*I go*) did then what continuous ones do today. For example, Chaucer says at the start of *The Canterbury Tales*, when he has arrived at the Tabard Inn in Southwark to embark on his pilgrimage, *at the Tabard as I lay*. We would say *as I was lying*. *I go* in Shakespeare can mean, in addition to modern *I go*, also *I am going, I do go* or *I will go*. Jesus on the cross in the King James Bible says *Father forgive them for they know not what they do*, where we would say *for they don't know what they are doing*. It is not always obvious, though, which is meant. **Passives** were also rarer in early English. Shakespeare could not write a construction like *that house is being built*, which is both continuous and passive. We can only really appreciate choices of expression when we know what the possibilities were at the time.

In this chapter, we shall look at aspects of the subject in progressively larger units: first words, then phrases, then whole sentences. Finally, we shall look at units larger than sentences, such as the rhetorical period, and at short passages of text.

3.1 Words

Inflections

Inflections are word endings which tell you what job the word is doing. With **nouns** and **adjectives**, they indicate **number** (whether it is singular or plural), **case** (for example, whether it is subject, object or possessive) and **gender** (masculine, feminine, neuter). Verb inflections can tell us about tense: *lift, lifted*. **Tense** can also be shown by the form of the word itself – *drive, drove* – and by non-inflectional means through the help of other, **auxiliary** verbs: *I have lifted*.

The greatest, and least lamented, change in English grammar has been the drastic reduction in a complex inflectional system. Old English, the term generally given to the language from the earliest written records to about 1100, is a **synthetic** language. That is to say, it uses inflections a great deal to show word function. Over the centuries, the language has become **analytic**: the logical connections between words are now mostly done by other little grammatical words, such as prepositions. This change has had important consequences for what writers can and cannot do. Here is the opening of an Old English poem which shows how the synthetic system works in practice:

Wrætlic is þes wealstan; wyrde gebræcon
Wondrous is this masonry [literally: wall-stone]; fates broke
Burgstede burston; brosnað enta geweorc.
The city smashed decays of giants the work [the work of giants decays]
Hrofas sind gehrorene, hreorge torras,
Roofs are fallen, ruinous the towers,
Hrimgeat berofen hrim on lime ...
The frosty gate ravaged frost on cement ...

(The Ruin, lines 1–4)

The italicised letters of the original are examples of inflections: several of them can have different meanings, but the context of the sentence usually makes it clear which is intended:

- The form of the **demonstrative** *þes* (line 1) indicates masculine singular, agreeing with the masculine noun *wealstan*. Today *this* covers all forms in the singular, and grammatical gender has disappeared. However, we still change it to *these* for the plural (though there is no strong reason why we should: we manage well enough with *the* for both singular and plural).
- *Wyrd-e* (line 1) tells us it is the plural *fate-s*; the *-as* in *hrofas* and *torras* (line 3) is the *-s* ending which survives today for the plural (*hreorg-e* (3) is a plural ending of an adjective in agreement).
- *ent-a* (2) is the plural **genitive** of *giant*: thus it means *giants'*.
- The ending *lim-e* (4) is for the dative, a case which has a wide range of functions. Here it shows the word is governed by a preposition, *on* (4). In a synthetic language, the lack of written inflection is also a signal: *wealstan*, *burgstede* and *geweorc* are all **nominative** singular, the basic form of the word without any added letters for the so-called 'oblique' cases. Verbs also change their form: *gebræcon* is past plural, *berofen* the past **participle** (modern equivalents are *broke*, *broken*).

Inflections and flexibility

For a language which uses inflections to indicate the functions of words, word-order is much more flexible: in the Old English, *decays of giants the work* is quite clear, since we know from inflections that *work* is the subject and that *giants* is in the genitive. Here, *of giants* must be telling us something more about the noun. This flexibility allows the poet to make effective arrangements, playing words off against each other: verbs can surround the noun they govern, as in *broke the city smashed* (lines 1 and 2). Two verbs of different colour can stand next to each other as in *smashed / decays*. There is a symmetry in *roofs are fallen, ruinous towers*.

These kinds of device are also helped by the absence of many **prepositions** and the lack of an **article**. (Strictly speaking, Old English has no **definite article** *the*; notice how *burgstede* stands alone – it could mean *a city* as well as *the city*). In the lines we have been discussing, lexical words predominate over grammatical ones, forming a dense texture: *city smashed*; *decays giants' work*. There is a compact, concrete texture to the writing, supported by the alliterative, four-beat sound framework.

Middle English

Over the tenth and eleventh centuries, the Old English inflections were largely lost. The vowels in unstressed positions like the endings of *wyrd-**e*** and *ent-**a*** were not pronounced with their full value and came to sound like schwa (matt*e*r). They were then written as they sounded: the final *-e* in Chaucer's verse, as we saw in the previous chapter, is a remnant of this eroded inflection. At the same time, prepositions were also in use in Old English. An example from *The Ruin* is the prepositional phrase *on lime*: since the preposition is doing the job of telling us what *lime* is doing in the sentence, then an inflectional ending is not essential.

Middle English literature therefore has considerably fewer inflections than Old English. A passage which illustrates this is the opening of the Middle English poem *Sir Gawain and the Green Knight* (c.1360):

Sithen the sege and the assaut watz sesed at Troye,
The borgh brittened and brent to brondez and askez,
The tulk that the trammes of tresoun ther wroght
Watz tried for his tricherie, the trewest on erthe ...

(Since the siege and the assault was ceased at Troy, / the town destroyed and burnt to brands and ashes, / the man that the schemes of treason there wrought / Was tried for his treachery, the truest on earth ...)

Loss of endings

Here we notice how the definite article has become regular. Nouns do not have separate genders so can all take *the*. Case endings are lost (*trammes* is an object but has no ending to indicate this), and *-e* endings which might look like inflections are simply French spellings (this is the case with *sege, trammes* and *tricherie*, which are all in origin French words).

Rise of prepositions

The loss of inflections certainly makes the English seem more familiar to us and thus easier. But it also has important consequences for how the language can be written. What was once done through inflections now has to be done with other instruments. The first such instrument is the preposition, heavily used here to show the relation of words to each other: ***at** Troye*, ***for** his tricherie*, ***on** erthe*. In doing this job, prepositions in older texts do not always work exactly like today. Below, we shall see examples of how prepositions can mislead us if we always interpret them in their contemporary sense.

Importance of word order

Together with prepositions, grammatical relations are expressed through word order: it is purely through word order that in Modern English we understand that *the boy loved the girl* and *the girl loved the boy* have different meanings. The order of elements in a sentence becomes more fixed: there is now only one plain way of saying 'the work of giants decays'. The kinds of symmetries and clashes which we considered in *The Ruin* are harder to achieve. There is still some remaining flexibility: we can say *we played in the park* or *in the park we played*. Choices like these are an important part of the style of English writers.

Surviving inflections

Noun inflections

Nominal inflections are the genitive and plural endings: *lady's, ladies', ladies*. These have remained constant for a long period and present no particular problems for the modern reader. There are two further forms which come up occasionally, and can seem quaint or 'wrong' unless we know they are grammatically regular. One is the survival of the 'silent' genitive *-e* ending without *'s*: an example is Chaucer's *In hope to stonden in his **lady** grace* (*General Prologue*, 88), where the meaning is 'his lady's grace'. This survives in words like *Ladychapel*, and can also occur in texts of Shakespeare's period, as when Hamlet talks of *all the region kites* (2.2.581). But this usage is comparatively rare.

The second older noun inflection is the irregular plural in *-n*, which we are used to in *children* and *oxen*. Several other words have also had this plural and since shifted to *-s*.

Verbal inflections

Verbal inflections which we find in medieval and Early Modern texts are those for the second person singular (*thou hast*) and third person singular (*he doth*): the *-st* ending accompanies the *thou* form, which will be discussed below.

Word class

Words can create effects not only through their lexical meaning, but also through their grammatical **class**, also known as **part of speech**. Words on their own do not have a grammatical class: *dog* on its own is simply a word without a function, just as a plank of wood in a shed is no more than a plank of wood. But when we use it for something, it takes on a grammatical property: *Do you like my dog? Don't dog my footsteps; These are the dog days; I'm dog tired.* Unlikely but not impossible: *this is my son, Dog.* In order, we have used the word as a concrete noun, a verb, an adjective, an adverb and finally a proper noun. These are so-called parts of speech, functions which come into being when the words form part of a speech or sentence. To press the analogy, we might use our plank of wood as a shelf, a tabletop, a deadly weapon and so on.

In reading, it is often a useful ploy to focus on one particular word class: what is the writer doing with verbs? Are there many **abstract** nouns (*art, courage*), or is the language chiefly **concrete** (*table, grease*)? Does one particular class predominate, and if so how does this affect the general texture of the passage? These questions can take us some way into a text and help us to understand the way it works on us. The following are examples of this line of critical enquiry. We shall look first at the lexical words, and then the grammatical ones.

Lexical words

Nouns

The opening of *Robinson Crusoe* (1719) has the style of a non-fictional work like a travel journal. Partly this is achieved through the heavy use of proper nouns (names of places and people), which we associate with the register of factual writing. Consequently, the effect is one of authenticity:

> I was born in the Year 1632, in the City of *York*, of a good Family, tho' not of that Country, my Father being a Foreigner of *Bremen*, who settled first at *Hull*: He got a good Estate by Merchandise, and leaving off his Trade, lived afterwards at *York*, from whence he married my Mother, whose Relations were named *Robinson*, a very good Family in that Country, and from whom I was called *Robinson Kreutznaer* ...

The sense that we are being given a lot of facts is added to by the lack of any description of internal experiences. These details would be what anyone can observe. There is also a feeling of loose arrangement in the syntax, which gives the impression that thoughts are being written down as they come, not in a planned manner. Details are added as second thoughts, attached by loose **conjunctions**: *tho' not, from whence, whose* and *from whom*. The phrase *a very good Family in that Country* has a particularly abrupt, improvised effect. This looseness may be a deliberate art on Defoe's part, or a reflection of the fact that he wrote quickly. The conversational feel certainly marries with the proper nouns dominating the lexis to make us believe we are listening to a true-life story.

Verbs

Verbs are the engines of English. The sentence has been defined as the domain of a **finite** verb (one which has tense). When well used, verbs can add precision as well as vitality to a piece of writing. Here is a passage from Marlowe's *Hero and Leander* (published 1598). It describes the arrival of the morning and the parting of the two lovers:

> Now had the Morn espied her lover's steeds,
> Whereat she starts, puts on her purple weeds,
> And, red for anger that he stayed so long,
> All headlong throws herself the clouds among.
> And now Leander, fearing to be missed,
> Embraced her suddenly, took leave, and kissed;
> Long was he taking leave, and loath to go,
> And kissed again, as lovers use to do.

Sad Hero wrung him by the hand and wept,
Saying, 'Let your vows and promises be kept.'

(571–80)

The description of the dawn gains a vividness and particularity from the choice of verbs: *espied, starts, puts on, throws*. The **personification** works through surprise: the slow and serene experience of dawn is defamiliarised and turned in our mind into a frantic, rather ungainly hurry. This makes us think of Leander suddenly realising what time it is and hurrying away. Without any comparison being explicitly made in the text, we see Leander spying the sun, throwing something on and hurrying off. The vigorous actions described in the verbs help the verse to continue its onward movement, against the brakes of couplet and syntactic endings. Verbs here also evoke feelings: Hero's grief is summed up by her actions of wringing his hand and then turning round in the door because she cannot bear to see him leaving. These dramatic, and psychologically convincing actions give an immediacy to this classical tale.

Adjectives and adverbs

These are generally termed the descriptive words. The opening stanzas of Hardy's poem *The Convergence of the Twain* (1912), on the sinking of the *Titanic*, demonstrate some of the effects of these word classes:

1

In a solitude of the sea
Deep from human vanity,
And the Pride of Life that planned her, stilly couches she.

2

Steel chambers, late the pyres
Of her salamandrine fires,
Cold currents thrid, and turn to rhythmic tidal lyres.

3

Over the mirrors meant
To glass the opulent
The sea-worm crawls – grotesque, slimed, dumb, indifferent.

The first stanza is a sentence, in which everything before the verb *couches* is adverbial. Though grammatically the adverbial element is second to the verb, this is not how the lines work on an imaginative level. The verb seems to recede into the background, as the magnificent phrases (*Deep from human vanity*) and the surprising *stilly* claim our attention. The repetitive rhyme contributes to the sense of stillness.

The second stanza contains several adjectives. We are reminded that it is *steel* chambers being threaded by currents, and we get in that detail an idea of human vanity and the scale of the destruction. Perhaps the most foregrounded word is the adjective *salamandrine*: a salamander is a lizard which in fable was supposed to live in fire; the ship's engines have a similarly fabulous ability to burn in water. *Salamandrine* links the ship to the world of myth, together with *pyres* and *lyres*; it also anticipates the serpents of the next stanza. In the next line, *cold* appeals to our imaginary sense, and the idea of cold is even sharper coming straight after *fires*. Images work together with sound, too: the pair of words *rhythmic tidal* evoke in their rhythm the steady, slow movement of the tides. The adjectives are often forms of words we would expect to see as nouns – *steel, salamander, tide* – and so the images of these objects are brought to mind through the adjectives. To put it another way, adjectives can go on doing their describing job but, just like nouns, they can also make us call to mind specific objects. The lines thus become rich with images, singly and in combination.

The third stanza ends in a remarkable series of four adjectives for the sea-worm. Normally a list of four adjectives would be a sign of overwriting, yet here each term contributes an important idea. The words also suggest themselves as adverbs, coming directly after the verb *crawls*: the worm crawls grotesquely and slimily. While *grotesque* and *slimed* are strong sensual terms, *dumb* and *indifferent* belong with the ongoing theme of futility: what was classy and opulent on earth has no value, and commands no respect, in the deep. The broken rhythm provided by the list of commas focuses our attention on the worm, while the range of ideas carried by the descriptive terms helps to convert the image of the ship and its present position into an allegorical picture on the vanity of human glory.

Grammatical words

Prepositions

We have seen how inflections decreased in English in the medieval period, with the result that prepositions took on the job of indicating relations between words: *the man **of** my dreams, the last **in** the race*. When reading literary texts, especially before the eighteenth century, we need to pay attention to prepositions. In sixteenth- and seventeenth-century texts, they have far more flexibility than we are used to today, and it sometimes takes a moment to see what they mean:

DOL	But I have spied sir EPICURE MAMMON –	
SUBTLE	Where?	
DOL	Comming along, *at* far end of the lane,	*at the*
	Slow *of* his feet, but earnest *of* his tongue,	*with*
	To one, that's with him.	
SUBTLE	FACE, goe you, and shift.	
	DOL, you must presently make readie, too –	
DOL	Why, what's the matter?	
SUBTLE	O, I did looke for him	
	With the sunnes rising: 'Marvaile, he could sleep!	*by means of*
	This is the day, I am to perfect for him	
	The *magisterium*, our *great work*, the *stone*;	
	And yeeld it, made, into his hands: *of* which,	*about*

He has, this month, talk'd, as he were possess'd.
And, now, hee's dealing peeces *on*'t, away ...   *of*
I see no end *of* his labours.   *to*

(Ben Jonson, *The Alchemist* (1610), 1.4.6–25)

Well into the eighteenth and nineteenth centuries, we find prepositions in uses
they have since lost:

'Well,' said Elinor, 'it is a comfort to be prepared *against* the worst. You have
got your answer ready.'

Miss Steele was going to reply on the same subject, but the approach of her
own party made another more necessary.

'Oh, la! Here come the Richardsons. I had a vast deal more to say to you, but
I must not stay away from them any longer. I assure you they are very genteel
people. He makes a monstrous deal of money, and they keep their own coach.
I have not time to speak to Mrs. Jennings about it myself, but pray tell her
I am quite happy to hear she is not *in* anger *against* us, and Lady Middleton
the same.

(Jane Austen, *Sense and Sensibility* (1811), vol. 3, ch. 2)

We, of course, would say 'prepared *for*' and 'angry *with*'. But if we modernised
the text in this way, would it still mean exactly the same? The *against* has its own
particular colour. To be prepared *against something* suggests a state of mind
which is active and defensive. To be *in* anger implies a strong state like 'he's in
a foul mood', and to be angry *against* carries an aggressive tone absent from
angry *with* (although, to add to the confusion, *with* originally meant *against*, a
sense which survives in *withstand*). A few lines later, Elinor thinks *Every thing
depended, exactly after her expectation, on his getting that preferment*, where
after means *according to*. Perhaps it carries some idea of time with it, too:
everything depended, exactly as she had expected.

It is hard to tell what the nuances of such words had for Austen's first readers.
It may be that *against* had become so normal that its literal sense of *anti-* was
lost, and the usages here do not seem to be pointed to as significant bearers of
meaning. We can certainly read too much in, because the words seem odd; but
equally, we should not assume that the changes in use from Austen's time to
ours have occurred without any shift in sense.

Pronouns

You, Ye

And Naomi said unto her two daughters in law, go, return each to her
mother's house: the LORD deal kindly with *you*, as *ye* have dealt with the
dead, and with me. The LORD grant *you* that *ye* may find rest, each of *you* in
the house of her husband. Then she kissed them; and they lifted up their
voice, and wept. And they said unto her, Surely we will return with *thee* unto
thy people.

(*King James Bible* (1611), *Ruth*, I.8–10)

Naomi speaks to her two daughters-in-law with the plural *you*. They address her with the singular *thou* forms: here we see *thee* (object, equivalent of *me*) and *thy* (genitive, equivalent of *my*). Another point to notice in the passage is the separate forms of *you*: *ye* for the **subject** (*ye have dealt*) and *you* for **object** (*with you*). This distinction had probably largely passed out of real speech by 1611, when the King James Bible was published, and would have had an old-fashioned flavour even then.

Thou, You

As well as *ye* and *you*, the *thou* / *you* distinction preserved in the King James Bible was also vanishing from actual speech. By 1575, there are documents showing *you* as the normal form for the singular as well as the plural. During the time when *thou* and *you* could both be used for the singular, speakers and writers therefore had a choice – and where there is choice, there is the chance to convey meaning.

Though it is lost in English, the choice of two words for singular *you* remains in many other languages: French has *tu* and *vous*, Spanish *tu* and *usted* and German *du* and *Sie*. Broadly speaking, the conventions are the same in each of them: *thou* (the *tu* form) is familiar, intimate and used with equals and inferiors; *you* (*vous*) is polite, respectful and used to elders and superiors. By deviating from these basic uses, speakers can express feeling: *thou* can be insulting when used to a superior (as Kent does to the King in *King Lear*), while *you* can be either notably respectful as a departure from an expected *thou*, or cold and distanced if *thou* would be the norm.

Some of these ranges of meaning are illustrated in the following episode from Malory's *Le Morte Darthur* (1469–70). King Arthur first rescues Merlin from three churls (peasants) who are pursuing him:

> 'Ah, Merlin,' said Arthur, 'here hadst *thou* been slain for all thy crafts had I not been.'
> 'Nay,' said Merlin, 'not so, for I could have saved myself and I had willed. But *thou* art more near *thy* death than I am, for *thou* goest to thy deathward and God be not thy friend.'

Arthur's use of *thou* to Merlin is appropriate. Merlin, like everyone else, is below the King, and he is not a powerful baron who needs to be treated with a formal *you*. Merlin's use of *thou* to the King is more surprising, as we might expect a deferential *you*: possibly it is a way of reminding Arthur that Merlin has superior knowledge beyond the young King's understanding, or perhaps it is a mark of friendship. The two then encounter a knight who is refusing to let anyone pass until they joust with him. The knight does not know he is talking to the King.

> 'Sir knight,' said Arthur, 'for what cause abidest *thou* here, that there may no knight ride this way but if he joust with thee? I rede thee to leave that custom.'

Again, Arthur's use of *thou* is normal for a king. We might read more into the knight's reply: when Arthur declares he will joust, his adversary replies with a defiant 'And I shall defend *thee*' (*defend* meaning 'prevent'). The *thou* forms add to the atmosphere of defiance and contempt: the same knight has jousted with a knight of the Round Table called Sir Griflet a few pages earlier, and in the preliminaries to this bout they addressed each other as *you*. It is likely, then, that there is some dramatic charge in the form chosen here.

The two fight, and after a while their spears are broken. Arthur pulls out his sword.

> 'Nay, not so,' said the knight, 'it is better that we twain run more together with sharp spears.'
>
> 'I will well,' said Arthur, 'and I had any more spears here.'
>
> 'I have enough,' said the knight. So there came a squire and brought forth two spears; and Arthur chose one and he another. So they spurred their horses and came together with all their might, that either broke their spears to their hands. Then Arthur set hand on his sword.
>
> 'Nay,' said the knight, '*ye* shall do better, ye are a passing good jouster as ever I met with; and once for the high order of knighthood let us joust again.'

Impressed by Arthur's skill at fighting, the knight shifts into *ye*: this seems to signal his respect. (Notice in this passage, too, the old use of *and*, meaning *if* in *and I had any more spears*. This occurs quite often in Shakespeare's plays over a century later, though by then it had probably become old-fashioned.) The battle rages on, and eventually Merlin has to save Arthur by putting the knight into a deep sleep.

> 'Alas, said Arthur, 'what hast *thou* done, Merlin? Hast thou slain this good knight by thy crafts? – for there liveth not so worshipful a knight as he was ...'
>
> 'Care ye not,' said Merlin, 'for he is wholer than *ye*; he is but asleep, and will awake within this hour. I told *you*,' said Merlin, 'what a knight he was.'
>
> (*Le Morte Darthur*, pages 27–8 (Oxford Classics edition))

Arthur continues to address Merlin as *thou*, as we would expect, but now Merlin changes to the *ye* form. (Notice again the ye / you distinction: *I told you* is objective.) It is hard to see why he uses the more formal word, for he is in just the same 'I know better' mode he was in a page earlier. But the change would not be accidental, and may have carried some tonal shift to an original audience which we cannot pick up today. In late medieval and Renaissance literature, reading the significance of *thou* and *you* is difficult. Sometimes the two are interchangeable, with no distinction in meaning. Often, though, we can uncover a further level of meaning in a passage of dialogue or a dramatic scene by investigating the *thou / you* choices at work.

His / Its

Another change in English grammar in the pre-modern period was the arrival of the word *its* for 'of it'. This form arrived around 1600, and its adoption was gradual. Spenser (1552?–99) does not use it at all. There is no example of *its* in Shakespeare's quartos (the earliest editions of his plays) though there are a few in the 1623 Folio. These may be by Shakespeare, or they may be the result of a little updating by the Folio editors and typesetters who prepared the texts. In the 1611 Bible there is just one *its* (*Leviticus* xxv.5), and even *Paradise Lost* (1667) has only two instances. *Its* did not become the normal way to say 'of it' until the end of the seventeenth century. Before the introduction and acceptance of *its*, the meaning *of it* had to be expressed in other ways. We find *it* in Shakespeare (*the cat had it head bit off by it young*), and the Bible makes much use of *thereof*. But the most common way of expressing *of it* was with *his*. This word can be used as a possessive determiner (*that's his seat* – the word is working as an adjective determining the particular quality of the seat), and as a possessive pronoun (*that's his*: here, *seat* is understood, and *his* is standing in for the noun, thus working as a pronoun).

> Ye are the salt of the earth: but if the salt have lost his savour, wherewith shall it be salted?
>
> (*Matthew* v.13)

It is tempting to assume that *his* in a literary text implies personification. This may often be the case, but there has to be other evidence for us to be sure. These lines by Herbert were published in his collection *The Temple* in 1633:

> Prayer, the church's banquet, angels' age,
> God's breath in man returning to his birth.
>
> ('Prayer', lines 1 and 2)

Prayer is the breath which God breathed into man, now returning to God. Are we meant to interpret it here as a personified *he*? It is hard to see how this beautiful idea is improved by the device. It may simply mean *its*, though it is hard to be certain. In these verses from Herbert's *Deniall*, *his* presents similar problems when it first appears. When we learn that each *would* (that is, wanted) to go somewhere, the sense of personification becomes stronger, and in the next stanza it is confirmed:

> My bent thoughts, like a brittle bow,
> Did fly asunder:
> Each took his way; some would to pleasures go,
> Some to the wars and thunder
> Of alarms.
>
> 'As good go anywhere,' they say,
> 'As to benumb
> Both knees and heart, in crying night and day,
> *Come, come, my God, O come,*
> But no hearing.' (verses 2 and 3)

The speech marks are put in by a modern editor, giving a signal that is not in the original version.

Constructions with pronouns

Objective genitive

Another use of a pronoun which we find in Early Modern English is the so-called **objective genitive**. Thus when Timon of Athens says *I am joyful of your sights*

(1.1.249), we would say *I am joyful at the sight of you*. The *you* referred to by Timon's *your* is the object of the verb: I see *you*. Another example is this:

LUCENTIO   And let me be a slave t'achieve that maid
            Whose sudden sight hath thralled my wounded eye.
                        (*Taming of the Shrew*, 1.1.217–18)

Lucentio means, of course, that he has seen her. This construction is not obsolete: we may still say 'His defence was conducted by a young barrister' or 'The Academy was responsible for her training,' but its use is restricted.

Ethic dative

A further feature of pronouns we may encounter is the so-called **ethic dative**. This is an extra object pronoun slipped in where it is not grammatically necessary, to emphasise and add an emotional colour to the action of the verb. A sentence like *Open the door* makes perfect sense; but if we add a pronoun to give *Open me the door*, then we can imply that we feel personally affected by the action. It is a subtle touch, slightly subtler than *Open the door for me*. In the latter, *for me* is not an add-on but a crucial part of the sense. The potential for misunderstanding caused by this construction is the source of the comedy in this passage:

PETRUCCIO   Here, sirrah Grumio, knock, I say.
GRUMIO   Knock, sir? Whom should I knock? Is there any man has
            rebused your worship?
PETRUCCIO   Villain, I say, knock me here soundly.
GRUMIO   Knock you here, sir? Why, sir, what am I, sir, that I should
            knock you here, sir?
PETRUCCIO   Villain, I say, knock me here soundly.
                        (*Taming of the Shrew*, 1.2.5–11)

Me + verb

In modern English, pronouns follow the verb: I like *you* (direct object), he talks *to me* (indirect). Learners of other languages become familiar with pronouns placed *before* the verb: *s'il vous plaît* is *If it to you pleases*. In Old English, pronouns can also be in this position: the speaker of *The Dream of the Rood* promises to recount *Hwaet me gemaette* (line 2). We must translate this as *what I dreamed*, making the *I* the agent, but literally it means *what to me it dreamed*, making the speaker the passive receiver of the dream vision. *I dreamed* and *it dreamed to me* convey different notions of dreaming.

This construction appears in certain set phrases in pre-modern texts. Here are two uses by the knight in the episode from Malory we considered above:

'That is me loath,' said the knight, 'but sithen I must needs, I will dress me thereto.'   (p.25)

'Thou art in my danger [power] whether me list to save thee or slay thee.'
                                                                        (p.28)

In the first *That is me loath* means *It is to me undesirable*. (This speech is also an example of the genitive *-s* at the end of *need* making an adverb: *I must needs* means *I must necessarily.*) In the second, *me list* means *to me it pleases.* A more familiar example is the word *methinks,* common in Shakespeare and later writers. In origin, this means *it seems to me* (*to me it seems*), a phrase crystallised in a word (from Old English *thynkan,* seem).

Deictic words

Deixis means pointing, and refers to the elements of a text which place it in a specific time and place. *Deictic* words can indicate:

- A space or location [*spatial*]: *here, there*
- Persons referred to [*personal*]: *me, you, them, us* etc.
- The speaker and listener [*personal*]: *I, you*
- Time [*temporal*]: *now, then, today, yesterday, tomorrow.* Verb tenses
- Things [also *spatial*: the objects form part of the spatial context]: *this, these / that, those.*

Words like *that* and *there* are often accompanied by gestures in real life: *Let's go there* or *Can you pass me that* lend themselves to real pointing. When they appear in stage writing, these words provide valuable suggestions for movement. *Antony and Cleopatra* starts with Antony in Cleopatra's court in Egypt. This is his first reaction to learning there is news from Rome:

> ANTONY   Let Rome in Tiber melt, and the wide arch
> Of the ranged empire fall. *Here* is my space.
> Kingdoms are clay. Our dungy earth alike
> Feeds beast as man. The nobleness of life
> Is to do *thus* ...
> (*Antony and Cleopatra,* 1.1.35–9)

Where is *here*? The spot Antony is standing on, or the country of Egypt? Similarly, *thus* must be accompanied by some action. He might kiss Cleopatra, but there are other possibilities, such as drinking something to show he prefers the pleasures of basic living to high office, of lying down to show his contempt for kingly action.

Another function of deictic words is to establish context. In a dialogue, it is important that participants know what words like *there* and *then* refer to. These point to the shared world we have in our minds. The sense of incomprehension if we do not pick them up can be used to powerful literary effect:

> *I* am in my mother's room. It's I who live *there now.* I don't know how I got *there.* Perhaps in an ambulance, certainly a vehicle of some kind. I was helped. I'd never have got there alone. There's *this* man who comes every week. Perhaps I got *here* thanks to him. He says not. He gives me money and takes away *the* pages. So many pages, so much money. Yes, I work *now,* a little like *I used to,* except that I don't know how to work *any more.* That doesn't matter apparently. What I'd like now is to speak of the things that are left, say my good-byes, finish dying. *They* don't want *that.*
> (Samuel Beckett, *Molloy* (1951))

We do not know who *I* refers to, or what time *now* indicates. The definite article *the* in *the pages* implies we know what pages he means, but of course we do not. Are they the pages we are reading? In the last sentence *they* suddenly appears, but we cannot know who *they* are. The combined effect of these uncertainties is to make us feel dislocated: we are listening to an unknown speaker, who is familiarly mentioning things outside our frame of reference. The deictic words also work on our imagination: our mind must turn *they* into some group of people to make sense of things. We collude in creating the world around the text.

Words – Exercises

1. Comment on the use and effect of different parts of speech in the following lines:

   Then sprang up first the golden age, which of itself maintained
   The truth and right of everything unforced and unconstrained.
   There was no fear of punishment, there was no threatening law
   In brazen tables nailèd up, to keep the folk in awe.
   There was no man would crouch or creep to judge with cap in hand,   5
   They livèd safe without a judge, in every realm and land.
   The lofty pinetree was not hewn from mountains where it stood,
   In seeking strange and foreign lands, to rove upon the flood.
   Men knew none other countries yet than where themselves did keep;
   There was no town enclosèd yet, with walls and ditches deep.   10
   No horn nor trumpet was in use, no sword nor helmet worn;
   The world was such that soldiers' help might easily be forborn.
   The fertile earth as yet was free, untouched of spade or plow,
   And yet it yielded of itself of every things enow.   [*enow*: enough]
                    (Arthur Golding (1536–1605), part of the description of the Golden
                    Age from his translation of Ovid's *Metamorphoses* (1567), Book 1.
                    Modernised spelling)

2. Read the following passage, and identify:

   (a) prepositions with different senses from modern English
   (b) a verbal inflection which is not used in modern English.

   As I fortuned to take my voyage into Thessaly, about certaine affaires which I had to doe (for there myne auncestry by my mothers side inhabiteth, descended of the line of that most excellent person Plutarch, and of Sextus the Philosopher his Nephew, which is to us a great honour) and after that by much travell and great paine I had passed over the high mountaines and slipperie vallies, and had ridden through the cloggy fallowed fields; perceiving that my horse did waxe somewhat slow, and to the intent likewise I might repose and strengthen my self (being weary with riding) I lighted off my horse, and wiping away the sweat from every part of his body, I unbrideled him, and walked him softly in my hand, to the end he might pisse, and ease himselfe of his wearinesse and travell: and while he went grazing freshly in the field (casting himself sometimes aside, as a token of rejoycing and gladnesse) I perceived a little before me two companions riding, and so I overtaking them made the third.

(Apuleius, *The Golden Asse*, translated by William Adlington (1566), beginning. Original spelling.)

3. Read *Othello*, Act One, Scene One, and suggest the significance of the different uses of *thou* and *you*.

3.2 Phrases

The noun phrase

Words combine to make phrases, and the two most important kinds of phrase are the **noun phrase** and the **verb phrase**. The noun phrase, which usually carries the main cargo of information in a sentence, consists of a head word and up to three other main parts:

Determiner	Modifier	Head	Qualifier
The	*old fat*	*cat*	*on the windowsill.*

The following notes complete the technical description of a noun phrase:

- All noun phrases have a head word. Proper, non-count and plural nouns have only this: *America, sugar.* Other singular nouns must take a determiner: *the bus, my cat, a house.*
- The modifier and qualifier (also sometimes called post-modifier) are not necessary for the grammar of the sentence: *the cat* could act as a subject or object without their help.
- Modifiers and qualifiers can consist of several words, and can contain their own phrases: *the windowsill* above is a noun phrase embedded in another: *the old lady's cat* contains a noun phrase in the modifier position.
- Sometimes we find a pre-determiner before the determiner: *all the old fat cats.*

Older noun phrases: flexibility

In older texts we often meet noun phrases taking shapes that would not normally be possible today. Here are just a few of these arrangements:

(a) *The Prologe of the Wyves Tale of Bathe* (Canterbury Tales)
The words *Wyves ... of Bath* together make up a modifier to the head word *Tale*: as we would say in today's English The [determiner] *Wife of Bath's* [modifier] *Tale* [head]. This is one of the commonest ways in which the modifier is broken up in texts of earlier periods. A more dramatic example is when Arthur swears by *my fadirs soule Uther!* Uther belongs in the modifiying group 'Uther my father'. Its displacement to the end of the phrase gives it an extra emphasis. It is important to recognise that the separation of the parts of

the modifier was a perfectly normal feature of English in Malory's time: the grammatical reason is that *'s* as an inflection can only belong to one word, like *Wife's*. In *Wife of Bath's*, the *'s* is an enclitic (stuck-on) particle marking the whole group of words as a phrasal unit. This use of *'s* occasionally appears in Middle English but only became regular by about 1800.

(b) *Faire Helene, flowre of beautie excellent* (*The Faerie Queene*, III, ix, stanza 35, line 1)

There are two noun phrases here: the first is *Faire Helene*; the second is in apposition to it, that is to say it sits beside it and tells us something more about it. We could add a 'who is' between them. In the second phrase, *flowre of beautie excellent*, we find an adjective after the noun it modifies in *beautie excellent*. This is a device common in poetry into the twentieth century and it still survives in some fossilised phrases (*court martial, crown imperial, heir apparent* etc.). But which noun does *excellent* refer to? It could describe all three nouns *Helen, flowre* and *beautie*. Rather than turn to a grammar rule-book, we simply have to reflect on the effect the line has had on us; the possible combinations – *excellent Helen* and so on – make such good sense that the words associate freely in our imagination.

(c) Of Mans First Disobedience, and the Fruit
    Of that Forbidd'n Tree, whose mortal tast
    Brought Death into the World, and all our woe ...

(Milton, *Paradise Lost*, Book 1, lines 1–3)

These lines give us examples of several kind of noun phrase, from that consisting of a single head word, *Death*, to the longer *Mans First Disobedience* (determiner + modifier + head), to *the Fruit of that Forbidd'n Tree*, in which *of ... Tree* is a qualifier containing its own noun phrase. These phrases are all bound together in a much larger one: in fact, the head *Fruit* is just the beginning of a gigantic noun phrase, for everything after it serves as a qualifier. It is possible in English to continue a noun phrase indefinitely in this way, a construction which Milton quite often explores.

One kind of qualifier is a **relative clause**: in 'the apple which I bought yesterday', the *which ...* clause tells us more about the head word *apple*. *Which* is the relative, and *apple* is the antecedent it refers to. To avoid ambiguity, we try to keep **antecedent** and relative close to each other: 'the apple which I bought yesterday' is clearer than 'the apple in the groceries I bought yesterday'. In the lines from *Paradise Lost*, though, the relative pronoun *whose* refers not to *Tree*, as we might at first assume, but to *Fruit*. A distance between relative and antecedent is another kind of flexibility which we meet in earlier texts.

Parallelism

Parallelism involves the repetition of structures within a text which brings the forms of its verbal arrangement to our attention. Noun phrases are often used to create parallelism, as in the following passage:

That such a Religion, in such a Time, by the Sermons and Conduct of Fisher-men, Men of mean breeding and illiberal Arts, should so speedily triumph over the Philosophy of the World, and the Arguments of the Subtle, and the Sermons of the Eloquent; the Power of Princes and the Interests of States, the Inclinations of Nature and the Blindness of Zeal, the Force of Custom and the Solicitation of Passions, the Pleasures of Sin and the busy arts of the Devil; that is against Wit and Power, Superstition and Wilfulness, Fame and Money, Nature and Empire, which are all the causes in this World that can make a Thing impossible; this, this is to be ascribed to the Power of *God*, and is the great Demonstration of the Resurrection of *Jesus*.

> (Jeremy Taylor (1613–67), Sermon preached at the
> Funeral of the Lord Primate)

This mighty sentence uses various parallel noun phrase shapes to great rhetorical effect. Here are the main shapes employed:

- *Such a Religion, such a Time*
- *Mean breeding, illiberal arts*
- *The Philosophy of the World*: this structure is repeated until *the busy arts of the devil*, which allows in the adjective *busy* as a variation
- Two phrases consisting of head only, joined by a conjunction: *Wit and Power* etc.
- After a brief pause, the sentence ends with a return to the dominant shape in the concluding *the Power of God* and *the Resurrection of Jesus*.

The noun phrases also work as rhythmic units, reminding us that our division of sound and grammar is artificial. As *the x of the y* is repeated insistently in the middle, we are held in suspense. We know that the enormous *that* clause has to be resolved for the sentence to make sense; but we are also expecting the rhythm to be brought to a close at the cadence. The end, when it comes, is thus doubly satisfying.

Formulae

The repetition of noun phrase structures does not guarantee an effective parallelism. Sometimes particular shapes become repeated in a rather formulaic way. Some common examples of such formulae are given below.

Doublets

In the doublet, two words or short phrases are joined by *and*: *Wit and Power* is an example of a doublet of nouns in the passage above. The device is frequent in sixteenth- and seventeenth-century writing, when English and Latin-derived words are tied together:

> And yet time hath his revolutions; there must be *a period and an end* to all temporal things, *finis rerum*, an end of whatsoever is terrene; and why not of De Vere? Where is Bohun, where's Mowbray, where's Mortimer? Nay, which is

more and most of all, where is Plantagenet? They are entombed in *the urns and sepulchres* of mortality. And yet let *the name and dignity* of De Vere stand so long as it pleaseth God.

(Sir Ranulph Crewe, Oxford peerage case, 1625)

In each case, the two words mean practically the same. The device may be needed for rhythm, though not for understanding: none of the Latinate words is particularly obscure. In this passage by Francis Bacon the device is taken even further, without the two parts of the doublet necessarily coming from different languages:

But the greatest error of all the rest is *the mistaking or misplacing* of *the last or furthest* end of knowledge. For men have entered into a desire of *learning and knowledge*, sometimes upon *a natural curiosity and inquisitive appetite*; sometimes to entertain their minds with *variety and delight*; sometimes for *ornament and reputation* ...

(*Advancement of Learning*, 1605)

Crewe and Bacon seem incapable of using one important noun without giving it another as a companion. This is a habit which still afflicts writers today. To Bacon, it may have seemed like an elegant ornamentation of the message with a rich accompaniment of words, emphasising the points with a scholarly air.

Noun phrases and meaning

Bacon's 'doubleting' also reminds us that extra words and phrases do not always deliver new ideas. This is particularly the case in Renaissance writing, when rhetoric manuals often encouraged writers to show off the fullness of their vocabulary. Thus, new phrases may be restatements of ideas we have already heard. It is useful to ask how much new meaning is being carried by a noun phrase, for it may have some other main function: it may be decorative, simply enlarging the vocabulary of the passage, or emotionally expressive, or chiefly rhythmic.

Stock phrases

Noun phrases can take various shapes. In theory, there is no limit to the number of modifiers one can put before the head or the number of qualifiers which may follow it. The opening of *Paradise Lost*, discussed above, is an example of a qualifier which is drawn out to unusual lengths. However, certain shapes often settle down into being stock formulae, both in the style of an individual author, or as one of the characteristics of a particular period. In English, perhaps the most common kind of noun phrase is the structure: [determiner] + adjective + noun. Examples can be found from all periods, but eighteenth-century verse seems to be particularly characterised by it:

In vain to me *the smiling mornings* shine,
And *reddening Phoebus* lifts *his golden fire*;

The birds in vain *their amorous descants* join,
Or *cheerful fields* resume *their green attire* . . .
(Thomas Gray (1716–71), 'Sonnet On the Death of Mr Richard West')

Only the birds are left alone without a modifier. This shape of phrase became so stock that it is still perhaps part of the general conception of poetry: *the bubbling brook, the rosy-fingered dawn* and so on.

Collocations

Combinations of words like those italicised above are **collocations**. Just as certain phrase structures are frequently repeated, so particular combinations of words can recur so frequently that it becomes hard to imagine one without the other: *auspicious occasion, sumptuous banquet, sour cream* are examples of collocations which have become virtually singular units of expression.

Authors can have their favourite adjectives, and their favourite collocations. Sometimes these are the formulaic epithets of individual characters, like *fleet-footed Mercury* in Homeric epic. At the beginning of *The Old Curiosity Shop* (1840), we can see such a collocation being created. In the space of a few lines, the narrator meets a *pretty little girl* who is *a little frightened* (an adjective phrase), so he decides to take *the little creature* home. The adjective *little* seems to be on the lookout for any noun it can stick itself onto. Over the next two pages, the narrator refers to her as the *little creature* two or three times, and this collocation sticks for the rest of the novel. But the adjective is still in the system: *I love these little people*, he confides in the reader; when we meet the girl's father, it is no surprise to learn he is *a little old man*. He tells the girl's father the *little story* of their meeting. He is invited into the front room:

> The old man kissed her; then turned to me and begged me to walk in. I did so. The door was closed and locked. Preceding me with the light, he led me through the place I had already seen from without, into a small sitting-room behind, in which was another door opening into a kind of closet, where I saw a little bed that a fairy might have slept in: it looked so very small and was so prettily arranged. The child took a candle and tripped into this little room, leaving the old man and me together.
>
> (*The Old Curiosity Shop*, Chapter 1)

This, we may feel, is a redundant modifier. If a bed is small enough for a fairy to sleep in, we do not really need to be told it is little as well; nor do we need to be informed that the room is little, three lines after learning it is small. The word seems to be imprisoning the man, the girl and the room and making them into what the narrator wants them to be – fairytale types rather than living characters.

Sometimes, though, apparent weaknesses are necessary for strengths to realise themselves. At the same time as *little* is turning up everywhere, Dickens conjures up an atmospheric picture of the curiosity shop, full of picturesque objects. And the sentimental and perhaps rather patronising attitude which *little* expresses is also part of the religious vision of the novel. It turns the old man and the girl into something saintly: *little* for Dickens implies vulnerability as well as size, and carries an echo of Christ's *Suffer the little children to come unto me*. The word seems redundant, yet it suggests a background of associations which form part of the narrator's perspective on his experience.

Evaluating noun phrases

Once we can notice and describe noun phrases, we can consider the use that a writer is making of them. Here, the modernist writer William Faulkner (1897–1962) uses long modifiers to mesmerising effect:

> From a little after two o'clock until almost sundown of the long hot weary dead September afternoon they sat in what Miss Coldfield still called the office because her father had called it that – a dim hot airless room with the blinds all closed and fastened for forty-three summers because when she was a girl someone had believed that light and moving air carried heat and that dark was always cooler, and which (as the sun shone fuller and fuller on that side of the house) became latticed with yellow slashes full of dust motes which Quentin thought of as bring flecks of the dead old dried paint itself blown inward from the scaling blinds as wind might have blown them.
>
> (William Faulkner, *Absalom, Absalom!* (1936))

In the phrase *the long hot weary dead September afternoon* the modifier has five elements. The dense feel of this helps us to imagine the stuffy scene, the sense of time dragging and things not changing. There is a sensation of unusually prolonged observation, the sort of noticing of objects which we do when we are stuck in a waiting room: *a dim hot airless room, the dead old dried paint*.

There is the same feel of concentrated attention, though this time with a different emotional tone, in D.H. Lawrence's description of a father looking at his new-born child in *The Rainbow* (1915):

> But he waited for the dread of these days to pass; he saw the joy coming. He saw *the lovely, creamy, cool little ear* of the baby, a bit of dark hair rubbed to a bronze floss, like bronze dust.

The long modifier – *lovely, creamy, cool little* – in this phrase here carries authority because it seems authentic. When we look at people or things we love, it is often a detail we focus on. Emotion (*lovely*) is mixed with fascinated discovery (*creamy, cool*). As in the passage from Faulkner, the long modifier catches a psychologically convincing moment of noticing.

Writers also introduce surprising variations on phrases, and create collocations in which the modifier or qualifier seems more prominent than the head. An example is Hopkins's phrase which opens 'The Wreck of the Deutschland': *Thou mastering me God!* Besides striking deviations such as this, economy is a hallmark of many great writers. Though there is perhaps a common idea that literature is a particularly descriptive use of language, it is often the case that writers are unusually restrained in their use of modifiers and qualifiers, and when they are used they add precision and focus rather than general atmospheric wrapping.

The verb phrase

The second type of phrasal group we shall look at is the verb phrase. In English, this consists of three parts: the auxiliary, the head and the extension.

(Subject)	Auxiliary	Head	Extension	(Obj)
I	have	spoken	to	him.
He	will	answer		me.

The auxiliary element can consist of several words, though this is a relatively modern development in the language. Auxiliaries can:

- Indicate time: *I **have** spoken, I **had** spoken, I **will** speak.*
- Reflect the view of the speaker toward the action. These are the so-called **modal** auxiliaries (*modal* coming from *mood*): *I **should** work tonight: I certainly **ought** to. But I **may** not. I **might** go to a party instead. I **can** always do it later. But I **must** finish it by Friday.*

As this simple example shows, auxiliary verbs can reflect subtle differences in attitude by the speaker, indicating such things as desire, probability and obligation. These meanings are not constant and have changed over time. In literary texts before roughly the eighteenth and nineteenth centuries we often find simple constructions, in which auxiliaries have a larger range of possible meanings than they do today.

The grammar of verbal constructions is fairly involved. We shall get a view of their importance in literature from considering their effect in certain passages.

Our first example is once again from Malory. It comes just before the passage we discussed in comparing *thou* and *you* in the previous section, and begins when Sir Griflet has defeated the mysterious knight in a joust:

> When the knight [Sir Griflet] saw him lie so on the ground, he alit, and was passing heavy for he weened he had slain him; and then he unlaced his helm and got him wind. And so with the truncheon set him on his horse and got him wind, and so betook him to God, and said he had a mighty heart; and said, if he might live, he would prove a passing good knight.

There is a difficulty here created by verbal forms. Does Sir Griflet think he has killed the knight or not? We are told he believed he did, and that he *betook* (commended) his adversary's soul to God. At the same time, he appears to make some effort to resuscitate him.

A further confusion occurs since we can take the speeches at the end as direct or indirect. With this, we are likely to be guided by editors, who must be guided by their best instincts. The line could be punctuated *'He had a mighty heart!'* Now, if Sir Griflet said *'He had a mighty heart'* then he clearly thought his opponent was dead. But if what he actually said was *He **has** a mighty heart* then it would still turn into *He had a mighty heart* in reported speech. If I say to you *I drive a blue car*, you might say to someone *He told me he drove a blue car*. Malory sometimes drifts in and out of speech in a way which modern authors cannot, and which may be related to techniques of aural storytelling. He is not alone in this, and the punctuation of early texts often raises questions about what verb forms were actually used by the speaker.

The situation is still harder in the next 'speech', which seems to us to indicate that Sir Griflet thinks the knight will live: *if he might live*. But this could be deceptive: *might* is the past of *may*, and *should* is the past of *shall*. That is, if this was direct speech, it would mean 'If he had been able to live, then he would have been able to become a very good knight', or, as we would say, 'If he'd survived, then he would have been ...'. The interpretation rests on the meaning of the auxiliaries: *might* and *should* are no longer used to refer to the past, but they were in Malory's time, and this seems to be the probable meaning here.

We can continue our examination of verbal meanings by continuing with the same story. This now takes us to Arthur's court. Twelve knights have come from the Emperor Lucius of Rome to demand *truage* (tribute). This is Arthur's reply:

'Well,' said King Arthur, 'ye are messengers, therefore ye may say what ye will, or else ye should die therefor. But this is my answer: I owe the emperor no truage, nor none will I yield him, but on a fair field I shall yield him my truage: that shall be with a sharp spear or else with a sharp sword. And that shall not be long, by my father's soul, Uther.'

Let us discuss the different **modals** here in turn.

May

Arthur tells the messengers *ye may say what ye will*. Probably we first take *may* in one of its most frequent modern senses as *are allowed to*. This makes good sense here: King Arthur is giving them permission to speak freely. But the word might have the sense of *can*, as in *are able to*: he is recognising that the knights' status as ambassadors gives them the right to say anything. This probably makes even better sense, as it makes the next part of the sentence more logical: of course you can say that as you're ambassadors, otherwise you'd die for it.

Shall and will

The lines above also illustrate some of the uses of *shall* and *will*. These used to be full verbs. Old English *sculan* means *must, have to, ought to* – it suggests that the future act is a matter of obligation, or is ordained and inevitable. *Willan* means *want to*. In '*ye may say what ye will*' we see *will* used in this original way as a verb: you can say whatever you want to.

Shall and *will* came to be used as auxiliaries because English has no separate form of the verb for denoting future time, which therefore has to be expressed in a so-called periphrastic form, with *shall* or *will* before the base form of the verb, that is the infinitive without *to* (*I shall **eat**, you will **stay***). This lack of a future tense is what makes modal auxiliaries so important, and in medieval and Renaissance texts *shall* and *will* frequently carry a modal value: they don't just express the future time, but bring their own associations with them, so that *I will go* can imply *I want to go*, and *you shall go* means *you ought to go*. Thus, when Arthur says *none will I yield him*, the *will* expresses *I don't want to*. Then, in *on a* *fair field I shall yield him my truage, shall* carries the idea of inevitability: it is going to happen. This notion that a conflict is not just Arthur's desire, but something destined and inescapable, is reinforced by the repetition of *shall* in *that shall be with a sharp spear ... that shall not be long.*

Naturally, there are times when it is helpful to be able to talk about the future in a neutral way, without implying desire or obligation. Sometimes *shall* and *will* appear interchangeable, and in the century after Malory *shall* became the usual educated form for many users. This sense of *shall* being more elegant and dignified partly accounts for its heavy use in the King James Bible. However, Shakespeare and other writers often observe the old distinctions and in their writings we can often detect modal colours adding further layers of significance to a sentence or passage.

To return to Malory, the next scene recounts Arthur's rescue of Merlin, mentioned earlier, and introduces us to more verbal nuances:

> And then was he ware of three churls chasing Merlin, and would have slain him. Then the King rode unto them, and bade them, 'Flee, churls!' Then they feared sore when they saw a knight come, and fled.
> 'Ah, Merlin,' said Arthur, 'here hadst thou been slain for all thy crafts had I not been.'
> 'Nay,' said Merlin, 'not so, for I could have saved myself and I had willed ...'

Would

Would, as we have already noted, is the past of *will*. In *would have slain him* it carries the original meaning of volition: they wanted to kill him. It is the same verb as Merlin uses at the end in its original use as a main verb: *and I had willed* means *if I had wanted to.*

Hadst

In *here hadst thou been slain*, the auxiliary *hadst* means 'would have'. This is unlikely to cause difficulty to a modern reader, though it helps to be aware that in older texts, one auxiliary can do a job which we need two or even more words to do today.

Our next passage illustrating changing aspects of the verbal phrase is taken from the King James Bible (1611). Its date does not mean it is typical of the English being written or spoken at that time. Bible translation was treated extremely cautiously, and translators were told to make as few changes as possible from earlier English versions. The result is that this, the so-called Authorized Version stays very close to the English of the great translator William Tyndale, whose first translation appeared in 1526. The King James Bible therefore preserves many forms of the language that had changed or disappeared from the time of Malory: for example, there is the *he sings / he singeth* ending, which we also find in Shakespeare, though the *-th* sound was rapidly dropping out of normal speech at that time. Its range of verbal constructions is illustrated by this passage from *Genesis*, Chapter 3:

1. Now the serpent was more subtil than any beast of the field which the LORD God had made. And he said unto the woman, Yea, hath God said, Ye shall not eat of every tree of the garden?
2. And the woman said unto the serpent, We may eat of the fruit of the trees of the garden:
3. But of the fruit of the tree which is in the midst of the garden, God hath said, Ye shall not eat of it, neither shall you touch it, lest ye die.

Past time: the perfect

Here we find the various past tenses with which we are familiar today: the **preterite** (*he said*) the **perfect** – sometimes called the **present perfect** (*God hath said*) and the **pluperfect** for events further in the past (*God had made*). Of these, the perfect can be exploited for subtle effect. It is used to refer to events in the past which take place in a time period that is still perceived as open. For example, the sentence *He has written twenty books* implies that *he* is still living. It means: he has written twenty books in the time period of his life, which is still going on. The event of writing is in the past, but the time period is continuing. The serpent could say 'Did God say', and Eve could reply 'God said, Ye shall not …'. Their use of the perfect instead of the preterite implies some ongoing time period such as 'in your time in the garden'. The effect is to make God's command more immediate and relevant. Notice the use of *shall* for a command, carrying the verb's original sense of obligation. The serpent conveys the same certainty when he reassures Eve:

4. And the serpent said unto the woman, Ye shall not surely die:
5. For God doth know that in the day ye eat thereof, then your eyes shall be opened, and ye shall be as gods, knowing good and evil.
6. And when the woman saw that the tree was good for food, and that it was pleasant to the eyes, and a tree to be desired to make one wise, she took of the fruit thereof, and did eat, and gave also unto her husband with her, and he did eat.

Do

These verses provide examples of the so-called 'dummy auxiliary' or 'expletive' *do*. *Do* has various uses in literary language: in poetry, it can be useful for filling the metre of a line. It is also used for emphasis, and this seems to be its function in verse 5: *For God doth know* is a little more forceful, and perhaps more dignified, than 'God knows'. The use in *did eat* is probably not emphatic but reflects uncertainty on the part of the translators as to the 'correct' past of *eat*: was it *eat* – not yet spelled *ate* – or *eated*? Various forms probably occurred in real speech. The phrase *did eat* solves the problem, making it clear it is in the past.

An older meaning of *do* which occurs in medieval texts is 'to cause', as in Chaucer's *The Merchant's Tale*: *Do strepe me and put me in a sak, And in the nexte ryver do me drenche* (Fragment IV, 2200–1). This means 'cause someone to strip me ... to drown me'. Another verb which does the same job is *let*, which comes up constantly in Malory: *he let make Sir Kay seneschal of England* etc. It is equivalent to modern English *have* as in 'I'll have someone call you' (and to French *faire* and *laisser*, and German *lassen*). In the biblical verses from *Genesis* there is an interesting similarity in *Unto Adam and his wife did the LORD God make coats*, though this is probably a slightly emphatic *did*, to point out God's care for man, rather than the older meaning.

We shall now move on in the *Genesis* story. Adam and Eve become aware they are naked and clothe themselves. God discovers what has happened, and punishes them. There is an interesting distinction between *will*, used for God alone, and *shall*, to denote the things which are destined to happen to the sinning mortals:

16. Unto the woman he said, I will greatly multiply thy sorrow and thy conception; in sorrow thou shalt bring forth children; and thy desire shall be to thy husband, and he shall rule over thee.

Phrasal and prepositional verbs

Verse 16 also illustrates some uses of the third part of the verb phrase, the extension: *bring **forth**, rule **over***. **Phrasal verbs** are extended by an adverb, as in *stand back*, while prepositional verbs are extended by a preposition, as in *stand in*. These extension words give the head verbs a wide range of extra meanings. We saw earlier some examples of prepositions which have changed. Similarly, several verb extensions have also shifted: *shall be to* means *shall be for*.

Now let us turn to God's words to Adam:

19. In the sweat of thy face shalt thou eat bread, till thou return unto the ground; for out of it wast thou taken: for dust thou art, and unto dust shalt thou return.
20. And Adam called his wife's name Eve; because she was the mother of all living.
21. Unto Adam also and to his wife did the LORD God make coats of skins and clothed them.
22. And the LORD God said, Behold, the man is become as one of us, to know good and evil: and now, lest he put forth his hand, and take also of the tree of life, and eat, and live for ever:
23. Therefore the LORD God sent him forth from the garden of Eden, to till the ground from whence he was taken.

Participle

English has two kinds of participle, the past and the present: The fruit *was **eaten*** is the past, the fruit *is ripening* is the present. The *-ing* is also used in continuous forms: *I was running* etc. These verbal forms easily work as modifiers: in the phrases *the **driven** snow* and *the **ripening** fruit* participle forms are modifiers in noun phrases. In verse 20, we see the process go a stage further: in *mother of all living*, the participle word *living* is not only adjectival but implies a noun as well: Eve is the mother of all living things. Participles have several other jobs – they can also be nouns (*Do you object to her **writing***) and modifying adjectives (*the **soldering** iron*). In texts of this period and earlier we often encounter strange uses, whose meaning takes some working out. In *Antony and Cleopatra*, we have *From his all-obeying breath I hear the doom of Egypt*, where the sense is in fact 'his breath which all obey', the opposite of its modern interpretation. Similarly, in *Troilus and Cressida* we are told *Women are angels, wooing: things won are done*, where *wooing* means when they are being wooed.

Subjunctive

The **subjunctive mood** is used to refer to actions which are not actually taking place except in the mind of the speaker: they may be feared, wished for, warned against and so on. In Old English, there were special endings to denote the subjunctive, but these gradually disappeared, making it hard to tell the difference between the subjunctive and the normal **indicative** mood. In modern English the subjunctive is obsolete except in certain phrases like *God save the Queen* (expressing the wish *may God save*), *if I were*, or, more rarely, *if there be any*.

In medieval and Renaissance texts the subjunctive occurs more frequently, but because it appears so similar to the indicative it is easy to miss. These biblical verses provide examples of its clearest use, which is in the second and third persons. In the present tense these lose their endings: *thou goest* becomes *thou go*, and *he goes* (or *goeth*) becomes *he go*. Thus in verse 19, *till thou return* is a subjunctive, indicating that the action of dying, though inevitable, is still in the future. Both verbs are subjunctive in *lest he put forth his hand, and take also of the tree of life*, where the action is a possibility to be avoided. The earlier use in verse 3, *neither shall ye touch it, lest ye die* is also subjunctive, but can easily pass unnoticed as there is no difference in the form of the verb between this and the normal indicative *ye die*.

In the modern period, the auxiliary part of verb phrases becomes more complex, while modals continue to mark important differences of meaning.

Samuel Richardson, *Clarissa* (1747–48)
I beg your pardon, my dearest friend, for having given you occasion to remind me of the date of my last. I was willing to have before me as much of the workings of your wise relations as possible; being verily persuaded that one side or the other would have yielded by this time: and then I should have had some degree of certainty to found my observations upon. And indeed what can I write that I have not already written? You know that I can do nothing but rave at your stupid persecutors: and that you don't like. I have advised you to resume your own estate: that you won't do. You cannot bear the thoughts of having their Solmes: and Lovelace is resolved you shall be his, let who will say to the contrary. I think you must be either the one man's or the other's. Let us see what their next step will be.

(Letter 37)

Long phrases: should, would

In Richardson's writing we find an easy use of longer phrases, characterising the 'speaker' (the novel is made entirely out of letters) as sophisticated and subtle: *would have yielded, should have had* etc. These same phrases show the use of *would* in the third person and *should* in the first, just as *shall* and *will* were given these tasks in the expression of future time. This is a concept of correctness which had not entered the language at the time of the two previous passages.

Auxiliaries: can, shall, will

We find *can* above, both in the sense of 'am able', and also its opposite, 'cannot'. There is an interesting use of *will* and *shall* with their colours of volition and obligation: in context, *that you won't do* implies 'you don't want to do it'. *Lovelace is resolved you shall be his* is stronger than 'will be his' would be. In the last lines we have *will* as a full verb in the subjunctive: *let who will say . . . .* The last *will* is the 'colourless' simple future: it seems unlikely that any conscious intention is implied.

Must

Finally, the word *must* in this passage demands interpretation. Some context is necessary here. Clarissa, to whom the letter is written, is faced by an unenviable choice: she must either marry Solmes, the husband her family has chosen for her (hence *their Solmes*), or Lovelace, a dubious character who is pursuing her. Now her friend says she *must* marry one or the other: does she mean *you have to marry one of them*, implying she has some duty to do this, or does she mean *You are fated to end up marrying one or the other*? Both meanings are possible in the passage, and both survive today. Since it is unlikely that Clarissa's friend would be so bossy, it seems likely that 'fated' is the meaning here. The passage as a whole illustrates the use that can be made of verbal phrases to talk about imagined or expected events with subtle degrees of certainty and shades of feeling.

Having explored noun and verb phrases, we can now go onto the next level, that of the clause / sentence.

Phrases – Exercises

1. The following sonnet was written by William Wordsworth (1770–1850) on the beach near Calais in 1802. The 'Dear child' he addresses is the ten-year-old Caroline, his daughter by Annette Vallon. Read the poem a few times, and then identify the noun phrases. What effects are created by the structure of the phrases and their various elements?

   It is a Beauteous Evening

   It is a beauteous evening, calm and free,
   The holy time is quiet as a Nun

Breathless with adoration; the broad sun
Is sinking down in its tranquility; 4
The gentleness of heaven broods o'er the Sea:
Listen! The mighty Being is awake,
And doth with his eternal motion make
A sound like thunder – everlastingly. 8
Dear Child! dear Girl! That walkest with me here,
If thou appear untouched by solemn thought,
Thy nature is not therefore less divine:
Thou liest in Abraham's bosom all the year, 12
And worship'st at the Temple's inner shrine,
God being with thee when we know it not.

Notes: Abraham's bosom is the resting place of the souls in heaven (see *Luke* xvi.22).

The Temple's inner shrine is the holy of holies of the temple at Jerusalem, where God is held to be present.

2. Here is another letter from *Clarissa*. The heroine, Miss Clarissa Harlowe, has just eloped with Lovelace. She is writing to her friend Miss Howe. Comment on the use and effect of verb phrases, particularly modals and other auxiliaries.

Oh my dearest friend!
After what I had resolved upon, as by my former, what shall I write? What *can* I? With what consciousness, even by *letter*, do I approach you! – You will soon hear (if already you have not heard from the mouth of common fame) that your Clarissa Harlowe is gone off with a man! –

I am busying myself to give you the particulars at large. The whole twenty-four hours of each day (to begin the moment I can fix) shall be employed in it till it is finished: Every one of the hours, I mean, that will be spared me by this interrupting man, to whom I have made myself so foolishly accountable for too many of them. Rest is departed from me. I have no call for that: and that has no balm for the wounds of my mind. So you'll have all those hours without interruption till the account is ended.

But will you receive, shall you be *permitted* to receive, my letters, after what I have done?

Oh, my dearest friend! – But I must make the best of it.

(Letter 92)

3.3 Clauses

SPCA analysis

Once we have a noun phrase (NP) and a verb phrase (VP) we have enough to make a grammatical clause or sentence:

NP	VP
Dogs	bite
The old man	was dying

'Noun phrase' and 'verb phrase' are grammatical terms. They describe these kinds of arrangements of words. If we then want to discuss what these phrases are doing within a clause, we need a different set of terms. In this section, we shall be dealing with a way of describing a clause in terms of the function of clause elements, rather than their grammatical composition. For example, in grammatical terms, *Dogs* is a noun phrase made up of a single headword: it would remain a noun phrase whatever it is doing in a sentence, whether subject (*Dogs bark*) or object (*I love dogs*). In the clause *Dogs bite* it is the **subject**. This is the first term we must look at more closely.

Subject (S)

What is a subject in a sentence? There are various ways of answering this question. First we might define a subject by its meaning: it is the agent of the verb, that which is performing the action (***Dogs** bite*). Or it may be the topic referred to (***my brother** is kind*). When we write a sentence, subject and verb have to agree in number (*The old man **was**, not **were***). The subject is also what we ask about if we turn the sentence into a question (*Do **dogs** bite?*).

Predicator (P) / predicate

In *Dogs bite*, then, we can say that *Dogs* is a noun (the part of speech), and also the head of the noun phrase, which is functioning as the subject. What, then, we might ask, is the function of the verb *bite*? In the method of analysis we are looking at in this section, *bite* is the **predicator**. It tells us what the subject is doing.

There is a potentially confusing overlap between the predicator, which refers to the verbal group accompanying the subject, and the grammatical term **predicate**, which is simply everything after the subject. The distinction should be clear if we look at a single sentence:

The old shepherd lived on the barren mountainside.

The predicator is the verb belonging to the subject: *lived*. The predicate is everything we are told about the subject: *lived on the barren mountainside*.

There is one important difference between noun phrases and verb phrases, and hence between subjects and predicators. That is, while the noun phrase cannot be broken up, the verb phrase can. Predicators, therefore, can consist of words which are slightly separated from each other. One way they can be interrupted is by an adverbial element, giving us more information about the verb: *he has **just** come in, I have **recently** been trying hard to get in touch with you*. The adverbial element, in bold in these examples, comes between auxiliary and main verb. Another common kind of disruption occurs when we ask a question: *Shall I compare thee to a summer's day?* Here, subject and auxiliary change places. When the predicator is interrupted in this way it is said to be discontinuous.

Complement (C)

The term **complement** can be used in two senses in grammar. The first sense is as subject or object complement. When we say something like *He is tall*, the word *tall* is said to be the subject complement, telling us what the subject is. In *He pronounced it delicious*, *delicious* is the object complement describing the object *it*.

The second use of *complement*, and the one we are concerned with here, is more general. It is simply the name given to anything which is needed to complete the sense of the predicator. For example:

S	P	C
She	is	kind
The young man	is making	cakes

In traditional grammar, *kind* is subject complement, and *cakes* is object, suffering the action of the verb. But in the SPCA system, both are regarded as a complement. In fact, when we analyse a sentence as SPCA, we do not use the term 'object'. Anything which we have to put after a verb to make sense – including direct or indirect object – is the complement. It will be seen that this system is in fact a very simple model of analysis, since it uses only four terms.

Adjunct (A)

The final term we are concerned with here is the **adjunct**. This is simply anything left over once we have identified the other three. An adjunct will commonly give more information about the circumstances of an action: *with a smile, quickly, at the end of the lane*. All of these are adverbial phrases, which would give more information about a verb. Adjuncts are very frequently adverbials, unsurprisingly since extra information about circumstances is exactly what adverbials are generally used for. Some grammarians also label as adjuncts other stuck-on elements like *however* and *actually*, which are usually labelled **conjuncts** because they join larger units of discourse together. Very often, though, an adjunct will be an adverbial. The term 'adjunct' describes its function in the sentence as something added, not grammatically essential.

A simple SPCA structure looks like this:

S	P	C	A
The old man	found	the message	on his doorstep

Of the four elements, the adjunct is the most dispensable as far as making grammatical sense is concerned. It is also the most movable in word order. There can, of course, be many adjuncts in a clause:

A	S	P	C	A
At last	I	could see	him	properly

A		A		S P
One evening in the middle of winter,		without any warning,		he died

Using SPCA

The SPCA system gives us a means of breaking down sentences into their constituent parts without going into too much technical analysis. This can help us in various ways:

- Looking for the subject and predicator gives us a path into the long and elaborate sentences which we often encounter in literary texts. In these, it is not always obvious what, or where, the S and P are. Once we have identified these elements, we are well on the way to understanding the sentence.
- An author's use of word order is an important aspect of style. Deviation from normal word order is often deployed to point a meaning or create an expressive effect. The terms of SPCA allow us to describe such stylistic devices.

Sentence structure: applying the SPCA system

Now we have learned the SPCA system, it is time to apply it to some sentences, to see how it can help us to notice some of the ways in which statements can be put together, and the effects which different sentence structures can achieve. Sentence structure is used for many stylistic purposes. We shall consider just two general headings under which word order can be studied: the relation of clause structure to information structure; and poetic inversion.

Ordering information

The structure of a sentence is the way the information in it is arranged. The shape as well as the content of a sentence affects the way we interpret it. Once we have identified subject and predicator, and, if there are any, complement and adjunct, we can ask the following question: where is the most important information, and how is the writer emphasising it?

In answering this, we might first look at the beginning and end of any sentence. Very often we will find at the beginning the **topic**, what the sentence is about. The end is important because it is natural for sentences to grow to a sort of climax and have their most important idea placed at the end: this is called **end-focus**. Consider the following examples:

S	P	A
He	died	in the middle of winter

A		S	P
In the middle of winter		he	died

Both sentences provide the same information, but they do so with a different ordering of elements. In the first sentence the subject is the topic (*He*), but the focus falls on the adjunct (*in the middle of winter*): it is *when* he died that seems to be the most important information. In the second version, the adjunct still seems important because it is in the topic position, but the real emphasis – unless the intonation of a speaker indicates otherwise – is on the predicator, *died*. The ordering of elements has affected the way we interpret the statements.

Suppose that we wanted to keep *died* in the end-focus position, but at the same time wished to give even more emphasis to the adjunct, *in the middle of winter*. Then we might turn to a common habit in English of chopping up a sentence and turning it into two:

It was in the middle of winter that he died

The relative *that* links the two clauses, the main to the subordinate. Effectively both *middle of winter* and *died* are now at the end of a clause and so seem to carry a special importance. This kind of construction is called a **cleft sentence**.

Here is an example of a literary writer ordering information so as to grade it in importance:

> Outside poetry, and, in lesser measure, his family life, Swinburne's interests were curiously limited. He had no 'small talk', and during the discussion of the common topics of the day his attention at once flagged and fell off, the glazed eye betraying that the mind was far away. For science he had no taste whatever, and his lack of musical ear was a byword among his acquaintances.
>
> (Sir Edmund Gosse, *Portraits and Sketches* (1912))

In the first sentence, the important point is that Swinburne had few interests. Thus, the complement *curiously limited* is placed at the end, and the adjuncts are used to build up to it. The sentence could equally have been written *Swinburne's interests were curiously limited outside poetry and, in lesser measure, his family life*, but the sense of leading up to the main point would then be lost. Alternatively, the end-focus could have been made even more dramatic by putting the adjunct between verb and complement: *his interests were, outside poetry etc., curiously limited*.

A similar effect is present in the second sentence, with the adjunct *during the discussion topics of the day* delaying the final *his attention* [S] *at once* [A] *flagged* [P] *and fell off* [P]. A little later we have *For science he had no taste whatever*. Why not *He had no taste whatever for science*? The author's arrangement, with *For science* in the topic position and the adjunct *whatever* at the final point in the clause, emphasises Swinburne's indifference. The movement of *For science* to the front of the sentence is an example of the process of *topicalisation*.

Clause structure: inversion

Topicalisation, cleft sentences and shifting into end-focus are regular ways of arranging sentence elements in English. They all occur in normal conversation as well as in literature. But we can find writers reversing the order of elements, or inverting, in all sorts of other ways. Undoubtedly the most extravagant inverter in English literature is Milton. Here he describes the angel Raphael's flight to earth:

> Down thither prone in flight
> He speeds, and through the vast ethereal sky
> Sails between worlds and worlds, with steady wing
> Now on the polar winds, then with quick fan
> Winnows the buxom air; till within soar   5
> Of towering eagles, to all the fowls he seems
> A phoenix, gazed by all, as that sole bird
> When to enshrine his relics in the sun's
> Bright temple, to Aegyptian Thebes he flies.
>   At once on the eastern cliff of Paradise   10

He lights, and to his proper shape returns
A seraph winged; six wings he wore, to shade
His lineaments divine.

(Paradise Lost, v, 266–78)

To begin with, though the phrases are unusual (*Down thither prone*), the basic construction is common. It is ASP, as in *with a big smile he accepted*. When we see this basic structure we can see that the first two clauses follow the same order. In the second clause the subject *he* is logically there – we understand it as part of the sentence – even though it is not written. It is a compound sentence with, as is usual, the pronoun elided in the second clause, as in *He opened the door and left*. Applying the SPCA analysis, we see the following repeated structural pattern:

A   [*Down thither prone in flight*]
S   [*He*] P [*speeds*], *and* A [*through the vast ethereal sky*]
S   [*he*, understood] P [*Sails*]

The plain subject *he* is sandwiched between the far richer adjunct, which is topicalised at the start of the construction, and the predicator, which is in the end focus slot. So we can say that the action and its description are brought vividly to our attention, while the subject is of less interest. In these lines, the adjuncts are further emphasised by their position in the verse line. Both come at the end of the line, which, like the end of a clause, is a natural focus point. So the focusing achieved by verse form is layered onto that provided by the grammar.

If we return to the passage from Milton, we can see that the basic structure we have just described is repeated as a recurring pattern. This structural repetition offsets the remarkable variety of rhythm and dazzling richness of imagery:

A	S	P	C
With steady wing ... with quick fan	[he]	winnows	the buxom air
To all the fowls	he	seems	a phoenix
To Aegyptian Thebes	he	flies	
At once ... Paradise	He	lights	

This structure, as used here, is also front-heavy: the longest, most informative element is shifted to the front, and this gives the verse a 'heavy' feel. The sentences at once become easier to follow, though much less compelling poetically, if we move the 'heavy' part to the end: *he winnows the air with steady wing ..., he flies to Aegyptian Thebes*.

Typical inversions occur in the last sentence quoted above:

six wings he wore, to shade
His lineaments divine.

Six wings he wore has the shape CSP, an inversion common in poetry and in some idioms of colloquial speech: *Two cars you've crashed!* Just as 'poetic' is the inversion of elements in the nominal group, with the modifier following the head word in *His lineaments divine* (another example is *A seraph winged*).

Inversion of subject and predicator

Another common inversion is PS – *say I*. This does not occur in these lines from Milton, though *to his proper shape returns A seraph winged* could in theory be construed in that way (i.e. meaning *A seraph winged returns to his proper shape*), but this seems very lame. It is more likely that *A seraph winged* is in apposition to *a proper shape* (as in *to my home town I went, Luton*). Elsewhere in *Paradise Lost* the PS order is quite usual. An example is *to whom soon moved with touch of blame thus Eve* (ix.1143). This has the order A (*to whom*) + A (*soon*) + P (*moved*) + A (*with touch of blame*) + A (*thus*) + S (*Eve*). The sheer quantity of adjuncts is typical of Milton, giving the impression that as much information as possible is being squeezed into the lines. As readers, we are forced to concentrate all the time as we try to take in so much detail.

Literary effects of reordering

Poetic licence

We cannot prove that Milton thought through consciously the grammar of his sentences as we have above: describing poetry is a different task from writing it, and there is no special reason to expect the two activities to coincide. It is also always possible to over-interpret syntax, as it is with any linguistic phenomenon. Many unusual shapes in poetry are no doubt there not to build in further meaning or effect, but to give the poet flexibility within the constraints of metre and rhyme. Sometimes, too, inversion is probably used because it is felt to be part of poetic language: deviation becomes, paradoxically, what is expected. In lazy verse, this kind of device is felt to assure a proper literary feel.

Style

Milton uses inversion and strange sentence structures so much, however, that they cannot only be explained as fitting the requirements of metre: indeed, at many points they make the metre more complicated. They are a feature of his grand style, echoing classical epic poems such as *The Aeneid*, in which Latin word order is notably freer than English. By using complex structures, Milton is associating his work with these great classical precedents, and so giving it a particular majesty and dignity.

As well as pointing back to Latin, Milton's syntax is also part of the contemporary style in the arts generally termed the Baroque. Baroque art favours bold, extravagant designs and colours: examples are the paintings of El Greco and the richly decorated architecture of Inigo Jones. Ordered and balanced sentences express classical harmony, while the short stabbing sentences of much writing today perhaps say something about a modern taste for speed and constant excitement. It is often fruitful to look for resemblances between sentence structures and the wider culture in which an author worked.

Poetic effects

As we have seen, writers sometimes reorder sentences from what we might normally expect to emphasise meaning. We have seen how in the first lines of the Milton passage the adjuncts are given prominence both by their position at the start of the clause and by their placing at line endings. This structuring helps us to imagine the scale of the voyage. If the poet had written *He speeds down thither prone in flight*, we would read the long phrase more quickly because the idea of speed would be in our mind. Delaying the verb makes us linger over the sensation of space created in this phrase and by *through the vast ethereal sky*. Similarly, *with steady wing* at the end of the line helps us to fix the image of the wing, before we see what it does.

Another effect created through syntactic order is that it brings words together, sparking new ideas. This is an important feature of Latin verse and Milton bends the rules of English word order to imitate it. An example above is the juxtaposition in *sky / Sails*, where contrasting ideas of sky and sea are brought together. Another example of juxtaposition at a line ending is *quick fan / Winnows*. We first interpret *fan* in its common modern sense of something you beat the air with to create a breeze. When the verb *Winnows* is revealed, another sense of the word is brought out, for a *fan* was also an instrument for winnowing grain: it was a basket used for separating the corn from the chaff. In the normal SPCA word order this would become *He winnows the buxom air with quick fan*, and the extra sense would be less clear.

So far we have been analysing the structure of single clauses. We can now move on to the next level and consider whole sentences, which often consist of several clauses tied together by conjunctions.

Clause structure – Exercises

1. Write an account of the effects of the grammatical structures of the passage below.

    - How does the ordering of the elements of the clauses emphasise certain ideas?
    - Select two or three sentences, and comment on the importance of the subject, predicator, complement and adjuncts.
    - What relation can you find between the sentence shapes used and the atmosphere of mystery and excitement?
    - Take some sentences and find other ways in which the elements could have been ordered. Then describe the particular effects of the ordering which the writer has used.

    The Child Angel: A Dream
    I chanced upon the prettiest, oddest, fantastical thing of a dream the other night, that you shall hear of. I had been reading the 'Loves of the Angels', and went to bed with my head full of speculations, suggested by that extraordinary legend. It had given birth to innumerable conjectures; and, I remember, the last waking thought, which I gave expression to on my pillow, was a sort of wonder 'what could come of it'.

    I was suddenly transported, how or whither I could scarcely make out – but to some celestial region. It was not the real heavens neither – not the downright Bible heaven – but a kind of fairyland heaven, about which a poor human fancy may have leave to sport and air itself, I will hope, without presumption.

Methought – what wild things dreams are! – I was present – at what would you imagine? – at an angel's gossiping.

Whence it came, or how it came, or who bid it come, or whether it came purely of its own head, neither you nor I know – but there lay, sure enough, wrapt in its little cloudy swaddling bands – a Child Angel.

Sun-threads – filmy beams – ran through the celestial napery of what seemed its princely cradle.

(Charles Lamb (1775–1834): from The Last Essays of Elia (1833))

2. Identify the inversions in the following lines, and comment on their effect:

The Pleasures of Retirement
When lavish Phoebus pours out melted gold,
And Zephyr's breath does spice unfold,
And we the blue-eyed sky in tissue vest behold,

Then view the mower, who with big-swollen veins
Wieldeth the crookèd scythe, and strains
To barb the flowery tresses of the verdant plains.

Then view we valleys by whose fringèd seams
A brook of liquid silver streams,
Whose water crystal seems, sand gold, and pebbles gems;

Where bright-scaled gliding fish on trembling line
We strike, when they our hook entwine;
Thence do we make a visit to a grave divine.

(Edward Benlowes (1603?-76), from Theophila (1652), Canto 13)

3.4   Sentences: types of sentence

Sentences divide grammatically into three types: simple, compound and complex.

Simple sentence

A simple sentence consists of a single clause, with a subject and a predicate. The contemporary crime writer James Ellroy has created an extraordinary style based on using short, simple sentences, clustered in brief paragraphs. With their use of standard structures, they form the sharpest contrast to Milton's style:

Littell leaned on his car. The façade expanded. He got the sun. He got Arden Smith's car. He got her U-Haul.

He borrowed a Bureau car. He ran Arden Smith. She came back clean. He got her vehicle stats. He nailed her Chevy.

She felt dirty. She saw the hit. She ran from the PD. That U-Haul said *RUNNER*.

(The Cold Six Thousand (2001), ch. 5, p. 28)

Conjunctions in the mind

In the passage above there are no conjunctions. Sentences laid together like this (or just joined with *and*) are said to be **paratactic**. Nevertheless, even though there are no conjunctions on the page, there may still be some in the mind. We have a strong instinctive desire to join together events and put them in logical relations. We may connect sentences like this: *She felt dirty **because** she saw the hit, **so** she ran* ... . In fact, unless we did something like this, the text would be meaningless. Of course, the passage above makes more sense in the context of the story, but the machine-gun prose makes serious demands on the reader to connect events. The style perhaps owes something to film, in which we are used to putting objects and events into logical patterns without the help of conjunctions.

Expanding a finite clause

Take a simple sentence like *She saw the hit*. Here, we have a subject (*She*), a predicator (*saw*) and a complement, the direct object *the hit*. The verb *saw* is said to be **finite** because it is marked for tense and mood, here past indicative. **Non-finite** forms are the participles (*seeing, seen*) and the **infinitive** (*see*). These are not marked for mood or tense.

The subject and finite verb are the basic elements of the clause. One of the things we find when reading earlier English is how one finite verb can go a long way. This is often in imitation of Latin, where finite forms are avoided and actions are referred to in other ways. A simple, single-clause sentence can easily be made complex in this way if we add dependent non-finite clauses, that is clauses which are introduced by one of the non-finite verb forms:

*Without quite **understanding** what was happening, she saw the hit*
(non-finite clause introduced by present participle)
***Unseen** by the gunman, she saw the hit*
(non-finite clause introduced by past participle)

Or we could keep the sentence simple but add a phrase in **apposition**:

*She, **usually the least observant of people**, saw the hit*

Another kind of expansion is to replace the subject with something much longer. This could even contain an embedded clause of its own:

***The last person you would have expected** saw the hit*

Here, *you would have expected* is a relative clause forming part of the subject.

The examples above (except the expansion with apposition) are technically complex, since non-finite clauses are dependent: a complex sentence, as we shall see later, is a main clause with one or more subordinate or dependent clauses. The point to be made here, though, is that in all the expansions we have made to *She saw the hit* there is still only that one finite verb *saw*, acting rather like the keystone in a building. Everything else is built around it. In reading literature of the nineteenth century and earlier, it can be a helpful exercise to identify the basic elements SPCA and the finite verb, to find the base structure within what can be very elaborate constructions. Here are some typical features of writing in a more verbose style than we are used to in the age of Ellroy:

(a) Long subject
Now, *the evil consequences of the acceptance of this kind of religious idealism for true*, were instant and manifold.

(John Ruskin, *Modern Painters*, III (1856))

(b) Adjuncts before subject and after predicator
Early on a cold and dark spring morning **Mr Nelson's servant arrived** *at this school at North Walsham with the expected summons for Horatio to join his ship.*

(Robert Southey, *Life of Nelson* (1813))

The finite verb is *arrived*. Elsewhere in the sentence we find the non-finite form, the infinitive *to join*, making a non-finite clause within an adjunct.

In the next example, there are a number of infinitives (*to look* etc.) coming before the main finite verb: there is a deliberate suspense in keeping us waiting for the finite clause, which comes after a long series of adjunct phrases:

(c) Altogether, with her meagre knowledge, her inflated ideals, her confidence at once innocent and dogmatic, her temper at once exacting and indulgent, her mixture of curiosity and fastidiousness, of vivacity and indifference, her desire to look very well and to be if possible even better, her determination to see, to try, to know, her combination of the delicate desultory flame-like spirit and the eager and personal creature of conditions: she would be an easy victim of scientific criticism ...

(Henry James, *Portrait of a Lady* (1881))

In this last example, the finite clause is so delayed that it is even introduced by a colon. One of the many demands being made on the reader is to retain all this information about the character, at the same time as the anticipation of the main verb induces us to read quickly. The lack of other finite verbs conveys the effect of a slow, reflective study of this character.

Compound sentence

Compound sentences are clauses tied together with the **co-ordinating** conjunctions *and, or* and *but*. The clauses in a compound sentence are said to be co-ordinate because they can exist independently: in *John bought oranges and Mary bought peaches* the two clauses are linked by *and* and do not depend on each other.

Co-ordinating conjunctions and narrative

Perhaps the most frequent use of *and* and *but* is to link separate events into narrative form: 'I went out *and* looked in the sales for some clothes *but* I didn't buy any' links three events in succession. The tone is simple, brisk and conversational:

> As I walked through the wilderness of this world, I lighted on a certain place, where was a den; and I laid me down in that place to sleep: and as I slept I dreamed a dream. I dreamed, and behold I saw a man clothed with rags, standing in a certain place, with his face from his own house, a book in his hand, and a great burden upon his back. I looked, and saw him open the book, and read therein; and as he read, he wept and trembled ...
>
> (John Bunyan, *The Pilgrim's Progress* (1678), beginning)

With these co-ordinate constructions Bunyan establishes a natural, conversational voice. We are at once inclined to trust the narrator and hold on to the story as it speeds along, event following event. At the same time, the use of *and* here has echoes of the Bible: *And God said Let there be light. And there was light.* By combining conversational freshness and biblical dignity, the narrative also suggests a high seriousness. The little word *and* is an integral part of this process.

Realistic *and*

The co-ordinating conjunctions suggest less analytical thinking on the part of the author. Bunyan's sentences seem to present an experience just as it happened, one thing after another, before the writer has shaped it into something more complex. For this reason, the compound sentence has attracted modern writers like Hemingway, who want to convey the immediacy of experience.

Compound sentences and ambiguity

The conjunctions of compound sentences, especially *and*, are so plain that they can easily escape our attention. Yet authors will sometimes use them in preference to a subordinating conjunction precisely because they are less attention-grabbing. The range of logical relations that can be expressed by co-ordinating conjunctions is wide. This is the beginning of Henry James's novel *The Spoils of Poynton* (1897):

> Mrs Gereth had said she would go with the rest to church, *but* suddenly it seemed to her she shouldn't be able to wait even till church-time for relief: breakfast was at Waterbath a punctual meal *and* she still had nearly an hour on her hands. Knowing the church to be near she prepared in her room for the little rural walk, *and* on her way down again, passing through corridors and observing imbecilities of decoration, the esthetic misery of the big commodious house, she felt a return of the tide of last night's irritation, a renewal of everything she could secretly suffer from ugliness and stupidity.

The *but* introduces Mrs Gereth's realisation of how fed up and impatient she is. As it takes us swiftly into the next clause it helps convey the suddenness of the thought. Another way of writing this would have been to use a **conjunct**, a linking word or phrase which starts a sentence: *However, suddenly it seemed,* or

Nevertheless, suddenly . . . . These would have a heavier feel, while *but* takes us into the world of a thought suddenly arriving in her mind. The first *and* implies 'and so', and the second one 'and then'. If we substituted them with *so* and *then*, though, the feel of the passage would be different. It would feel more like we were with the author analysing her from the outside, rather than inside the character, experiencing her feelings along with her.

Complex sentence

Complex sentences are clauses linked by subordinating conjunctions. The following construction contains several examples:

> *Though* his father's death brought no other convenience to him but a title to redeem an estate mortgaged for as much as it was worth and *for which* he was compelled to sell a finer seat of his own, *yet* it imposed a burthen upon him of the title of a viscount and an increase of expense, *in which* he was not in his nature too provident or restrained, having naturally such a generosity and bounty in him *that* he seemed to have his estate in trust for all worthy persons *who* stood in want of supplies and encouragement ... *which* yet they were contented to receive from, *because* his bounties were so generously distributed ...
>
> (Clarendon, *The History of the Rebellion*, description of Falkland)

In this construction, the main clause is *it imposed a burthen upon him*. (The *yet* which introduces it does not make the clause subordinate, but reminds us of the opening *Though* which is now some way away.) Other clauses are subordinate to, or dependent on, the main clause. **Subordinate** clauses expand elements in the main clause: they might further define or describe them, or explain them, or add further information.

We saw earlier in this chapter how the logical relations between words can be signalled by inflections (*the king's throne*) and by prepositions (*the throne of the king*). At the level of the clause, logical relations are shown by the order of elements (*the rebels burned the king's throne*: SPC). Subordinating conjunctions represent logical relations at the next level, in indicating the relation of subclauses to the main one in the sentence. The following sentence by Clarendon (1609–74) gives an idea of the complexities of thought which subordination can express. Here it allows us to keep moving from one idea to the next without the heavy pause that a full stop would bring.

> The person whose life this discourse is to recollect (and who had so great an affection and reverence for the memory of the prelate, [archbishop Laud,] that he never spake of him without extraordinary esteem, and believed him to be a man of the most exemplar virtue and piety of any of that age) was wont to say, the greatest want the archbishop had was of a true friend, who would seasonably have told him of his infirmities, and what people spake of him; and he said, he knew very well that such as friend would have been very acceptable to him; and upon that occasion he used to mention a story of himself: that when he was a young practiser of the law, being in some favour

with him, (as is mentioned before,) he went to visit him in the beginning of a Michaelmas term, shortly after his return from the country, where he had spent a month or two of the summer.

(From *The History of the Rebellion*, published 1702)

Here is the same sentence set out clause by clause with co-ordinators and subordinators in bold:

1. The person **whose** life this discourse is to recollect
2. (**and who** had so great an affection and reverence for the memory of the prelate,
3. **that** he never spake of him without extraordinary esteem,
4. **and** believed him to be a man of the most exemplar virtue and piety of any of that age)

5. was wont to say,
6. the greatest want the archbishop had was of a true friend,
7. **who** would seasonably have told him of his infirmities,
8. **and** what people spake of him;

9. **and** he said,
10. he knew very well
11. **that** such a friend would have been very acceptable to him;

12. **and** upon that occasion he used to mention a story of himself:
13. **that when** he was a young practiser of the law, being in some favour with him,
14. (**as** is mentioned before,)
15. he went to visit him in the beginning of a Michaelmas term, shortly after his return from the country,
16. **where** he had spent a month or two of the summer.

This is a compound–complex sentence, because it contains complex constructions linked by *and*: 1–8 form a complex sentence, with the main clause elements being *The person was wont to say the greatest want.... .* A conjunction joins it to another in 9 and 10, followed by a third in 11–15. Within these three independent sentences we also find a tendency to use groups: at the start, there are two 'who' clauses, followed by two clauses reporting things he said; and within that we find groupings of phrases into two: *affection and reverence, virtue and piety*. The architecture of the sentence allows the account to run at an even pace, taking us from one idea to the next without hurry or confusion. The style conveys the idea of a certain kind of conversation, learned but also leisurely.

Syntax and thought

Syntax expresses thought. It allows us to link single ideas together into larger structures of narrative, description and argument: the sentence above does all three of these. Sometimes the syntax may not be strictly grammatical or logical, but will give us a clear impression of the flow of ideas; this flow of information, carried by a graceful rhythm, usually seems to be more important to writers like Browne and Milton than does strict grammatical agreement.

We have seen that co-ordination is well suited to story telling. Subordination is particularly suited to the articulation of a complex sequence of thoughts. It is the linguistic equivalent of a filing cabinet, putting every piece of information in its proper place. There are many possibilities not illustrated by the sentence above, such as concession (*although*), cause (*because, since, as*), opposition (*whereas*) and possibility (*if, whether*). *Complex subordinators* consist of more than one word: 'in order that', 'depending on whether' and so on.

Conjuncts and conjunctions

In modern grammar there is a difference between **conjuncts** and **conjunctions**. A conjunct is something that links a sentence, or a paragraph, with what has preceded it: *nevertheless, however, on the other hand*. (Confusingly, these are also sometimes classed as adjuncts in SPCA analyses.) Conjuncts do not contain a clause, whereas subordinating conjunctions always introduce a clause. Thus we can say as a complete statement *Nevertheless, the King resigned* but not *Although, the King resigned*. Both types of word are very similar, though, in providing the logical framework of a discourse.

Subordination and end-focus

Subordinate clauses can work with end-focus to create similar effects of expectation, emphasis and resolution. In these lines from a sonnet by Shakespeare, subordinate *when* clauses accumulate, making us expect *then* to appear and complete the sense. This is a frequent device in the sonnets, and tests how many such clauses we can keep in our mind at one time.

> When I do count the clock that tells the time,
> And see the brave day sunk in hideous night;
> When I behold the violet past prime,
> And sable curls all silvered o'er with white;   4
> When lofty trees I see barren of leaves,
> Which erst from heat did canopy the herd,
> And summer's green all girded up in sheaves,
> Borne on the bier with white and bristly beard,   8
> Then of thy beauty do I question make ...
> (Sonnet 12)

Multiple subordination here gives a dramatic shape to the thought being expressed. It also contributes to the sense we have of intellectual control in the shaping of the text. The language of this poem may spring from spontaneous thought, but it is superbly controlled on every level: the formal frame of metre and rhyme; the architecture of the large sentence; parallelism within lines and clauses (*When ... and, When ... and*; parallel noun phrases like *brave day* and *hideous night*); and the choice and sequences of images to convey both the thought of time passing and the emotion which the thought evokes. The use of subordination here, keeping us moving until the resolution in a main clause, also creates a rhythm: the images follow in a continuous flow, all belonging to one syntactic structure and one unified mental reflection.

Suspended syntax

Shakespeare's sonnet is an example of suspended syntax. It keeps us in suspense until the end of the sentence. This is done through expansion of elements of the main clause, building in delays. Suspended syntax is not always achieved through subordinate clauses: it can be done through the arrangement of adjunct phrases in a simple sentence as well. In each sentence of this passage from an essay by the nineteenth-century writer Thomas de Quincey (1785–1859), we sense that the 'best', or most important, is being kept until last. In this example, it is phrases rather than clauses which are used to achieve the suspense.

> With respect to William's murders, the sublimest and most entire in their excellence that ever were committed, I shall not allow myself to speak incidentally. Nothing less than an entire lecture, or even an entire course of lectures, would suffice to expound their merits. But one curious fact, connected with his case, I shall mention, because it seems to imply that the blaze of his genius absolutely dazzled the eye of criminal justice.
>
> ('On Murder Considered as one of the Fine Arts' (1827))

Suspended syntax gives writing like this a particularly strong feel. The sentences feel as if they know where they are going, and are leading us towards something interesting. Sentences end with strong ideas and images – *the eye of criminal justice* – which also make sense of the whole statement.

Sentences – Exercises

1. Take the following simple sentences and build around them, without adding any more finite verbs. Pronouns like *it, he, they* can be changed into different subjects: for example, *he* can become *the man from the bank*. When you have expanded the sentences, try to describe what you have added using the correct grammatical terms, and comment on the stylistic effects achieved.

Example
The neighbour phoned.
At last, three months after arriving here, the neighbour, a man in his forties, apparently unmarried and perhaps feeling the need for company, phoned.

> They stole the car.
> She wept.
> They climbed the mountain.
> Bert called.

2. Read the following passage and paraphrase the author's argument in your own words. Then comment on how the syntax and style of the original contribute to its effect. What kinds of sentences are used, and what use does the author make of conjuncts and subordination?

> After considering the historic page, and viewing the living world with anxious solicitude, the most melancholy emotions of sorrowful indignation have depressed my spirits, and I have sighed when obliged to confess, that either nature has made a great difference between man and man, or that the civilization which has hitherto taken place in the world has been very partial. I have turned over various books written on the subject of education, and patiently observed the conduct of parents and the management of schools; but what has been the result? – a profound conviction that the neglected education of my fellow-creatures is the grand source of the misery I deplore; and that women, in particular, are rendered weak and wretched by a variety of concurring causes, originating from one hasty conclusion. The conduct and manners of women, in fact, evidently prove that their minds are not in a healthy state; for, like the flowers which are planted in too rich a soil, strength and usefulness are sacrificed to beauty; and the flaunting leaves, after having pleased a fastidious eye, fade, disregarded on the stalk, long before the season when they ought to have arrived at maturity.
>
> (Mary Wollstonecraft (1759–97), *A Vindication of the Rights of Woman* (1792))

3.5 The period

Modern grammar has helped us to analyse the long, complex sentences which we often find in older literature. Writers like Milton and Clarendon, however, did not see their writing in exactly these terms. To them, a very important concept was the period. The period is like a sentence in that it ends in a full stop (in North America, *period* still means full stop), but it often contains many statements which we would recognise as sentences, divided by colons or semicolons rather than full stops. The period represents one single, unified line of thought and is governed by rhythm as much as by syntax. It is more like a paragraph than a sentence, gathering together all the thoughts within the exploration of an idea. The full stop at the end of a period marks a heavier point of finality than a stop at the end of a sentence like the ones in this paragraph.

Within a period, then, the various clauses are regarded as belonging together. Rhetoric books often describe the sections of a period as limbs: like the bones in a finger or leg, these sections are separate units which make up something greater. To continue the analogy, conjuncts are like joints. They continue a line of thought rather than mark a new departure. The main punctuation points mark the chief limbs which make up the body, or composition, of the period. These limbs are designated **commata** or **cola**, depending on whether they end with a comma or a colon (or semicolon).

Here is an example of a period by the seventeenth-century writer Sir Thomas Browne (1605–82). I have made the *commata* and *cola* clearer by dividing the text into numbered sections. On the page, of course, it is continuous prose.

1. Thus there are two bookes from whence I collect my Divinity;
2. besides that written one of God, another of his servant Nature, that universall and publik manuscript, that lies expans'd unto the eyes of all;
3. those that never saw him in the one, have discovered him in the other:
4. This was the Scripture and Thelogy of the Heathens;
5. the naturall motion of the Sun made them more admire him, than its supernaturall station did the Children of Israel;
6. the ordinary effect of nature wrought more admiration in them, than in the other all his miracles;
7. surely the Heathens knew better how to joyne and reade these mysticall letters, than wee Christians, who cast a more carelesse eye on these common Hieroglyphics, and disdain to suck Divinity from the flowers of nature.

(Religio Medici, Section 16 (1643))

Here the divisions show how Browne's thought is advancing step by step. Nature is a sign of God as much as the Bible (1 and 2); some have perceived God through Nature who have not even read the Bible (3): This is what the Heathens did (4). Nature revealed more of God to heathens than miracles did to the children of Israel (5 and 6). So the Heathens can teach Christians something when it comes to adoring God through Nature (7). With this, the period comes to an end.

The period pivots around the first colon, which ends 3. On either side, we find *semicola*, further divided into *commata*. This arrangement is looser than modern grammar allows. We would have to start a new sentence at several points here; but if we did so, we would lose the visual sense that they belong together. To some extent, the paragraph has come to take over this function. What a paragraph cannot do, however, is indicate, for example, that 5 and 6 are exactly equivalent statements: they are not co-ordinated or subordinated, but are still part of the period, as they could not be grammatically part of a modern sentence.

Punctuation

The modern reader is often deprived of the experience of reading periods because the punctuation of older texts is regularly modernised. This editorial practice may make texts from different periods accessible, but, unless we are aware of it, it can be misleading, in at least two ways.

First, modern punctuation squeezes older kinds of writing into modern-type sentences. It makes Chaucer and Browne obey the rules of modern grammar. We seem to be disinclined to accept the apparent looseness of the syntax of much medieval and Renaissance writing. Along with spelling, the grammar – through punctuation – is regularised to fit modern preconceptions of writing. Yet what might seem loose according to the structures of grammar which we recognise today may be very effective by other criteria. The period by Browne above, for example, suggests a spoken voice, picking up thoughts as they come to the mind before tidying them into compartmentalised sentences.

As well as 'correcting' pre-modern grammar, modernised punctuation also has the effect of misleading us about the nature of punctuation itself at earlier periods in literature. Today, punctuation is chiefly used to indicate logic. For example, a colon indicates that what follows has a particular relation to the sentence before, such as a list or explanation. Originally, though, punctuation was practical and rhetorical rather than grammatical. It was used to indicate pauses and vocal emphases rather than logical connections: an exclamation mark still does this today.

In many of the quotations in this book, I have used modern editions which have 'tidied up' punctuation, since confronting everything for the first time in its original presentation may make it harder to concentrate on the specific point being made. But serious study of the language of literary texts needs to take account of how those texts appeared to their first readers.

Here is how a speech from *Antony and Cleopatra*, which we have already seen, appears in the First Folio (1623).

ANTONY   Let Rome in Tyber melt, and the wide Arch
                Of the raing'd Empire fall: Heere is my space,
                Kingdoms are clay: Our dungie earth alike
                Feeds Beast as Man; the Nobleness of life
                Is to do thus: when such a mutuall paire,
                And such a twaine can doo't, in which I binde
                One paine of punishment, the world to weete
                We stand up Peerelesse.   (1.1)

This is not Shakespeare's punctuation. It is the system used by the compositors of the book, which was put together after his death. But it shows us another way of thinking about structures in language. The 'sentence', which we think of as the chief unit of sense in grammar, is evidently less important than the unity of thought expressed by the period. We have four *cola*, the third with a central pause on the semicolon. In each *colon*, Antony is saying in a different way that he cares nothing for Rome or Roman ideas of nobility. The colons make each statement seem of equal importance in the sequence, and indicate suitable pauses and emphases to the actor. The closing period marks it as a whole.

Now let us read the speech again, in the modern punctuation of the Oxford edition:

                Let Rome in Tiber melt, and the wide arch
                Of the ranged empire fall. Here is my space.
                Kingdoms are clay. Our dungy earth alike
                Feeds beast as man. The nobleness of life
                Is to do thus; when such a mutual pair
                And such a twain can do't – in which I bind
                On pain of punishment the world to weet –
                We stand up peerless.

This modern layout undoubtedly brings Shakespeare into our time, and gives us a text which helps the contemporary reader and actor. But there are also disadvantages. The sense of the *cola* forming part of something larger is lost. The emphasis on *thus* implied by the colon is lost, and it is not clear why a semicolon is preferred here. Where the First Folio has a sequence of four *cola*, with the longest coming in a climactic position at the end, the modern text gives a succession of sentences with no obvious feel of a final destination.

Punctuation has also been used to bring the writing into line with modern grammar: the clause *in which I bind / On pain of punishment the world to weet* has been put in dashes to mark it as an interruption of the main clause. Yet it may be that the Renaissance reader would not have sensed this as an aside or interruption. In the Folio it is one of three *commata* in the last colon, and works as a second step in an ascending sequence towards the climactic word *Peerless*. The punctuation suggests aspects of rhythm and intonation. If we stop worrying about grammatical correctness and listen for rhetorical effectiveness, then it makes considerable sense. Much of the feeling of gradation in delivery, through semicolons, colons and the full stop, has been lost in the modern presentation.

Beyond the sentence

We have proceeded from words to phrases to clauses, and then to sentences which link clauses either through co-ordination or subordination. In discussing the period, we have seen how punctuation and conjuncts, as well as sub-ordinators, can build a still larger unit of sense.

But even when markers such as punctuation and conjunctions are not present, sentences link together to form larger units, or texts. How do they do this? Two approaches to text analysis are cohesion and coherence. Cohesion is achieved through linguistic devices on the page which show how sentences refer to each other. Coherence, which lies beyond grammar, involves whether a text seems logical, consistent and makes sense in terms of our normal experience of language use. We shall look briefly at each.

The period – Exercise

The following is a passage from Milton's *Paradise Lost* (1667). It keeps the punctuation of the earliest editions, and the original spelling. At this point in the poem, the fallen angels in hell have just been addressed by Beelzebub, who has suggested that one of them should make the dangerous journey to earth to corrupt mankind.

First, read the passage, using the punctuation as a guide to performance. Pause at the punctuation marks, and at any line endings which seem to demand a pause. When you have read the lines aloud, comment on what effect the punctuation has on the way you read and interpret the lines.

> This said, he sat; and expectation held
> His look suspense, awaiting who appeerd
> To second, or oppose, or undertake

The perilous attempt: but all sat mute,   4
Pondering the danger with deep thoughts; and each
In others count'nance red his own dismay
Astonisht: none among the choice and prime
Of those Heav'n-warring Champions could be found   8
So hardie as to proffer or accept
Alone the dreadful voyage; till at last
Satan, whom now transcendent glory rais'd
Above his fellows, with Monarchal pride   12
Conscious of highest worth, unmov'd thus spake.
O Progeny of Heav'n, Empyreal Thrones,
With reason hath deep silence and demurr
Seis'd us, though undismaid: long is the way   16
And hard, that out of Hell leads up to Light;
Our prison strong, this huge convex of Fire,
Outrageous to devour, immures us round
Ninefold, and gates of burning Adamant   20
Barrd over us prohibit all egress.

(Book 2, lines 417–37)

3.6   Cohesion: joining sentences

Cohesion is the study of the linguistic elements of a text which weave the various parts together. It can be observed within the sentence and between sentences. There are five kinds of cohesive device:

• **Reference**: a personal or demonstrative pronoun refers to something else: Do you like *cycling*? I do. Why not take *it* up? No *bike*? No problem! I've got a spare one. How does ***this*** suit you? The best two-wheeler ever made! You'll need ***these***, too: *pump, helmet, repair kit* ...
  [*it* is a pronoun referring to *cycling*; *this* is a demonstrative which refers to *bike*; *these* refers to the nouns which follow – *pump* etc.]

There are two types of reference:

Exophoric reference. *Exophoric* terms refer to things *outside* the text, such as political or cultural context. Some of the most important exophoric words are those which fall under the heading of *deixis*. Mutually understood exophoric reference is an important element of coherence – literally, it is knowing what someone is talking about.

Endophoric reference. *Endophoric* words refer to things *inside* the text. They might refer back to something already mentioned, or forward to something about to mentioned.

References back are *anaphoric*:

Do you like *cycling*? I do. Why not take *it* up?
[*cycling* ← ***it***]
No *bike*? No problem! I've got a spare *one*. How does *this* suit you?
[*bike* ← ***one*** ... ***this***]

References forward are *cataphoric*:

And you'll need **these**, too: *pump, helmet, repair kit* ...
[**these** → *pump* etc.]

- **Substitution**: other words besides pronouns stand for something:

  Do you *like cycling*? I **do**. Why not take it up? No *bike*? No problem! I've got a spare **one**. How does this suit you?
  [**do** is a substitution for *like cycling* – **do** used in this way is sometimes called a *pro-verb*; **one** is a substitute for *bike*]

- **Ellipsis**: an element is omitted, because we can fill it in from something already mentioned, or simply understand it (this is a special case of substitution, and can be called 'substitution by zero'):

  Do you like cycling? I do. Why not take it up? **No bike**? **No problem**! I've got a spare one. How does this suit you?
  [i.e. [You have] no bike? '[That is] no problem!']

- **Lexical**: the same object or idea recurs. A word might be repeated, or there may be many synonyms for it, or words which belong to the same topic.

  Do you like **cycling**? I do. Why not take it up? No **bike**? No problem! I've got a spare one. How does this suit you? The best **two-wheeler** ever made! You'll need these, too: **pump, helmet, repair kit** ...
  [All the words in bold italics belong to the topic of cycling]

- **Conjunction**: in *cohesion*, 'conjunction' refers to *any* element which indicates that a statement is linked in some way to another: thus *then*, an adverb, is a conjunction in cohesion, because it has this connecting function. Conjunctions as cohesive devices are grouped according to their function:

  (i)   *Temporal*: says something is happening next – *and, then*.
  (ii) *Additive*: next sentence provides more information – *and, moreover*.
  (iii) *Adversative*: introduces a contrast or opposition – *but, yet, nevertheless, however*.
  (iv) *Causal*: something occurs because of something else – *if ... then, because, since, so*.
  (v)   *Correlative*: *when ... then*, other formulations which 'bring together' two segments. (For *when ... then* as a tying device, see Shakespeare, Sonnets 12, 15, 29, 30 and 106.)

  Sometimes conjunctions are not spoken or written down, but are *understood*. This logical link is immediately picked up by the listener. There is an *implicit causative* between the two.

Example

Here are the first three sentences of Francis Bacon's essay 'Of Revenge' (1625):

Revenge is a kind of wild justice, which the more man's nature runs to, the more ought law to weed it out. For as for the first wrong, it doth but offend the law; but the revenge of that wrong putteth the law out of office. Certainly, in taking revenge a man is but even with his enemy, but in passing it over he is superior, for it is a prince's part to pardon.

Sentences 1 and 3 could stand alone as single observations. Cohesive devices make us perceive them as part of a sequence:

Reference: *anaphoric reference*
Sentence 1: '*Revenge ... it*'. Notice also that the relative pronoun *which* refers to *Revenge*, not to *wild justice*.
Sentence 2: '*the first wrong, it*'. This construction is not usual in modern English, but is common in Early Modern texts: the reference word here helps to emphasise *the first wrong* (this means the crime which motivated the revenge, and thus sparked off the whole sequence). Other examples are *The first wrong ... **that** wrong*, and sentence 3: in taking *revenge ...* passing *it* over; *a man ... **he***.

Ellipsis: Sentence 3 ... *in passing it over, he is superior* [to him].

Lexical: *Revenge* occurs in each sentence. With the referent *it*, then the *idea* of revenge has come up five times. *Law* is also repeated; *justice* belongs to the same topic, and links with *even*; reiterated *wrong* helps to tie the two parts of sentence 2.

Conjunction. This is best illustrated if we look at the passage as a whole:

1. Revenge is a kind of wild justice, which *the more* man's nature runs to, *the more* ought law to weed it out. [*correlative*]
2. *For* [*causal: introduces explanation of last statement*] as for the first wrong, it doth but offend the law; *but* [*adversative, introducing a contrast*] the revenge of that wrong putteth the law out of office.
3. *Certainly* [*additive, introducing further explanation; means 'unquestionably' – an adverb functioning logically as a conjunction*], in taking revenge a man is but even with his enemy, *but* [*adversative*] in passing it over he is superior, *for* [*causal*] it is a prince's part to pardon.

These cohesive elements, particularly the wide range of conjunctions, mark the text as a piece of concentrated argument, demanding the reader's careful attention. Besides cohesion, other unifying devices are at work. We are drawn in by the pattern of balanced sentences, leading us to expect the second half to answer or resolve the first. Ideas are also fashioned through the rhetorical device of antithesis, whereby ideas are made clearer through being held in contrast: *nature* and *law*; *offend* and *putteth out of office*; *taking ... even, passing it over ... superior*.

Cohesion – Exercise

What are the devices of cohesion in the following passage? (All the names mentioned are those of inventors.)

'Tis frivolous to fix pedantically the date of particular inventions. They have all been invented over and over fifty times. Man is the arch machine, of which all these shifts drawn from himself are toy models. He helps himself on each emergency by copying or duplicating his own structure, just so far as the need is. 'Tis hard to find the right Homer, Zoroaster, or Manu, harder still to find the Tubal Cain, or Vulcan, or Cadmus, or Copernicus, or Fust, or Fulton, the indisputable inventor. There are scores and centuries of them. 'The air is full of men.' This kind of talent so abounds, this constructive tool-making efficiency, as if it adhered to the chemic atoms, as if the air he breathes were made of Vaucansons, Franklins, and Watts.

(Ralph Waldo Emerson (1803–82), from 'Experience', *Essays, Second Series* (1844))

3.7 Coherence

Cohesion does not guarantee coherence. 'I saw a ship. Ships please Henry. He likes me' contains the cohesive markers of lexical repetition and pronouns. But in most circumstances it would be incoherent. Equally, a discourse can be coherent even if it is not cohesive. Let us imagine a dialogue like the following:

A: Did you see the gardens?
B: It was raining

This does not contain cohesive markers, but it would not be difficult to imagine a situation in which this exchange made perfect sense to the speakers. The surrounding circumstances and shared understanding of what is being referred to would make it coherent.

Coherence is an important element in literature as well as real speech, and there are many ways in which texts, like conversations, may be coherent. There is narrative coherence, whereby one episode follows another in a way which seems to make sense – for example, by cause and effect. As we have just seen, conversational coherence can apply in even the most apparently fragmented dialogue if the participants share mutual understandings. Whatever we read or hear we tend to fit into familiar language usages: sense may be made of a sequence of sentences once we know it is a joke, or an attempt at seduction, or a prayer or a veiled threat and so on.

A use of language which does not fit into these usages, or which upsets our picture of things, can soon seem incoherent: *yesterday I saw the moon climbing the mountain which politicians wrote that symphony about.* Even here we would try to find some connecting thread to make the statement coherent: we do not like pure nonsense.

Logical coherence

In the study of literature we often place a high value on the expressive qualities of language, or its use in characterisation and description and other literary topics. The consistency of these forms part of our impression of a text's coherence: for example, a character seems consistent if he or she presents the same qualities throughout, or changes and develops in an understandable way.

Literature also involves logical discourse, whereby the sequence of statements in some way makes sense. The most starkly logical speeches are perhaps those which present rational arguments, and literary texts are rich in examples of these. There are arguments of many kinds in *The Canterbury Tales* and in Shakespeare's plays, while *Paradise Lost* is thick with debate and explanation. Attending to the logical construction of speeches can also be a great aid to understanding the relation that the sentences have to each other. The following examples suggest some ways of exploring this aspect of literary works.

What's the point?

One question we can ask of a passage is 'what point is being made, exactly?' If we try mentally to reduce a passage to its logical core, we may find that a simple point is wrapped up in a great deal of rhetorical decoration. Here is the beginning of *Richard III* (in older punctuation):

> Now is the Winter of our Discontent,
> Made glorious Summer by this Son of Yorke:
> And all the clouds that lowr'd vpon our house
> In the deepe bosome of the Ocean buried.
> Now are our browes bound with Victorious Wreathes,
> Our bruised armes hung vp for Monuments;
> Our sterne Alarums chang'd to merry meetings;
> Our dreadfull Marches, to delightfull Measures.
> Grim-visag'd Warre, hath smooth'd his wrinkled Front:
> And now, in stead of mounting Barbed Steeds,
> To fright the Soules of fearfull Aduersaries,
> He capers nimbly in a Ladies Chamber,
> To the lascivious pleasing of a lute.

The basic point is that 'A grim time of War has changed to a pleasant one of peace'. The writing is in the rhetorical tradition we have already considered in the discussion of noun phrases: it illustrates the practice of using language plentifully, showing off the number of ways one can say the same thing. This is why it is easy to follow the drift of a Shakespeare play or speech, even if we haven't read it. We are often given another chance to take in an idea if we weren't listening the first time.

Argument

There are numerous types of argument, and many kinds of fallacy: some writers, like Milton, expect their readers to pick these up, while many medieval and Renaissance authors were influenced by the training in logic which was then standard in schools and universities. Even the most emotive lines in literature sometimes have reference to this background logic. To some of its first audience, Hamlet's 'To be or not to be' may have suggested an echo of the schoolroom, where Aristotle's *on kai me on* (being and not being) was a well-known text. Marlowe's Doctor Faustus, bored of academic study, decides to *Bid on kai ma on farewell*, and Hamlet is of course a university student.

An argument is a point supported by reasons. This point + supporting argument or evidence is a basic form of coherence. Here is how Juliet's mother introduces the topic of marriage in *Romeo and Juliet*:

> Well thinke of marriage now, yonger than you
> Heere in Verona, Ladies of esteeme,
> Are made already Mothers. By my count
> I was your Mother, much vpon these yeares
> That you are now a Maide, thus then in briefe
> The valiant Paris seekes you for his loue.
>
> (1.3.71–6)

I have used old punctuation again here, to show that it had not yet reached its present functions. Today we would turn the comma in the first line into a colon, since it is introducing an argument explaining why Juliet should get married.

The same shape can occur over a longer passage. In these lines from *Henry IV Part Two*, Hotspur is trying to prove to the King that Mortimer is not a traitor:

> Reuolted *Mortimer*?
> He neuer did fall off, my Soueraigne Liege,
> But by the chance of Warre: to proue that true,
> Needs no more but one tongue. For all those Wounds,
> Those mouthed Wounds, which valiantly he tooke,
> When on the gentle Seuernes sedgie banke,
> In single Opposition hand to hand,
> He did confound the best part of an houre
> In changing hardiment with great *Glendower*.
> Three times they breath'd, and three times did they drink
> Vpon agreement, of swift Seuernes flood;
> Who then affrighted with their bloody lookes,
> Ran fearefully among the trembling Reeds,
> And hid his crispe-head in the hollow banke,
> Blood-stained with these Valiant Combatants.
> Neuer did base and rotten Policy
> Colour her working with such deadly wounds;
> Nor neuer could the Noble *Mortimer*
> Receiue so many, and all willingly:
> Then let him not be sland'red with Reuolt.
>
> (1.3.92–111)

The proposition is that Mortimer has never failed the King, except through the mischances of war. Everything that follows is adduced as proof of this point: he fought to his utmost, and would never have undergone such punishment out of deceit. The last line restates the proposition. The interest of the speech is partly in how the emotive language undercuts the logic and makes it seem a little untrustworthy. But beneath the passion, the speech is extremely coherent because of its logical shape.

Logic is not grammar, but it is a close neighbour. It is frequently helpful in understanding literary texts to ask 'What is being argued? How does this sentence relate to the one before? Is it supporting the point, or restating it, or drawing a conclusion from it?' There is a tendency today to separate argumentative from 'creative' writing. Yet much of the most creative literature is full of argument: indeed a text could hardly have any coherence if we could see no reason why one sentence is following another. Shakespeare's sonnets, many of the lyrics of Hardy and Yeats – all are in some ways pieces of argument. Analysis of the logical form of texts may seem dry next to savouring their emotional force; yet it can also be an aid to appreciation. The underlying logic takes us into emotional logic. We can best respond to the emotive and expressive qualities of a text when we have a clear idea of what it is arguing.

Coherence – Exercise

Summarise in about fifty words the argument of the following lines. Describe what logical job each statement of the original is doing: for example, is it stating a point, restating a point in a different way, illustrating with an example and so on? Comment on the use the poet makes of the rhyming couplet form in driving his argument home.

> They, who have best succeeded on the stage,
> Have still conform'd their genius to their age.
> Thus *Johnson* did mechanic humour show,
> When men were dull, and conversation low.
> Then, *Comedy* was faultless, but 'twas coarse: 5
> *Cobb's* tankard was a jest, and *Otter's* horse.
> And, as their *Comedy*, their love was mean;
> Except, by chance, in some one labour'd scene,
> Which must atone for an ill-written play:
> They rose, but at their height could seldom stay.   10
> Fame then was cheap, and the first comer sped;
> And they have kept it since, by being dead.
> But, were they now to write, when critics weigh
> Each line, and ev'ry word, throughout a play,
> None of them, no, not *Johnson* in his height,   15
> Could pass, without allowing grains for weight.
> Think it not envy, that these truths are told;
> Our poet's not malicious, though he's bold.
> 'Tis not to brand 'em that their faults are shown,
> But, by their errors, to excuse his own.   20
> If Love and Honour now are higher rais'd,
> 'Tis not the poet, but the age is prais'd.
> Wit's now arriv'd to a more high degree;
> Our native language more refin'd and free.
> Our ladies and our men now speak more wit   25
> In conversation, than those poets writ.

Then, one of these is, consequently, true;
That what this poet writes comes short of you,
And imitates you ill (which most he fears),
Or else his writing is not worse than theirs.   30
Yet, though you judge (as sure the critics will),
That some before him writ with greater skill,
In this one praise he has their fame surpast,
To please an age more gallant than the last.
                (John Dryden (1631–1700), epilogue to the
                Second Part of *The Conquest of Granada* (1670))

Commentaries

The two commentaries for this section are both medieval texts. The first is by Chaucer, from the late fourteenth century, and the second is by Malory, from about a century later. Together, these texts illustrate some of the points raised in the chapter, and show how the grammar of different periods of English has important consequences for the meaning and reception of texts.

Commentary I

Chaucer, *The Prologue of the Prioress's Tale* (c.1390)

The Prologue of the Prioress's Tale occurs in *The Canterbury Tales* (c.1387–1400) after *The Shipman's Tale* and the words of the Host. It is a hymn of praise to God and the Virgin, which establishes the religious tone of the tale which follows. The text is from the Riverside Chaucer, which employs a modern system of punctuation.

	O Lord, oure Lord, thy name how merveillous	
	Is in this large world ysprad – quod she –	[spread]
	For noght oonly thy laude precious	[praise]
	Perfourned is by men of dignitee,	[celebrated]
5	But by the mouth of children thy bountee	[excellence]
	Parfourned is, for on thy brest soukynge	[sucking]
	Somtyme shewen they thyn heriynge.	[declare thy praise]
	Wherfore in laude, as I best kan or may,	
	Of thee and of the white lylye flour	
10	Which that the bar, and is a mayde alway,	
	To telle a storie I wol do my labour;	
	Nat that I may encressen hir honour,	[increase]
	For she hirself is honour and the roote	
	Of bountee, next hir Sone, and soules boote.	[soul's remedy]
15	O mooder Mayde, O mayde Mooder free!	[gracious]
	O bussh unbrent, brennynge in Moyses sighte,	[unburned, burning]

That ravyshedest doun fro the Deitee,
Thurgh thyn humblesse, the Goost that in th'alighte, [Holy Spirit]
Of whos vertu, whan he thyn herte lighte, [power]
20 Conceyved was the Fadres sapience, [wisdom]
Helpe me to telle it in thy reverence!

Lady, thy bountee, thy magnificence,
Thy vertu and thy grete humylitee
Ther may no tonge expresse [language of human
in no science; learning]
25 For somtyme, Lady, er men praye to thee, [before]
Thou goost biforn of thy benyngnytee,
And getest us the lyght, of thy preyere,
To gyden us unto thy Sone so deere.

My konnynge is so wayk, O blisful Queene, [skill, weak]
30 For to declare thy grete worthynesse
That I ne may the weighte nat susteene; [sustain]
But as a child of twelf month oold, or lesse,
That kan unnethes any word expresse, [scarcely]
Right so fare I, and therfore I yow preye,
35 Gydeth my song that I shal of yow seye. [guide]

The syntax of the passage is complex: several clauses are linked together by conjunctions, relatives and subordinators, making each stanza a complete period:

> **Wherfore** in laude, **as** I best kan or may,
> Of thee and of the white lylye flour
> **Which that** the bar, **and** is a mayde always,
> To telle a storie I wol do my labour;
> **Nat that** I may encressen hir honour,
> **For** she hirself is honour and the roote
> Of bountee, next hir Sone, and soules boote.

In these lines, we can see syntax and verse form in close agreement: for example, the first statement, which seems to conclude with *labour*, corresponds to the ending of the first **quatrain** (we shall consider a possible alternative reading below). In lines 4 and 5 of the stanza a clause is enclosed in a verse line. By these points of correspondence, the sense becomes easier to follow within the artistic pattern.

At other moments, syntax and form diverge: the noun phrase *the white lylye flour / Which that the bar* (9–10, itself a pentameter) is spread over two lines, focusing our attention on *flour* and so giving that idea extra force. A similar effect is created over lines 6 and 7. The presence of the two ordering schemes of verse and syntax works to the benefit of the reader: the visual help of line endings helps us find our way through the labyrinth of clauses – written out as prose this would be far harder to read – while the frame of metre and rhyme holds each part of the construction together. The complex syntax here seems more assured, and is certainly much easier to follow, than non-narrative prose works by Chaucer such as *Boece* and *The Parson's Tale*. This raises the possibility that in Chaucer's literary culture, verse in English was actually found an easier medium of expression than prose, a claim which could be made for English literature until the seventeenth century.

The stanza in this passage corresponds with a long sentence or period. However, they are also so closely linked that one could also perceive larger constructions going across them: for example, the connective *Wherfore* at the start of stanza 2 makes it virtually a continuation of the preceding sentence; and the start of stanza 3, *O mooder mayde*, which is an invocation to the Virgin, could also be joined to the line before, as an exclamation qualifying *she*.

The analysis of grammar for the modern reader is closely affected by punctuation. The modern system, which I have preserved in the passage above for ease of reading, also divides up the sentences visually, and guides our understanding of the sequence of thought. In the Ellesmere manuscript, which is one of the earliest texts of Chaucer, we find a different system. A caesura appears within each line, but the modern repertoire of punctuation marks is largely absent. Stress and inflection are left more to the speaker's judgment. Seeing the lines without editorial help in these matters may suggest quite different articulations of the clauses.

> To telle a storie / I wol do my labour
> Nat that I may / encreesen hir honour
> For she hir self / is honour and the roote
> Of bountee next hir son / and soules boote
>
> O mooder mayde / o mayde moder free

The absence of a semicolon after *labour* takes away the pause and allows us to take the next line as a direct continuation rather than the start of a new idea. The absence of punctuation alters our response, weakens the sensation of closure, and so places on us an onus of interpretation, a duty which we normally delegate to an editor.

Another example of how punctuation affects interpretation in these lines is the effect of not seeing an exclamation mark where we would expect one. The word *Oh* immediately signals to us an exclamation, a calling out. But with the exclamation mark removed we can see more clearly that what is being said here is primarily an *invocation*, a calling in, as the speaker summons up the virtues of the Virgin in her mind and soul. The rhetorical term for the *Oh* statements, to God in stanza 1 and here to the Virgin, is **apostrophe**. While this must involve a heightening of tone of some kind, this is not necessarily the same as the modern notion of exclamation, signalled by the exclamation mark.

A further detailed point to note is that the speaker addresses both God and Mary in the familiar singular pronoun *thee*, until the plural imperative of *Gydeth* (35). Within the context of a prayer this familarity conveys not disrespect but the intimacy of devotion (and perhaps is influenced by the singular form of the Latin, which does not have the same *thou / you* distinction). No special meaning need be attached to the switch to the plural in *Gydeth*, which is probably there because of the metre.

Finally, we note the cohesive use of lexical repetition. This occurs not only through repeated words, but also ideas which are reiterated in some way. For example, *laude* is introduced in stanza 1 and taken up in the next stanza and *mayde* links 2 and 3. *Bountee* occurs in 1, 2 and 4, and a variant on the idea is *free* in 3. Stanza 4 picks up *vertu* from 3 (here in the sense of moral virtue), and *expresse* is repeated in 5, while *preyere* is taken up by *prey*. Repetition on this scale is unlikely to be the result of accident, and added to the repetitive patterns of the rhyme scheme and the elaborate syntax it adds to the impression of a language elevated above normal expression in its effort to express the perfection of its subject and the devotion of its speaker, a task which is admitted to be impossible: *Ther may no tonge expresse . . . .*

The chain words also create a cohesive structure beyond the level of the sentence. For while each stanza / sentence has its particular sense, the chains of words and ideas make up a larger 'sentence' articulating the virtues of God and His mother the Virgin: bounty, humility, magnificence, honour, worthiness and other attributes are foregrounded beyond the individual statements in which they occur. As we read, a picture of God and the Virgin emerges, beyond the specific statements encompassed in each stanza or grammatical period. We may well remember these words, and the vivid images around them, better than the specific arguments and propositions of the poem. Hence the lexis does not only work within the grammatical sentence: cumulatively and through cohesion it builds up in our mind an object of contemplation which transcends the frame of syntax altogether.

Commentary 2

Sir Thomas Malory, *Le Morte Darthur* (c.1470)

The following passage is taken from near the end of the great book known as *Le Morte Darthur*, several fragments of which we have seen in this chapter. For reasons which will be explained below, the text is a transcript of the single surviving manuscript copy of this work. (Some shorthand abbreviations have been normalised.)

Situation: King Arthur is abroad at war against Sir Lancelot. He has left Sir Mordred in charge of England in his absence, and entrusted him with the safety of Queen Guinevere.

As sir Mordred was rular of all Inglonde he lete make lettirs as thoughe that they had com frome beyonde the see And the lettirs specifyed that kynge Arthur was slayne in batayle with sir Launcelot / Where fore sir Mordred made a parlemente and called the lordys to gydir and there he made them
5 to chose a kynge and so was he crowned at Caunturbyry and hylde a feste there xx. dayes And aftirwarde he drew hym unto Wynchester / And there he toke quene Gwenyuer and seyde playnly that he wolde wedde her which was hys unclys wyff and hys fadris wyff / And so he made redy for the feste and a day prefyxte that they shulde be wedded where fore quene Gwenyuer
10 was passyng hevy but she durst nat discouer her harte but spak fayre and aggreed to sir Mordredys wylle And anone she desyred of sir Mordred to go

to london to byghe all maner thynges than longed to the brydale And by
cause of her fayre speche sir Mordred trusted her and gaff her leve And so
whan she cam to london she toke the towre of london and suddeynly in all
15 haste possyble she stuffed hit with all maner of vytayle and well garnysshed
hit with men and so kepte hit / And whan sir Mordred wyst thys he was
passynge wrothe oute of mesure and short tale to make he layde a myghty
syge a boute the towre and made many assautis and threw engynnes unto
them and shotte grete gunnes but all myght nat prevayle for quene
20 Gwenyuer wolde neuer for fayre speache nother for foule neuer to truste
unto sir Mordred to com in hys hondis agayne Than cam the bysshop of
Caunturbyry whych was a noble Clerke and an holy man And thus he seyde
unto sir Mordred sir what woll ye do Woll ye firste displease god and
sytthyn shame youre selff and all knyghthode / ffor ys nat kynge Arthur
25 youre uncle and no farther but youre modirs brother And uppon her he
hym selffe be gate you uppon hys owne syster there fore how may ye wed
your owne fadirs wyff And there for sir seyde the bysshop leve thys
opynyoun othir ellis I shall curse you with booke belle and candyll / Do
thou thy warste seyde sir Mordred and I defyghe the / Sir seyde the bysshop
30 wyte you well and I shall nat feare me to do that me ought to do And also ye
noyse that my lorde Arthur ys slayne and that ys nat so and there fore
ye woll make a foule warke in thys londe Peas thou false pryste seyde sir
Mordred for and thou chauffe me ony more I shall stryke of thy hede /
So the bysshop departed and ded the cursynge in the moste orguluste wyse
35 that myght be done And than sir Mordred sought the bysshop off
Caunturbyry for to haue slayne hym Than the bysshop fledde and tooke
parte of hys good with hym and wente nyghe unto Glassyngbyry and there
he was a preste Ermyte in a chapel and lyved in pouerte and In holy prayers
ffor well he undirstood that myschevous warre was at honde.

Background

I have presented the text in its medieval form, because this helps us to see the
way our perception of its grammar is conditioned by the way it is edited. Malory
completed *Le Morte Darthur*, a collection of interlocking tales of King Arthur
and the Round Table, in 1469–70, at about the same time as printing arrived
in Britain. Caxton duly produced a printed edition in 1485. In 1934 a manuscript was discovered in Winchester College (still commonly referred to as the
Winchester manuscript), which is now in the British Library. This manuscript is
clearly earlier than Caxton, and it has been shown that it was in Caxton's studio
(along with at least one other version, since lost). The manuscript is not written by Malory, though, and was probably preceded by even earlier manuscript
copies: it is not, therefore, 'the original'. It is, though, undoubtedly a medieval
manuscript book, which is something significantly different from a printed book,
of Caxton's age or later. Up until now, we have been reading medieval texts in
modern editions, which add punctuation and paragraphing. This is because
the problems created by seeing them in their original form, added to their
linguistic difficulty, would have made them extremely difficult on a first reading.
With Malory the vocabulary is much easier to understand, and we can allow

ourselves to investigate the language in something like the state in which it appears in a genuine medieval book.

Two modern editions have been made of the manuscript. The first is by Eugène Vinaver in 1947. Vinaver was the first to use the Winchester text, which he puts alongside Caxton to create a composite edition, drawing on both early versions. The two are not always the same: for example, in the manuscript version of this passage Mordred tells the lords to choose *a kyng*; but in Caxton he orders them to choose *him kyng*. This seems to make better sense, as Mordred obviously only has one candidate in mind, but there is no way of knowing for sure what Malory wrote. Perhaps Caxton had a more accurate manuscript, which said *him*, or perhaps he saw *a king* as a mistake to be corrected. The reading *a kyng* is equally viable, though. It conveys the menace of Mordred's seemingly innocent shotgun question. Vinaver's edition notes differences such as these, adds modern paragraphing and punctuation, and sticks to the original spelling. Vinaver also divided the text up in a way which he believed reflects the author's intended structure.

A more recent edition by Helen Cooper is based on the Winchester manuscript, using Caxton when he is correcting an obvious error, and for the opening and closing sections, which are missing in the manuscript. Both spelling and punctuation are modernised to help contemporary readers, while the paragraphing and division of the text into sections are very different from Vinaver's. While it is tempting to think of editions as rivals competing to present the best or more accurate text, it is perhaps more fruitful to see them as offering us different ways of reading the work. Editors interpret works in the way they present them; and the existence of different textual interpretations, just like different critical interpretations, can only be of benefit to us, especially when the original author's scheme is lost.

The passage above is not an edition, but a transcription. While a transcription aims to give an accurate account of the medieval text, there are still 'accidentals' which cannot be represented, and which may in some way affect the meaning: the obsolete character 'yogh', which looks a bit like a z with descending tail below the line, is here replaced by *gh*. The style of handwriting, the colour of ink (red is used for proper names), lineation and even the quality of the book itself are all aspects of the 'reading experience' which do not appear in a printed transcription as this. Getting back to the real text is as hard as getting back to nature.

Grammar

One of the most striking features of the syntax is the frequent use of the conjunction *and*. This device of consecutive sentences without any linking connectives or subordination, or simply joined by *and*, is called **parataxis**. Sometimes *and* is used to start a sentence or period, but there is no way we could tell this without looking: listening to this passage, we would barely be aware of it as being made out of sentences at all. Chronology, rather than grammar, is the factor which dictates the organisation of material. While *and* in speech can mean many things – *and what's more, and therefore* etc. – here it has its most basic storytelling sense of *and then*. This 'resumptive and', which simply kicks the story onward, has an important effect in making the narrative sound authentic. It has all the immediacy of spoken anecdote (*and I went there, and I told him,* as we might say), and it also suggests the non-judgmental historian, giving us the facts without commentary. This aspect of Malory's syntax has been associated with the 'chronicle style' of his narrative writing.

Malory's use of parataxis puts quite a strain on the reader. The effect is of things not being put in perspective, as it makes all the events seem equally important: nothing is subordinate to anything else. It can help to treat *and* as something which separates clauses as well as joins them. If we pause slightly when we come to it, as we would for a full stop, this keeps each episode distinct in its own little grammatical frame, with space to shine clearly. To take one example, there is a whole story told in the last sentence. The *and*s invite us to take it in a rush, but another way to read it is as a succession of miniature paintings in a manuscript book, or a series of stained glass images. Each clause is an action, and each action conveys a strong picture, and with it a strong emotional resonance as we imagine the Bishop's fear, piety and sense of looming disaster. The time lapses between events do not matter, and the simple past embraces it all:

> Than the bysshop fledde and tooke parte of hys good with hym and wente nyghe unto Glassyngbyry and there he was a preste Ermyte in a chapel and lyved in pouerte and In holy prayers ffor well he undirstood that myschevous warre was at honde.

That *and tooke parte of his good with him,* a touch of detail not needed for the story, adds a vivid realism to this bare, private drama.

And is the dominant conjunction, but not the only one. Subtler relations are sometimes suggested without changing the 'naïve' impression of the narrative:

> And so he made redy for the feste and a day prefyxte that they shulde be wedded where fore quene Gwenyuer was passyng hevy but she durst nat discouer her harte but spak fayre and aggreed to sir Mordredys wylle.

And so at the start here hardly means anything other than *and* – an idiom still common in conversational speech today. However, *where fore* carries a much stronger suggestion of 'as a result'. The *but* is used very effectively: for a brief moment, we are inside Guinevere's mind, experiencing what she is feeling and thinking. It is just enough to convey her cleverness, making her later action credible.

The sense of definiteness and truthfulness conveyed by the simple para-tactic syntax is emphasised by other devices. One is the fairly frequent use of the definite article *the* in noun phrases. The story is full of references to *the see, the lettirs, the feste, the brydale, the tower* and others. The deictic function of the word, pointing to specific things, works also with the place names and stray details, such as the length of the feast: together, these draw us into the world of the text and make it feel very real, even though it is only given a minimal physical description. The simple past tense which is relied on has a similar function, but for a different reason. Here it is the lack of definiteness which draws us in. In reading this story, we experience the events as we often do things in life, as a series of memorable episodes with only the vaguest notion of the time that passes between them. The remarkably inexact time frame – How long did the siege last? When exactly did the Bishop arrive? – gives us a sense of being inside the story as it whirls along.

Together with a sense of immediacy, of being there as it happens, we also feel a vigorous energy in the writing. This is not surprising given that so much happens, but it is at least partly achieved through the use of verbs. Malory uses numerous strong and vivid verbs for key actions. In the section dealing with Guinevere's flight and the siege we have *desyred ... trusted ... toke ... stuffed ... garnysshed ... layde syge ... made ... threw ... shotte*. From these it is possible to reconstruct mentally the sequence of events. The relatively simple noun phrases, which are often simply names, allow the verb phrases their full force.

In the verb phrases, active is almost always preferred to the passive – *he was crowned* is the exception simply perhaps because there is no way of saying this in the active without introducing another agent who would get in the way of the dominant Mordred ('the Bishop crowned him' etc.). *Arthur was slayne in battle* could be taken as an approximation to the pluperfect passive (*had been slain*) but it is simpler to take *slain* as an adjective. The normal preponderance of the active may strike us more than a medieval reader, since we are far more used to passive constructions. Nevertheless, the continual use of verbs to convey strong active meanings is part of the texture of bold, concise storytelling, and contributes to the sense of the powerful wills of the participants, and of things happening quickly.

Auxiliary verbs lend specific senses which we have to do some work to recover: when Mordred tells the assembled lords *he **wolde** wedde her*, the *will* verb conveys the idea of Mordred's *wylle* mentioned later: not just 'he was going to marry her', but 'he wanted to marry her'. This sense of volition is more obviously present in the Archbishop of Canterbury's question *What **woll** ye do?*, meaning 'what do you desire to do?' . It is notable that both he and Mordred use *shall* to refer to future time: *I shall nat feare me*, and *I shall stryke of thy hede*. Both speakers have an interest in depicting these future events as inevitable. The passage also gives examples of *may* in the present tense, referring to what is possible – *how may ye wed youre owne fadirs wyfe?* – and of its past form *might*: *all myght nat prevayle*.

A final grammatical point concerning small words is the use of *thou* and *you* in the verbal exchange. Canterbury consistently addresses Mordred as *ye*, and this is clearly part of his courtesy, going with *sir*; Mordred by contrast uses the *thou* form frequently, as a sign of his contempt.

Suggestions for Further Reading

Introductory

Geoff Barton, *Grammar in Context* (Oxford: OUP, 1999). A textbook aimed at GCSE Level. A clear textbook introduction to the grammatical analysis of texts.
David Crystal, *Discover Grammar* (Harlow: Longman, 1996). Systematic course, with exercises. Ideal for readers of all ages.

Intermediate

The following books also provide introductions to the subject, but may be more appealing to readers past school age:

Peter Collins and Carmella Hollo, *English Grammar: an Introduction* (Basingstoke: Palgrave Macmillan, 2000). A good introduction to some modern terminology (keyed to the work of Huddleston; see below).

David Crystal, *Rediscover Grammar* (London: Longman, 1988). A useful guide to the subject, without exercises. Handy for reference.

Nigel Fabb, *Sentence Structure*, Language Workbooks (London: Routledge, 1994).

Dennis Freeborn, *A Course Book in English Grammar*, Studies in English Language, 2nd edition (Basingstoke: Palgrave Macmillan, 1993).

Jim Miller, *An Introduction to English Syntax* (Edinburgh: Edinburgh University Press, 2001).

Advanced and reference

M.A.K. Halliday, *An Introduction to Functional Grammar* (London: Edward Arnold, 1985).

Rodney Huddleston and Geoffrey K. Pullum, with others, *The Cambridge Grammar of the English Language* (Cambridge: CUP, 2002).

Historical

The books above all describe the structure of English as it is today. For a guide to its change over time, and thus to the grammar of earlier texts, the following are of great use to the student of literature:

G.H. Vallins, *The Pattern of English*, The Language Library (London: André Deutsch, 1956). An older book which gives a clear and readable account of structural developments.

Jeremy J. Smith, *Essentials of Early English* (London: Routledge, 1999). Traces the development of English grammar up to the modern period.

Smith's book may be followed up by the following recent introductions to specific periods in the Edinburgh Textbooks on the English Language series:

Richard Hogg, *An Introduction to Old English* (Edinburgh: Edinburgh University Press, 2002).

Jeremy Smith and Simon Horobin, *An Introduction to Middle English* (Edinburgh: Edinburgh University Press, 2002).

On Shakespeare and Early Modern English, see:

E.A. Abbott, *A Shakespearian Grammar* (London: Macmillan (now Palgrave), 1872). Exhaustive study using traditional grammar.

N.F. Blake, *The Language of Shakespeare*, The Language of Literature (Basingstoke: Palgrave Macmillan, 1983). Mostly devoted to grammatical issues.

N.F. Blake, *A Grammar of Shakespeare's Language* (Basingstoke: Palgrave Macmillan, 2002). Comprehensive study using modern linguistic methods. Useful
for reference.
Manfred Görlach, *Introduction to Early Modern English* (Cambridge: CUP, 1991).

The following contain useful guides to features of grammar together with discussions of other features of language of particular periods:

Norman Blake, *The English Language in Medieval Literature* (London: J.M. Dent,
1977).
Manfred Görlach, *English in Nineteenth-Century England* (Cambridge: CUP,
1999).
Gert Ronberg, *A Way with Words: the Language of English Renaissance Literature*
(London: Edward Arnold, 1992).

Grammar and criticism

The following critical works pay close attention to syntax and punctuation in
texts:

Donald Davie, *Articulate Energy: An Inquiry into the Syntax of English Poetry*
(London: Routledge, 1955).
John Lennard, *The Poetry Handbook* (Oxford: OUP, 1996). Chapter 4 (Punctua-
tion) and Chapter 8 (Syntax), with bibliography.

For a full and sumptuous study of punctuation, demonstrating its importance
for interpretation, see:

M.B. Parkes, *Pause and Effect: Punctuation in the West* (Aldershot: Scolar Press,
1992). Many of the examples are, inevitably, in Latin (with translations). In the
course of this book, a full picture of the rhetorical period emerges.

◪ 4 Lexis

Lexis and literary criticism

In this chapter we shall concentrate on lexical, or open class words, and thus the meaning and expressive value of single lexical items, as they appear in texts. We shall start by looking at how the vocabulary has accumulated over history.

4.1 Word stock

English has a vast lexicon. Usually we can state the same idea in many different ways: for example, a guide like this might be called a *handbook* (from German) or a *manual* (Latin). At one time it might even have been referred to as an *enchiridion* (Greek, literally 'in the hand'). This possibility of expressing ideas in different ways gives English a remarkable richness: the same thought can be expressed in a manner which is posh or slangy, poetic or down-to-earth, polite or insulting. This is a result of history, through which words have come into English from many different sources.

The English word stock is built up of two main parts – Germanic and Romance. These arrived at different stages of the history of the language.

Germanic

English is a Germanic language. It originates in the speech of the Germanic tribes who invaded and settled Britain in the fifth century AD. Aspects of the language, such as pronunciation, inflections and grammatical structure, all follow a Germanic pattern. Old English poetry and prose show an extensive Germanic vocabulary, capable of sophisticated literary expression. The Old English period is conventionally dated 449–1066, although of course stages in a language never fall into such neat borders.

Another source of Germanic vocabulary is Scandinavia. Viking invasion and settlement brought with it words from another Germanic language, which added to the native stock. Some were new words, others variants of the same Germanic term: for example, *shirt* is Old English and *skirt* is the Scandinavian version of the same word. In time, these took on different meanings, so adding to the possible distinctions which could be made. Scandinavian words do not appear much in writing until 1100, and are naturally more frequent in regions where Scandinavian settlement was more dense. *Sir Gawain and the Green Knight* (c.1350), composed in the West Midlands where many Scandinavians had settled, is an example of an English text particularly rich in lexis from this source.

Germanic vocabulary, drawn mainly from Old English and added to by Scandinavian, forms much of the core lexis of modern English. This Anglo-Saxon vocabulary is often said to be characteristically earthy and vivid. Certainly, it has a rich lexis to describe such highly physical worlds as battle, agriculture, animals and geography. Because of this earthiness, coarse expressions are sometimes termed 'Anglo-Saxon' although several swearwords are of a different origin. Old English poetry and other writing does often deal with concepts, but it frequently does so through a densely concrete, visual expression.

Romance

Romance languages are those derived from Latin, spoken by the Romans. English has derived these Latin-based words both indirectly, mainly through French, and directly from Latin, chiefly through religion and scholarship.

French words were added to the native Germanic word stock in great quantities after 1066. The Norman invasion and occupation relegated English to a second-class language, spoken but not written for official functions. The Middle English period is dated 1066–1476; the latter is roughly the date when printing started in Britain. During this time, a huge number of French words came into the language (which also underwent dramatic changes in pronunciation and grammar). These words were associated broadly with the world of the aristocracy: the court, the arts, and the worlds of law and the Church through which much power was exercised. To this day, French-derived words often carry an aura of sophistication and high class.

Latin words, in addition to those which came to us through French, were added in great numbers in the period known as Early Modern English, which covers roughly 1476–1700. During the sixteenth and seventeenth centuries the classical languages were studied and felt to present a superior model of language, which English should imitate. Latin words were used to express old ideas, but also became the natural lexis for science, theology and philosophy. The general association of Latin lexis is with learning and abstraction.

Many other languages have contributed to the English word stock, particularly during the period of imperial expansion in the seventeenth, eighteenth and nineteenth centuries. The two main groups, though, remain Germanic and Romance.

Words and associations

We can summarise the general associations of these strands of lexis like this:

Germanic:	Old English and Scandinavian	concrete, vivid, plain
French:	Normans	aristocratic, sophisticated
Latin:	World of learning	abstract, learned, polysyllabic

These general associations allow a writer to paint an idea in different colours, and to make subtle distinctions: for example, we can *see, watch* or *look at* something (Old English), *regard, examine, view* or *perceive* it (French), or we can *spectate, inspect* and *scrutinise* it (Latin). No two of these words are interchangeable: each one conveys a certain kind of experience.

Below are two passages written roughly a century apart. Both are translations of the same lines from Virgil's *Aeneid*, one from the sixteenth and one from the seventeenth century. They could be compared in several ways, not least for their use of verse: Surrey's is the first use of blank verse in English, Denham's an example of the heroic couplet form perfected by Dryden and Pope. They also suggest different approaches to translation, and a different notion perhaps of the language suitable for the classics. We shall concentrate, though, on how vocabulary drawn from different sources affects the representation of the same basic idea.

(Aeneid 2.506–)
Translation 1
Parcase yow wold ask what was Priams fate.
When of his taken town he saw the chaunce,
And the gates of his palace beaten down,
His foes amid his secret chambers eke,
Th'old man in vaine did on his sholders then,
Trembling for age, his curace long disused,
His bootelesse swerd he girded him about,
And ran amid his foes ready to die.
   Amid the court under the heven all bare
A great altar there stood, by which there grew
An old laurel tree, bowing therunto,
Which with his shadow did embrace the gods.
Here Hecuba with her yong daughters all
About the altar swarmed were in vaine,
Like doves that flock together in the storme;
The statues of the gods embracing fast.
(Henry Howard, Earl of Surrey (?1517–47). Text published 1557)

Translation 2
Now Priams fate perhaps you may enquire,
Seeing his Empire lost, his Troy on fire,
And his own Palace by the Greeks possest,
Arms, long disus'd, his trembling limbs invest;
Thus on his foes he throws himself alone,
Not for their Fate, but to provoke his own:
There stood an Altar open to the view
Of Heaven, near which an aged Lawrel grew,
Whose shady arms the houshold Gods embrac'd;
Before whose feet the Queen her self had cast,
With all her daughters, and the Trojan wives
As Doves whom an approaching tempest drives
And frights into one flock.
(Sir John Denham (1615–59). First published 1656, revised 1668)

Among the Anglo-Saxon words are those for family members, and for many concrete physical things: *wives, daughters, gate, shoulder, sword, tree, shadow.*

Heven for sky is also from Old English, as are *King* and *Queen*. The vivid verbs *ask, beat, run, gird, bow, stand* and *swarm* were all known to the Anglo-Saxons. 'Idea' words of Germanic stock are *foe* and *bootless* (vain). Core words like these had become so established in English speech that they were not pushed aside by French or Latin substitutes. (Though they were subject to those influences in other ways: the *qu* spelling of *Queen* is a French form replacing Old English *cw-*, which, of course, represents the sound actually made.)

Some of the French words in Surrey's translation suggest the aristocratic world: *curace, palace* and *chambers*. Others are more conceptual: *fate, age* and *chaunce*. *Parcase* is a variant of French *perchance*. By Denham's time the French *per-* has been attached to Germanic *haps* to give the modern word *perhaps*.

When we turn to Denham's version, the chief difference we find is the increase in the Romance element: in the first lines *ask* becomes *enquire, town* becomes *Empire* and *his foes amid* is crystallised in the Latin *possest*. Clothes in Denham's version *invest* rather than *gird*, and the ladies are like doves driven by a *tempest* rather than a *storm*.

The desire for accuracy and the demands of rhyme and metre partly explain such differences. But the general effect seems to be to lessen the immediate vividness of the scene: the splendid line *And ran amid his foes ready to die* is replaced by the somewhat obscure *Not for their fate, but to provoke his own*, which draws our attention to the Latin verb and the poet's skilful use of balance, but dampens any excitement. The strong visual imagery of the lines still comes largely from Old English, and from French words introduced so much earlier that they had lost their foreign feel: the *aged Lawrel, shady arms, trembling limbs* and *frightened flock* are of this pre-Latinate stock. This abstraction contributes to the general air of dignity and sophistication for which Denham is presumably aiming. There is probably a different idea of what Virgil represents at work here, as well as a theory of the sort of speech which English verse should enshrine – polished, civilised and measured rather than rushed and excited. The Latinate vocabulary which Denham has at his disposal allows him to reshape the material to achieve these various aims.

Abstract and concrete

The use of a Germanic or a Latinate term can be an important part of the meaning of a text: *storm* and *tempest* offer differing moods as well as different metrical possibilities. *Storm* is more concrete and more a part of everyday speech; *tempest*, with its classical background, is a little more abstract. It suits Denham's lofty, elegant **register**.

The balance of abstract and concrete is an important feature of literary texts. It is not the case that Anglo-Saxon words are always concrete and Latinate words are always abstract: as we have seen, the abstract *foe* is Anglo-Saxon and the concrete *palace* is a Romance word. The important point is that the English word stock allows writers to move between concrete and abstract with great dexterity. In this passage from *An Apology for Poetry* (1595), Sidney moves from abstract propositions (those who attack poetry are being ungrateful) to clear and vivid illustration of the idea in concrete images:

And first, truly, to all them that, professing learning, inveigh against Poetry, may justly be objected that they go very near to ungratefulness, to seek to deface that which, in the noblest nations and languages that are known, hath been the first light-giver to ignorance, and first nurse, whose milk by little and little enabled them to feed afterwards of tougher knowledges. And will they now play the hedgehog that, being received into the den, drave out the host?

Profess, inveigh, object, ungrateful, deface and *ignorance* are the learned terms of Latin (*Poetry* is from Greek). *Light, nurse, milk, hedgehog* and *den*, all very concrete, are Germanic. Part of the life of the prose comes from this dynamic movement between different parts of the lexicon, which enables different kinds of statement: classical aphorism (a memorable saying of a universal nature) and proverbial folk wisdom cohabit in a prose of a marvellously varied texture.

Constantly in English writing we find this movement from abstract to concrete, as bare ideas are followed, or fleshed out by pictures. Keats's *When I have fears that I may cease to be / Before my pen has gleaned my teeming brain* follows a purely abstract line with one of great visual power. In this, he is perhaps learning from Shakespeare:

> To be or not to be, that is the question;
> Whether 'tis nobler in the mind to suffer
> The slings and arrows of outrageous fortune ...
> (*Hamlet*, 3.1.57–9)

Slings and arrows have particular force as they suddenly arrive into this philosophical contemplation. These lines also illustrate Shakespeare's tendency to use Latinate terms not only as intellectual counters but for their emotional energy: when Macbeth is confronting the monstrous thought of killing King Duncan he wishes that *th'assassination / Could trammel up the consequence and catch / With his surcease, success* (1.7.2–4). In these lines, he is using very marked Latinate diction (this is the first recorded instance of *assassination* in English). Yet the words, far from evoking a mood of detached learning, somehow catch in their sound, rhythm and trappings of high seriousness, the intensity of Macbeth's emotional state. Later in the play, we see abstract and concrete working together. When Macbeth learns of the death of Lady Macbeth, he reacts with a magnificent evocation of futility:

> She should have died hereafter.
> There would have been a time for such a word.
> Tomorrow and tomorrow and tomorrow
> Creeps in this petty pace from day to day
> To the last syllable of recorded time,
> And all our yesterdays have lighted fools
> The way to dusty death.
> (5.5.17–22)

Abstract terms for time sit next to a few, flickering concrete words – *creeps, lighted, dusty*. By sitting next to each other, they take on each other's qualities.

The concrete words like *dusty* suggest an abstract significance while *tomorrow* is emphasised until it seems to stand for something felt physically and immediately.

Word stock – Exercise

Using a dictionary

Many dictionaries will give you information about the origin of a word. For example, the *Concise Oxford Dictionary* has this as the last item in its entry for the word *crucial*:

[F f. L *crux, crucis* cross]

This means that the word comes into English from French, and that the French word is based on Latin *crux* (*crucis* is the Latin genitive, which is a case normally included when citing Latin words as it gives the root form before inflections: *cruc-*.)

A larger historical dictionary like the *Shorter Oxford English Dictionary* will tell us roughly when words came into English. This gives us the added information that French *crucial* was 'XVI in medical use' – that is, it was used as a medical term in the sixteenth century (to describe the ligaments in the knee-joint).

The great *Oxford English Dictionary* provides examples of the different senses of a word from texts across history. Here we can see that the English took the medical term from the French: texts referring to *crucial incisions* are found from the start of the eighteenth century. The term had entered philosophy rather earlier in the writings of Francis Bacon in 1620, and was swiftly rescued from the philosophers to give us useful common phrases such as *crucial decision*.

This kind of study has a great interest in its own right. For the close reading of literary texts, it is also extremely valuable in suggesting how a word may have felt to its readers: Latinate and learned, or Anglo-Saxon and common? New or old? Scientific, novel, or long since settled into common speech?

Exercise

Use a dictionary to find which of the important words in this sonnet by Donne are Anglo-Saxon and which are Romance. Comment on the effects the poet achieves through lexical variety.

> O my black soul! now art thou summoned
> By sickness, death's herald and champion,
> Thou'rt like a pilgrim which abroad hath done
> Treason and durst not turn to whence he is fled,
> Or like a thief which, till death's doom be read,   [*doom*: judgment]
> Wisheth himself delivered from prison,
> But damn'd and hal'd to execution,
> Wisheth that still he might be imprisoned.
> Yet grace, if thou repent, thou canst not lack;
> But who shall give thee that grace to begin?

O, make thyself with holy mourning black,
And red with blushing, as thou art with sin;
Or wash thee in Christ's blood, which hath this might,
That being red, it dyes red souls to white.
(John Donne (1572–1631). From *Holy Sonnets*, in *Poems*, published 1633)

4.2 Word origin: etymology

Etymology, the study of the origins of words, can also help us to understand the meanings intended in older texts. In Denham's translation above, for example, *invest* has its earliest, Latin sense of 'to clothe, dress, robe': it comes from *investire, in + to dress, clothe*. The word, which is first recorded in English writing from the 1580s, had already taken on a range of further meanings by Denham's time, but he seems to expect his readers to recognise this original sense. Here are some other examples of English words keeping their Latin meanings. They give some idea of how our understanding of texts can change dramatically if we understand something of the origins of key words.

Reduce

At the end of Shakespeare's *Richard III*, King Henry VII talks of traitors *That would reduce these bloody days again* (5.8.36), where *reduce* means 'bring back' from Latin *re-ducere*. When Adam in *Paradise Lost* beseeches God to *reduce me to my dust* (Book 10, line 748), he means he wants to be returned to the dust from which he was made, though the idea of being made smaller is also present.

Comfortable

The *comfortable words* of the Lord cited in the burial service in *The Book of Common Prayer* are, in their Latin sense, strength-giving: *con* (*with*, implying making or giving) + *fortis* (strong).

Secure

When Shakespeare's King Henry VI yearns for the life of a shepherd who takes *His wonted sleep under a fresh tree's shade, / All which secure and sweetly he enjoys* (*Henry VI*, 3, 2.5.50), *secure* has the original Latin sense of 'without care': *se* (from) + *cura* (care).

Immediate, commodity

Sith a man is made of the body and the soul, all the harm that any man may take, it must needs be in one of these two, either immediately, or by the mean of some such thing as serveth for the pleasure, weal, or commodity of the tone [one] of these two.

(Thomas More, *A Dialogue of Comfort*, III.iii)

Immediate here means 'without mediation' and *commodity* means 'benefit': it is placed alongside French *pleasure* and English *weal* (well-being): the three words help to define each other, reminding us that a word's meaning is established by the text as a whole, as well as from the historical senses it carries with it.

Affixes

The 'etymological sense' – the sense a word carried in its earliest use – is present not only in whole words in older texts, but in the many affixes which have built up over time. We can see one example in the use of *overwhelm* in these passages, one from the sixteenth and one from the seventeenth century:

> Whosoever seeks by headlong meanes to enter into Heauen, and disanull Gods ordinance, shall with the Gyaunts that thought to scale heauen in contempt of *Iupiter*, be ouer-whelmed with Mount *Ossa* and *Peleon*, and dwell with the diuell in eternall desolation.
>
> (Thomas Nashe, The Unfortunate Traveller (1594))

> There the companions of his fall, orewhelmd
> With Floods and Whirlwinds of tempestuous fire,
> He soon discerns ...
>
> (Paradise Lost, 1.76)

Here the prefix *over* refers to space rather than amount: the giants literally have mountains placed on top of them, and Milton's fallen angels are physically engulfed with floods and whirlwinds. The image is a more concrete one than we normally get in everyday expressions such as 'I'm overwhelmed with work'.

Dangers of using etymology

The use of etymology in the interpretation of literary texts also carries risks. It is possible to think that the earliest sense of a word, as recovered by etymology, is its 'true meaning'. This is the so-called etymological fallacy. It is fallacious because it fails to recognise that change at all levels, including meaning, is a fundamental aspect of language. In any case, even if the original meaning were the 'true' one, we could rarely know what it was: etymology can only give us the first recorded senses of a lexical item. In lost documents, and in speech, words may have had other senses which are lost for ever. Once a word is in the language it is subject to change in sound, spelling and meaning, but these changes are not necessarily corruptions. 'With care' and 'full of care' are both equally valid meanings of *careful*: they merely exist at different times. One sense is weakened, but another is introduced.

More directly relevant to literary criticism is the problem of deciding how word origins affected writers and readers at the time when texts were written. Just because we can find out a word in Chaucer was of French origin, that does not necessarily mean it *felt* French, or foreign or courtly, to Chaucer's audience: some might have had a new tinge, while others would have been long settled into everyday speech. The 'flavour' of words again has to be considered in the light of whole texts and other writings of the time.

Word origins – Exercise

Read the passage below, and then use dictionaries to find out the origins and meanings of the italicised words at the time the passage was written. Which meanings have changed most?

> This *excellent* and peerless man, whose life we have to *indite*, besides all other great and beautiful outward and *perpetual arguments* that God and nature adorned him withal, was beautified (if such things may add any weight to his *commendation*, as they do in the eyes and commendations of many) as well by the place of his birth, being born in London, the chief and notable principal city of this our noble Realm, as by the *heritage* and *worshipful* family from which he sprang. His father, Master John More, was very *expert* in the laws of this Realm, and for his worthiness *advanced* to be one of the Justices of the King's Bench, and to the worshipful degree of knighthood. Who, besides his learning, was endued with many notable and *virtuous* qualities and gifts. A man very virtuous, and of a very upright and *sincere conscience*, both in giving of counsel and judgment; a very merciful and *pitiful* man; and, among his other good qualities and *properties*, a *companionable*, a merry and *pleasantly conceited* man.
>
> (Nicholas Harpsfield (?1519–75), beginning of *The Life and Death of Sir Thomas More*, written c.1557)

4.3 Word types: neologism and archaism

We have seen how English vocabulary has built up over the centuries to become hybrid, absorbing words from several other languages. Individual words enter the language as new terms (**neologisms**). If they survive beyond the first few uses, they are liable to change in sound, spelling and meaning. When they fall out of daily use, and sound distinctly old-fashioned in the standard vocabulary (though they may persist in dialect), they have become **archaisms**.

Writers have made artistic use of both newborn and 'dead' words, to achieve effects which the current standard vocabulary would not be able to produce.

Neologisms

There are three main kinds of neologism (also termed a *coinage*):

Type 1 A *completely new* word, which does not seem to have an etymology.

Type 2 A *word which is a new formation*, made from other words or prefixes already in existence. To take a recent example, the word *homophobe* is derived from the Greek words *homo* (the same) and *phoebe* (fear).

Type 3 A word which is well-known, but is given a *new meaning*. An example is the slang use of *bad* and *wicked* to mean *excellent*.

Macbeth's use of the word *assassination*, which we encountered earlier, is an example of a Type 2 neologism, a word formed from elements already known.

It would not necessarily have caused great confusion: the word 'assassin' for political killer had already been in existence for about a century. The degree of newness felt in the word has to be judged against other factors:

- Dictionaries generally only record the first *written* use of a word (recorded speeches and broadcasts are an occasional exception). A word might therefore have existed in the *spoken* language for some time before an author used it.
- Dictionaries also draw on a select range of texts: it is impossible to look at all the English books ever written, even with the help of modern databases. It is always possible, then, that there is some earlier example of a usage (word being used), not yet discovered. Some neologisms formerly thought to be coined by Shakespeare were later found to have been used already by another Elizabethan writer, Thomas Nashe (1567–1601).
- When new words were entering the language at a great rate, as they were in Elizabethan English, the entrance of a word like *assassination* might have appeared quite normal, especially in the context of a verse play. New is not always surprising.

Neologisms and interpretation: Example

Latin words poured into English in the Renaissance period. One author who used them a great deal was the learned doctor Sir Thomas Browne (1605–82). We shall look at the beginning of his work *Pseudodoxia Epidemica* (1646), which was written to point out and correct many of the false and superstitious beliefs of his age:

PSEUDODOXIA EPIDEMICA, Bk. 1, ch. 1
'Of the Causes of Common Errors'

The First and Father-cause of common Error, is, The common infirmity of Human Nature; of whose *deceptible* condition, although perhaps there should not need any other *eviction*, than the frequent Errors we shall our selves commit, even in the express *declarement* hereof: yet shall we *illustrate* the same from more infallible constitutions, and persons presumed as far from us in condition, as time, that is, our first and *ingenerated* forefathers. From whom as we derive our Being, and the several wounds of *constitution*, so may we in some manner excuse our infirmities in the depravity of those parts, whose *Traductions* were pure in them, and their Originals but once removed from God. Who notwithstanding (if posterity may take leave to judge of the fact, as they are assured to suffer in the punishment) were grosly deceived, in their perfection; and so weakly deluded in the clarity of their understanding, that it hath left no small obscurity in ours, How error should gain upon them.

For first, They were deceived by Satan; and that not in an invisible *insinuation*, but an open and *discoverable apparition*, that is, in the form of a Serpent; whereby although there were many occasions of suspition, and such as could not easily escape a weaker circumspection, yet did the unwary *apprehension* of Eve take no advantage thereof.

Of the italicised words *deceptible* (able to be deceived), *declarement* and *ingenerated* are first recorded in this text. *Depravity* (corruption) is first recorded a few years earlier, in 1641 while *traduction* (handing down) is recorded before, but used here in this sense apparently for the first time. Several other words had only recently been introduced into English: *eviction* (proof), *illustrate*, *apparition* (form in which something appears) and *constitution* (general character) in their sense here all appear in the early seventeenth century. Going a little further back, *apprehension* (understanding), *insinuation* and *discoverable* appear in the last thirty years of the sixteenth century, and so may still have felt fairly new in 1646, when *Pseudodoxia* was published. There are also some words which may seem very new but in fact are not: *infallible* and *circumspection*, for example, are recorded as far back as the writings of Caxton (c.1422–91).

Browne is evidently deliberately using a formal vocabulary, very different from ordinary speech. The Latinate vocabulary is associated with weighty subjects, and with the world of scholarship. Browne is making it clear that he is addressing a great theme, and will do so in a learned manner. By employing new Latin-based words, he also indicates a liberation from old ways of thinking, which were wrapped up in old native language. The resulting tone is a curious mixture: the text sounds both self-consciously modern, but at the same time it carries the aura of ancient learning. The voice makes readers feel sophisticated and enlightened.

However, some readers of the period found such language irritating and pretentious, and called the introduction and invention of long words, principally from Latin, *inkhorn terms* (an inkhorn was a vessel for holding ink, and carried around on one's clothes). Opposition to inkhorn terms went back to the sixteenth century. The Elizabethan George Puttenham called them a 'peevish affectation … of clerks and scholars' (*The Arte of English Poesie*, 1589), and Thomas Wilson advised writers and speakers not to use 'any straunge inkhorn termes, but to speak as is commonly received' (*Art of Rhetorique*, 1553).

The anti-inkhorn protestors had a strong point when they said that ideas could be expressed in the language 'as is commonly received'. This is borne out by the large number of neologisms which did not survive. The passage contains several examples of these. They are rather like flowers which did not flourish in English soil. *Deceptible* vanishes without trace, perhaps rather surprisingly, as it seems a useful word (*gullible* was not used until the nineteenth century, though *gull* for someone who can be deceived is a very Elizabethan word). *Declarement* did not survive the seventeenth century, while its rival *declaration* did, though it lost its earlier sense (the one used in the passage) of 'elucidation'. *Traduction* meaning 'derivation', however, lasted until the nineteenth century. By contrast, *illustrate* and *insinuate*, relatively new words in this text, are still part of the vocabulary of current English.

Words getting older: antiquated and archaic language

Words become archaic for many reasons. Some belong to a defunct subject, like medieval alchemy; and some are made redundant by new words able to do the same job. Archaisms can sometimes, however, find new employment in literary writing. They have several attractive features:

- They can have a technical use, especially in poetry, helping the author to fit the metre or rhyme scheme.
- They create a special atmosphere. An ancient word can seem charming or quaint by its remoteness from ordinary talk: *Ye Olde Tea Shoppe*. Archaisms can also sound solemn and mysterious, and are used a good deal in religious writings. The King James Bible (1611) contains much archaic lexis besides the conservative grammatical features we noted earlier.
- Because they are confined to writing (except for survival in dialects), archaisms can seem especially literary. They are a normal part of poetic **diction** (language considered suitable for poetry) until well into the nineteenth century, because they suggest a world of feeling and experience 'above' the everyday. In this way they easily become stale. A great deal of eighteenth-century poetry with its repertoire of meads, brooks and rills shows language in this stale, habitualised state.

Literary works therefore conserve many words which are now extinct. Famous lines can sometimes be obscure for this reason: in Juliet's 'O Romeo, Romeo, wherefore art thou Romeo?' *wherefore* means not *where* but *why*: why are you Romeo, our family's enemy? Today we only meet this sense in the phrase *the whys and wherefores*.

It is often hard to determine exactly how archaic a word is. Dictionaries can only record written usages: just as a neologism may have existed in speech before a writer used it, so words may continue in everyday conversations, particularly in older generations, for an indefinite period. At the same time, the standard dictionaries chiefly record the standard language. In the medieval and Early Modern period, when standardisation was either non-existent or slowly developing towards the present situation, there cannot have been such an acute sense of a word surviving 'only in dialect', and thus having a range of comic or charming effects. For example, the (now) archaic word *geck*, meaning 'fool', appears in Shakespeare's *Twelfth Night* (5.1.355), then resurfaces centuries later, in George Eliot's novel *Adam Bede* (1859, ch. 9): this novel is set in the eighteenth century, so uses deliberately old-fashioned speech; but the word had evidently survived in the West Midlands dialect long after Shakespeare's time. It may have sounded peculiar to some members of a London audience, but it was not an archaism.

A famous supposed user of archaic vocabulary is the Elizabethan Edmund Spenser (c.1552–99). In these lines from the first part of *The Faerie Queene* (1590), Spenser states his decision to change his subject from pastoral poetry (his last work was *The Shepheardes Calendar*, about the seasons of the year) to the lofty world of knights and ladies:

> Lo I the man, whose Muse whilome did maske,
>   As time her taught, in lowly Shepeards weeds,
>   Am now enforst a far unfitter taske,
>   For trumpets sterne to chaunge mine Oaten reeds,

And sing of Knights and Ladies gentle deeds;
Whose prayses having slept in silence long,
Me, all too meane, the sacred Muse areeds
To blazon broad emongst her learned throng:
Fierce warres and faithfull loves shall moralize my song.

(Canto 1, Stanza 1)

There are other features of this text which seem archaic besides the words: spelling, frequent inverted word order and images like *Oaten reeds* for the Pan-pipes of the pastoral poet all point to an idea of the past. Besides that, the transmission of the book – its layout, printing and binding – might also have contributed a suggestion of great age.

The following words are generally glossed in modern editions: *whilome* (formerly, once); *weeds* (garb, clothing); *areeds* (appoints); *blazon* (announce, proclaim). Such a high frequency of obsolete words gives this text a very archaic feel, though this is not necessarily the atmosphere they conveyed to a reader of the time.

From *The Oxford English Dictionary* (*OED*), we learn that all the words listed above are medieval in origin, so they may well have felt old to Spenser's first readers, though those readers would no doubt have had a different sense of 'the medieval' from us. But only *whilom* (a variant of *while*) seems to be isolated to the medieval period, at any rate in this sense of 'Once upon a time'. It seems to have become a special word for use in poetry, belonging to poetic diction.

Whilom, then, might have felt archaic to Spenser's readers, preserved in poetry. But here we are faced by another problem. The association of poetic and archaic was an important one in the Romantic movement: we can see this in the deliberately antiquated language of Keats's 'La Belle Dame sans Merci', in Sir Walter Scott's works and in William Morris's romantic tales. The antiquated language partly works because it can be felt as deviating from a standard. The Romantic movement has had a great influence on modern sensibility, and is associated with ideas of heritage. But even faced by a true archaism, an Eliza-bethan reader may have reacted differently: there was less sense of a standard lexicon from which archaic or dialectal terms might deviate. The notion of the medieval for the Elizabethans was not necessarily that of the Romantics. We cannot, then, assume that even this word had the effect on its first readers as archaic things have on us today.

On the evidence of the *OED*, besides *whilom*, all the words listed above were in use at the time the poem was written. The first readers may have found them quite normal: a word like *blazon*, for example, which comes from heraldry, might have seemed perfectly up-to-date to an aristocratic reader obsessed by coats of arms and family trees. Indeed, this word might help to place the poem directly in the aristocratic world for which Spenser was writing. Others would have heard such words spoken by an older generation, and many would have been familiar with much of Spenser's diction through reading the printed romances, which provided a direct and popular link with earlier English. The English which people use actively at any one time is not the same as the English they read. Besides these romances, readers of *The Faerie Queene* had no means of looking up strange English words. A long poem full of genuine archaisms which could not be guessed from context would simply have been incomprehensible.

Nevertheless, even after making these allowances, the sheer accumulation of older words does seem to give these lines an archaic feel. It is certainly a very different kind of language from that in ordinary use, as recorded in letters of the time. These seem refreshingly modern by comparison. The device of archaism, even if it is less strong than it first appears, suggests some wider aims of the poet.

One such aim might be to create a sense of tradition and continuity. In this stanza, Spenser is deliberately comparing himself to the great Roman poet Virgil, who began his epic *Aeneid* after he had completed two earlier works set in the countryside. An antique language helps to establish this link from the Latin to the English poet, and establishes Spenser as a grand poet using the highest epic form.

Secondly, by using the *English* language, and drawing on words from Chaucer, Spenser is also placing himself deliberately in an *English* poetic tradition (rather against the current of his time, when Italian poetry was in vogue). The poem has the same reverence for the English past as did Spenser's noble readers, who were equally anxious to prove their ancient ancestry. The old words would have had a patriotic flavour, and help to give the impression that the poem expresses older values, from the 'good old days'.

The sense of tradition and patriotism also carries political implications. Here the language is part of Spenser's support of Queen Elizabeth I and the Church of England, which had only recently been established following the Reformation and England's break with Rome. Throughout *The Faerie Queene*, Spenser is stating through his allegory that Anglicanism, not Catholicism, is the true ancient religion which follows the teaching of Christ. He places Elizabeth – in the allegorical guise of Gloriana, the Faerie Queene – in a world of ancient events and ancient words: this suggests that she is the true representative of old values and beliefs. The lexis emphasises this sense of a wisdom passed down over generations.

Archaism and taste

Archaic or neologistic language is closely connected with taste. There is a similarity in this respect between archaisms in poetic language and 'revivalist' styles in architecture. While many eighteenth-century poets were using archaisms, their aristocratic patrons constructed 'follies' or fake Greek temples in their country parks. In the nineteenth century many writers (most notably Sir Walter Scott) continued to excavate old words, just as architects and designers were building in the classical and medieval Gothic manner. In both architecture and literature, there is often a tension between reaching out to the past on the one hand and being contemporary on the other. Poetic language reflects this: Wordsworth, for example, argues in the Preface to the *Lyrical Ballads* (1800) that poetry should be made out of the speech of living men, and was very much against the practice of using archaisms as 'poetic' furniture, a practice which was popular at that time, though of course archaisms may occur in the dialectal speech of living men. Archaisms can express a deep wish to make contact with the spirit of another age, and are consequently frustrating to readers from an age which is excited by the present and the future. The way we react to very new or very old words is a guide to our own sensibility.

Archaisms and neologisms – Exercise

Read the following stanzas from Sir Walter Scott's *Lay of the Last Minstrel*. Then find out as much as you can about the history of the italicised words, and comment on Scott's use of lexis, in particular archaism, neologism and dialect. Which words in the stanzas have become archaic since Scott's time?

> Away in speed Lord Cranstoun rode;
> The *Goblin* Page behind *abode*;
> His lord's command he ne'er withstood,
> Though small his pleasure to do good.
> As the corslet off he took,   5
> The dwarf *espied* the Mighty Book!
> Much he marvell'd a knight of pride,
> Like a *book-bosom'd* priest should ride:
> He thought not to search or staunch the wound,
> Until the secret he had found.   10
>
> The iron band, the iron clasp,
> Resisted long the *elfin* grasp:
> For when the first he had undone,
> It closed as he the next begun.
> Those iron clasps, that iron band,   15
> Would not yield to unchristen'd hand,
> Till he smear'd the cover o'er
> With the Borderer's curdled *gore*;
> A moment then the volume spread,
> And one short *spell* therein he read,   20
> It had much of *glamour* might,
> Could make a ladye seem a knight;
> The cobwebs on a dungeon wall
> Seem tapestry in lordly hall;
> A nut-shell seem a gilded barge,   25
> A *sheeling* seem a palace large,
> And youth seem age, and age seem youth –
> All was delusion, nought was truth.

> Sir Walter Scott (1771–1832), *The Lay of the*
> *Last Minstrel* (1805), Canto 3, Stanzas 8 and 9)

As well as dictionaries, a critical edition of the work should help. Much information in particular is to be found in Scott's own notes, as published in the first complete edition of his works in 1841.

4.4 Word meaning

Denotation and connotation

A word has sense and associations. To take an example, a cereal farmer and I both know what is meant by the word *harvest*: it is both the process, and the season, of gathering in crops. This is its dictionary definition, and the *denotative* sense of the word. It is the basic concept which as language users we identify with that particular word.

However, in the life of the mind, the word *harvest* will not work in a neat dictionary way. As someone who has never done a stroke of agricultural work in my life, I understand *harvest* within a pleasant conception of combine harvesters, golden fields and stacks of hay. The farmer might share some of these romantic pictures, but he will probably also think of matters such as work, payment, the technical aspect of machines and so on. These various ideas, which make up the different conceptions of *harvest* which the two of us have, are its *connotations*. As long as the word has the same denotative sense for both of us, we will be able to communicate; but at the same time the word will play on our minds and memories in different ways. A seventeenth-century farmer would have a different set of connotations again. In fact, the conception in the mind of a word will be different for every person: even a neighbouring farmer to our hypothetical one will have some different idea called up in the mind by 'harvest' in the form of personal significances (that was when my dog died etc.), sensual recollections and much else besides.

Words build up connotations not only through personal experience but also by cultural and literary tradition. Thus, the connotations of *harvest* in our mind may include biblical images, expressions about the corn and the chaff, paintings, the Grim Reaper and the harvest as a traditional image of death, harvest festivals and many other cultural artefacts. Around the central denotative sense of *harvest*, therefore, circle an infinite number of private connotations and a rich stock of shared cultural ones. The existence of private associations, unique to every individual, gives some truth to the idea that a text has a different meaning for each of us. The body of associations which is part of the common culture presents us with the challenge of discovering as far as we can the connotative aspect of words which a writer may be exploiting in a text. To continue with the idea of harvesting and farming, here is Chaucer's description of a ploughman, brother to the parson:

> With him ther was a Plowman, was his brother,
> That hadde ylad of dong ful many a fother;   [*fother*: load]
> A trewe swinker and a good was he,   [*swinker*: worker]
> Livinge in pees and parfit charitee.
> God loved he best with al his hoole herte
> At alle times, thogh him gamed or smerte,   [in pleasure or pain]
> And thanne his neighebor right as himselve.
> He wolde thresshe, and therto dike and delve,
> For Cristes sake, for every povre wight,
> Withouten hire, if it lay in his might.

His tithes paide he ful faire and wel,
Bothe of his propre swink and his catel.   [*catel*: chattels, possessions]
In a tabard he rood upon a mere.   [*tabard*: tunic]
                    (*General Prologue*, 531–43)

With the help of some glosses, the denotations of the words become clear: the ploughman spreads manure (*dong*), threshes, makes ditches (*dike*) and digs. He loves his neighbour, pays his tithes and works hard.

It is when we consider the connotations of the lexis, and imagine the conceptions that may have formed in the minds of medieval readers, that we uncover further significance in the passage. In terms of personal conception, *dong* would not have had the disgusting associations it has for many modern readers: it was simply manure, fertiliser. More generally, although we can understand the sense of tasks like *thresh*, *dyke* and *delve*, we are clearly left with a rather detached idea of these if we have never even seen these activities, let alone participated in them. In writings of Chaucer's time, and for centuries afterwards, images of animals and agriculture appeal to the direct experience of many of their original readers. Medieval and Renaissance literature is full of the tang and touch of things: riding horseback, the weight of a hawk on the wrist, the labours of the seasons. These things do not lend themselves to intellectual analysis, but they suggest a world of immediate connotations around words and images which has become weak or sentimentalised.

In reading the works of a writer like Chaucer, we can do something to recover connotations which belong to the culture around the text. The word *Ploughman*, for example, has a very clear denotative sense. In Chaucer's time it had also an association with the life of the Christian, pictured as a good, humble worker. *Piers Plowman*, by Chaucer's contemporary Langland, develops this idea, which is common to many medieval texts and images. Another Christian reference is in the direct allusion to Christ's commandment to love thy neighbour as thyself, an allusion being a device to point our minds very firmly to one particular idea surrounding a term. Other connotations in the passage include the Ploughman's tabard – a tunic, associated with poverty and humility – and his mare, a similarly humble horse. The denotative meaning is simply that he wears cheap clothes and rides a cheap horse: in the context of the passage, the associations add the deeper meaning that he is a picture of Christian humility.

The connotations of words allow us to evoke ideas and feelings without naming them: the meanings of Chaucer's descriptions of the ploughman thus go beyond the definitions of the words on the page. Writers will summon up strong feelings not by describing them, but by giving us pictures which work on us through their associative force. Even the words which pose no problems of basic sense for us will still summon up different associations. To turn to another literary text for a moment, Dante begins *The Divine Comedy* by saying he is 'midway through the journey of our life': for a medieval reader the idea of a *journey* would have carried with it memories of arduous, perhaps dangerous trips on foot or horseback. The Collect at Evensong praying for God's protection against 'the perils and dangers of this night' reminds us that for a sevententh-century audience *night* started at dusk, and was full of terrors.

Semantic change

A word can change both its denotative sense and its connotations. While connotations are ultimately unique to each person, communication with words is possible as long as the same core sense exists within them: an Elizabethan and I would know what we mean by *night*, even though we have different conceptions of it (including when it begins and ends). We would not understand one another if the word had changed its sense, or taken on new senses since the Elizabethan's time.

This shift of sense, or semantic change, is a natural phenomenon of language. A phrase like *make love*, first denoting courtship then more recently sexual intercourse, is an example of a quite dramatic change of sense which has occurred relatively recently. Change does not happen universally or at a steady rate. By contrast to *make love*, another **euphemism** for sex, *sleep with*, was known to the Anglo-Saxons. Literature conserves for us words used in senses which have since diminished or vanished. Here is an example of how our understanding of a literary text may be affected by this:

> Yet once more, O ye Laurels, and once more
> Ye Myrtles brown, with Ivy never sear,
> I come to pluck your Berries harsh and crude,
> And with forc'd fingers rude,
> Shatter your leaves before the mellowing year.
> Bitter constraint, and sad occasion dear,
> Compels me to disturb your season due.
>
> Milton, *Lycidas* (1645)

Here we find change both of connotation and denotation. The significance of plucking berries is only comprehensible once we remember the associations of the plants mentioned, associations here which have a symbolic force: laurels, myrtles and ivies are all evergreens and so associated with immortality. They also connote poetic inspiration, and have their own particular meanings: laurels are the crown of poetry, myrtles are associated with undying love granted by Venus, and ivy is connected both to Bacchus and wine, and to learning. Thus the first lines convey a desire to compose in verse which is both learned and loving.

The lines also contain numerous examples of shifted denotative sense: the *brown* myrtles are dark and the ivy is never *sear* (withered). The berries are *crude* (unripe) and the poet's fingers are *rude* in the sense of being uncivil, not lewd. The phrase *sad occasion dear* makes no sense with its modern significations: how can something be sad and dear the same time? Here, *dear* carries a number of possible senses, and it is hard to tell which if any is primary: the occasion of the death is severe, while that of plucking the berries is heartfelt. There is a strong sense of *grievous* and *dire*. *Sad*, meanwhile, means what it does today, only more strongly: it is distressing, lamentable.

We learn about semantic change through reading texts and using glosses. This process, which of course never ends, can be supported by some knowledge of the classifications which linguists have made. By studying the phenomenon of semantic change, we also find ourselves looking out from the text at the wider cultural context. Through changes in meaning we can trace changes in general outlook.

Four basic types of semantic change cover a great many instances. These are extension, narrowing, pejoration and amelioration. In all cases, we often find that it is not the case of a story in which a word moves from one sense to another. It is more like a branching effect, in which a new sense can emerge while an original one is still active.

Extension

Extension of meaning is also known as *generalisation*. As these terms suggest, it occurs when a word has a particular meaning which is taken over by one which is more general. An example is *fact*, which for Elizabethans often meant a deed or an act, particularly a wicked one. This is the sense in which Gloucester uses it when he blames Sir John Fastolf for running away from battle:

> To say the truth, this fact was infamous
> And ill beseeming any common man,
> Much more a knight, a captain and a leader.
> *(Henry VI* 1, 4.1.30–2)

This use of the word to describe something contemptible, or evil, is illustrated in *Macbeth*:

> LENNOX   Who cannot want the thought how monstrous
> It was for Malcolm and for Donalbain
> To kill their gracious father? Damnèd fact,
> How it did grieve Macbeth! Did he not straight
> In pious rage the two delinquents tear ...
> (3.6.8–12)

Since *fact* implies a deed which is notable in some way, it is also used in a positive sense, for a praiseworthy action. In a reference in *Paradise Lost* to *hee who most excells in fact of Armes* (2.124), *fact* implies deed, and *Armes* refers not only to weapons but to feats of arms.

If *fact* can denote both a hateful deed and an outstanding one, then it can simply refer to any deed, in a neutral sense. In this usage, it is opposed to speech. In Jane Austen's *Emma*, when the Churchill family at Enscombe let their adoptive son Frank stay away from home a little longer, we are told that *Enscombe however was gracious, gracious in fact, if not in word* (vol. II, ch. xii).

From this general sense of any action it is an easy step to the sense 'anything which has really occurred, or is really the case', the main sense today.

Religion

Religion retains in early English some specialised senses alongside the general one. We find at least three senses in Chaucer. First, there is the sense of being 'in religion', as in taking monastic vows and living in an order. In the *Prologue of the Monk's Tale*, this is what the Host means when he declares that the well-built Monk should be married, and breeding:

> I pray to God, yeve him confusioun
> That first thee broghte unto religioun!
> (Fragment VII, 1943–4)

A few lines later he develops his theme: religion, or the monastic life, has taken the best part of procreation, and we laymen are puny creatures:

> Religioun hath take up al the corn
> Of tredyng, and we borel men been shrympes.   [*borel*: coarse]
> (1954–5)

Religion in this sense does not necessarily denote a godly life: even Chaucer's conspicuously worldly monk could nonetheless be described accurately as *religious* in the language of his time. In the description of the exemplary Parson, *A good man was ther of religioun* (I.478) the word appears to mean 'the true religious life', a godly existence, not necessarily one spent in a monastery:

From a specialised sense of a life in orders, to the Christian life, we come to the more general sense which prevails today, a set or system of beliefs:

> 'I axe thee,' quod he, 'though it thee greeve,
> Of thy religioun and of thy bileeve.'
> (Chaucer, *Second Nun's Tale*, VIII.427)

Desperate

This is an example of a word whose specialised sense is made clear by its etymology: *de-spair* is from *de-spero*: *de*, a negative prefix, and *spero*, 'I hope'. In a Christian context, at least of the pre-modern period, one who loses hope in God has committed a mortal sin. The action accompanying this sin is suicide, and it is suicides to whom Donne refers when he is despising Death: *Thou art slave to Fate, Chance, kings, and desperate men* ('Death be not Proud', *Divine Poems*). This specific sense has extended and the word can now denote reckless actions with no reference to losing hope.

A scene in *Hamlet* puts the specialised sense close to an extended one. Horatio warns Hamlet against following the Ghost, saying *The very place puts toys of desperation, / Without more motive, into every brain* (1.4, in Q2 only). *Toys of desperation* are the suicidal impulses or whims which an evil spirit might induce. A more extended sense occurs when Hamlet ignores these pleas and goes with the Ghost. Horatio comments *He waxes desperate with imagination* (1.4.64), where *desperate* seems to mean reckless, careless – not only of God, but of anything.

Sometimes, the balance of specialised and general is hard to discern. At the end of *King Lear*, the deaths of the wicked sisters is reported like this:

> Your eldest daughters have fordone themselves,
> And desperately are dead.
>
> (5.3.267)

This seems to imply that they committed suicide, though in fact Goneril poisoned Regan before killing herself. The more general sense of 'in despair, hopelessly' is operating here as well: they not only killed themselves, but were also in a hopeless state, politically and spiritually.

Narrowing

Narrowing or specialisation is naturally the opposite to extension. A more general sense of the word has been taken over by a particular one.

Disease

The general sense is simply *dis-ease*, lack of ease and comfort, trouble. It does not denote any illness or physical pain. We meet the word in this sense, when Chaucer's Knight reacts to the Monk's tale, which has been an anthology of tragic incidents:

> I seye for me, it is a greet disese,
> Whereas men han been in gret welthe and ese,
> To heeren of hire sodeyn fal, allas!
> (*Prologue of Nun's Priest's Tale*, 5–7; VII.2771–3)

The word is equally general in sense in another instance of a noble person sorrowfully contemplating another's tribulations:

> The kynges herte of pitee gan agryse,
> Whan he saugh so benigne a creature
> Falle in disese and in mysaventure.
> (*Man of Law's Tale*, II.614–16)

Shakespeare's Richard Plantagenet follows Chaucer's Knight in balancing the word against its antithesis. Here, mental discomfort, what we might call stress, is contrasted to physical ease:

> First lean thine agèd back against mine arm,
> And in that ease I'll tell thee my disease.
> (*Henry VI* 1, 2.5.43–4)

Shakespeare would have been familiar with the usual modern sense of 'illness, sickness', which is recorded from the last years of the fourteenth century. The older general sense continues into the seventeenth century, though interestingly the *OED* records it as being revived with the spelling *dis-ease* in the early twentieth century.

Ghost

A general sense of this word, which occurs often in earlier texts, is soul, spirit, principle of life. This sense survives in the expression *Holy Ghost*. In medieval texts a *ghostly father* is a priest who cares for your soul.

The expression for dying as yielding or giving up the ghost is an early one. In a fifteenth-century play, Herod berates his knights for not seeing the three Kings on their way to Jesus: *I wole I yelde my gast / so sore my hert it grefys* (*The Towneley Plays*, 16.155, c.14th century).

The specialised sense of *ghost* as a supernatural emanation or apparition, which we are familiar with today, was also in use by the time of the Towneley plays. In Chaucer's *Legend of Good Women*, Aeneas answers Queen Dido when she fears that he is about to leave her:

> 'Certes,' quod he, 'this nyght my faderes gost
> Hath in my slep so sore me tormented ...'
>
> (1295–6)

Affection

The general sense of this word is emotion or feeling of any kind. The Elizabethan writer Roger Ascham (1515/16–68), in his treatise on archery, is not impressed by archers who swear when things go wrong:

> Such woordes be verye tokens of an ill mynde, and manifeste signes of a man that is subiecte to inmeasurable affections.
>
> (Roger Ascham, *Toxophilus* (1544), p. 146)

After Hamlet has behaved to Ophelia in a way which seems to contradict her father Polonius's theory that he is in love with her, Claudius, who has spied on the conversation says *Love? His affections do not that way tend* (3.1.165). The sense here is Ascham's general one of feeling. This general sense is preserved in the King James Bible (1611), where we are told *For this cause God gave them up unto vile affections* (*Romans* 1.26).

The modern specialised sense of 'loving feeling' is the most common one in Shakespeare. Presumably since other words were available to denote a general feeling and emotion, then *affection* was free to take on a more specific meaning.

Hint

With the examples above, we might guess that some change had occurred, and the context would take us some way towards working out which sense is employed. Other semantic changes are more subtle. An example is the word *hint*, which has undergone specialisation. Othello uses this word twice in one speech, in which he is explaining how he wooed and won the fair Desdemona. He recounts how Desdemona's father, Brabantio, loved to hear tales of his military campaigns: of *Rough quarries, rocks, and hills whose heads touch heaven, / It was my hint to speak* (1.3.140–1). When Desdemona says that any man telling such stories would have the power to woo her, Othello says *Upon this hint I spake* (1.3.165). Although the modern sense of 'veiled suggestion' fits the context, the sense of the word here is an earlier general one: it means occasion or opportunity, a meaning which has since disappeared.

Pejoration

Sometimes words can take on negative associations, which become so strong that they drag the denotation down with them. An example is *villain*, which originally denoted a peasant, but soon became associated with behaviour expected of someone of that status. By pejoration and generalisation, it then came to its modern sense of anyone behaving criminally. *Churl*, an Old English word which the French *villain* replaced, suffered the same fate. Thus Chaucer apologises for using *churles termes*, and we might criticise someone today for churlish behaviour. Meanwhile other status words like *noble* and *courtly* have gone in the opposite direction.

Knave

An interesting case of a status word shifting in connotation and denotation is *knave*. By taking all our examples from Shakespeare, we can see again how different meanings can branch out at the same time.

The most innocent sense of *knave* is simply boy (German *knabe*), and it can be used affectionately, as when Brutus bids the sleeping Lucius *Gentle knave, good night* (*Julius Caesar*, 4.2.320). Pejoration creeps in when the word denotes a male servant. The worthless but well-born Roderigo tells Brabantio that Desdemona has absconded with Othello and is *Transported with no worse nor better guard / But with a knave of common hire, a gondolier* (*Othello*, 1.1.126–7). From Roderigo's contemptuous reference to the serving classes it is a short distance to a sense of 'rogue, scoundrel', as in Falstaff's *Strike, down with them, cut the villains' throats! Ah, whoreson caterpillars, bacon-fed knaves!* (*Henry IV* 1, 2.2.81).

Words denoting a lack of worldly knowledge seem especially liable to pejoration: *simple* and *innocent* have taken on negative senses alongside the positive ones; *silly*, which used to mean blessed, has passed through meaning simple and pitiful to meaning stupid. At the same time, words denoting knowledge and skill are similarly debased: *cunning, sly, crafty, ingenious, smart* and *intellectual* have all taken on strong pejorative senses. From the evidence of language, it would appear that the English regard ignorance with contempt and cleverness with suspicion.

Both kinds of word are illustrated in Chaucer's *Canon's Yeoman's Prologue and Tale*. In this tale, the Yeoman describes, with boiling hatred, the exploits of his former master the Canon, who has cheated money from people by practising alchemy. Having heard something of this man, the Host invites the Yeoman to begin:

> 'Ther-of no fors, good Yeman,' quod oure Hoost;
> 'Syn of the konnyng of thy lord thow woost,
> Telle how he dooth, I pray thee hertely,
> Syn that he is so crafty and so sly.'
>
> (Fragment VIII, 652–5)

Cunning, crafty and *sly* all seem to be used in their positive denotations here, though the *OED* cites the last line as an instance of *crafty* in its bad sense of deceitful. This pejorative use was emerging, and it is difficult to be sure how Chaucer's readers would have taken it. Possibly the sheer accumulation of terms, as well as the context, carries some negative atmosphere.

There is certainly nothing negative about the word when a poor priest, one of the Canon's dupes, asks to learn *this noble craft and this subtilitee* (1247), or when the Canon himself calls it *this discipline and this crafty science* (1253) and promises his victim that *though poure I be, crafty thou shalt me fynde* (1290). *Sleight* appears alongside *craft* in a non-pejorative sense when the Yeoman describes the failed efforts of the Canon's apprentices: *For al oure craft, when we han al ydo, / And al oure sleighte, he* [gold] *wol nat come us to* (866–7). Meanwhile the priest, who loses all his money, is pitied as *O sely preest! O sely innocent!* (1076). *Silly* and *innocent* mean 'inviting compassion' and 'harmless' respectively.

Counterfeit

The process of pejoration has meant that this word has today only its negative sense of forgery. Recorded instances of this appear from the thirteenth century. But a specialised, positive sense of 'likeness, image' remains in some texts long after this date. Thus Bassanio, regarding a portrait, says *What find I here? / Fair Portia's counterfeit* (*Merchant of Venice*, 3.2.114–15). Hamlet uses the word as a verb when he shows his mother two painted, or *counterfeited*, representations of Claudius and Hamlet senior.

Amelioration

With amelioration, a word loses its negative senses and the positive meaning prevails. The word *luxury* illustrates both amelioration and generalisation, as it has moved away from an earlier sense of sinful sensual appetite. *Luxury* is from Latin *luxuria*, and *lechery* is from the Old French version of the same Latin word. In medieval and early modern texts, the first often carries the meaning of the second:

> GHOST If thou hast nature in thee, bear it not.
> Let not the royal bed of Denmark be
> A couch for *luxury* and damnèd incest.
>
> (*Hamlet*, 1.4.81–3)

Luxury here means sexual lust. Later, we find it meaning 'voluptuous', a sensual appetite but not an exclusively sexual one. The word has generalised to include any excessive, self-indulgent desire, but the pejorative force is still strong.

Luxurious man, to bring his vice in use, [to popularise his own vices]
  Did after him the world seduce,
And from the fields the flowers and plants allure,
  Where Nature was most plain and pure.
(Marvell, 'The Mower Against Gardens' (1681), 1–4)

Eventually, the word signifies anything desirable, and as its moral connotations fall away, it is used as a term of approval, though not without a suggestion of desire:

> Mrs Slocum had a bruise on her cheekbone, barely visible under a heavy coating of suntan powder. She wore a green wool dress which emphasized the *luxury* of her figure.
>
> (Ross Macdonald, *The Drowning Pool* (1950))

Nice

Nice is a dramatic example of amelioration, and an extraordinarily complex one. The *OED* gives sixteen main senses for this word, and a seventeenth for combinations (*nice-looking* etc.). Nine senses are itemised in the Crystals' Shakespeare glossary, none of them the usual modern one.

What is clear is that the root of *nice* is Latin *nescius*, meaning ignorant. In its journey from foolish to excellent, the main steps seem to be as follows:

(i)   First there is the straightforward sense of 'foolish', as in this account of a brawl:

> And doun he fil bakward upon his wyf
> That wiste no thyng of thus nyce stryf.
> (*Reeve's Tale*, I 4281–2)

(ii) From 'foolish' we move to 'scrupulous', in a negative sense – foolishly fussy about trifles:

> Ful many a draughte of wyn had he ydrawe
> Fro Burdeux-ward, whil that the chapman sleep.
> Of nyce conscience took he no keep.
> (*General Prologue*, I, 396–8)

This is also the meaning when Shakespeare's Henry V complains to Katherine of 'the nice fashion of your country in denying me a kiss' (5.2.272).

(iii) The word now moves from people to objects. From being foolishly particular about things it denotes things it would be foolish to be particular about because they are of such slight importance:

> BENVOLIO   Romeo, that spoke him fair, bade him bethink
> How nice the quarrel was, and urg'd withal
> Your high displeasure.
> (*Romeo and Juliet*, 3.1.144)

The essential meaning here is how trivial and pointless the fight was.

Then the idea of foolish falls away, and that of particularity remains. So it denotes being fastidious, accurate, a discriminating judge. In this sense we have Shakespeare's description of a painting of Troy as showing 'Some high, some low, the painter was so nice' (*Rape of Lucrece*, 1412).

(iv) *Fastidious* can also mean over-fastidious. Austen's Mr Woodhouse criticises himself for this in his appraisal of a new acquaintance, Mrs Elton:

> 'Well, my dear,' he deliberately began, 'considering we never saw her before, she seems a very pretty sort of young lady; and I dare say she was very much pleased with you. She speaks a little too quick. A little quickness of voice there is which rather hurts the ear. But I believe I am nice; I do not like strange voices; and nobody speaks like you and poor Miss Taylor.'   (*Emma* (1816) vol. 2, ch. 14)

(v) From 'discriminating and accurate' the word generalises to being a general commendation of anything. We can catch this shift causing some debate at the time of Jane Austen, in this discussion from *Northanger Abbey*:

> 'But now really, do not you think Udolpho the nicest book in the world?'
> 'The nicest – by which I suppose you mean the neatest. That must depend upon the binding.'
> 'Henry,' said Miss Tilney, 'you are very impertinent. Miss Morland, he is treating you exactly as he does his sister. He is for ever finding fault with me, for some incorrectness of language, and now he is taking the same liberty with you. The word "nicest", as you used it, did not suit him; and you had better change it as soon as you can, or we shall be overpowered with Johnson and Blair all the rest of the way.'
> 'I am sure,' cried Catherine, 'I did not mean to say any thing wrong; but it *is* a nice book, and why should not I call it so?'
> 'Very true,' said Henry, 'and this is a very nice day, and we are taking a very nice walk, and you are two very nice young ladies. Oh! It is a very nice word indeed! It does for every thing. Originally perhaps it was applied only to express neatness, propriety, delicacy, or refinement; people were nice in their dress, in their sentiments, or their choice. But now every commendation on every subject is comprised in that one word.'
> 'While, in fact,' cried his sister, 'it ought only to be applied to you, without any commendation at all. You are more nice than wise.'
>   (Jane Austen, *Northanger Abbey* (written 1798–1803, published 1818), ch. 14)

Mixed semantic change

Very often a word will follow more than one of the processes. *Enthusiasm* and *enthusiastic*, for example, originally referred to divine possession, denoting the fine line between mystical knowledge and insanity. From here, it could be used to describe poetic inspiration: according to Dryden, *Poetry, by a kind of enthusiasm or extraordinary emotion of soul, makes it seem to us that we behold* ... (*Discourse on Satire*, Preface to *Translation of Juvenal*, 1693). In the eighteenth century, the word was sometimes used in a strongly pejorative sense to mean fanaticism. Since then, both generalisation and amelioration have occurred to give the usual positive modern meaning. *Zeal*, a word originally meaning any strong state of mind, was specialised to 'ardent desire', and is often used in a negative sense to suggest excessive passion. The history of such words is part of a wider story of varying attitudes to certain states of mind and their demonstration, and of the secularisation of once strongly religious terms. In much premodern writing words like *devotion, adoration, worship* and *idol* remain closer to their original religious context.

Multiple senses: polysemy

Semantic change is not a simple narrative, but more a matter of branching. Different senses often exist at the same time. Another way of illustrating the various senses of a word, though still a simplified one, is in a family tree like this:

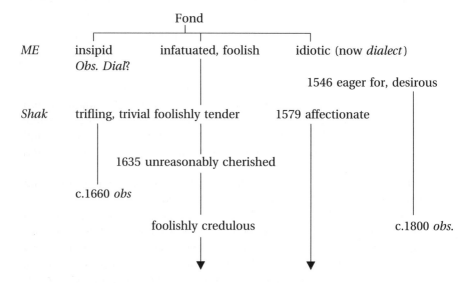

A 'family tree' also raises the question of how far words really do occupy distinct 'senses'. The difference between *foolish* and *idiotic* is one of degree. Dictionaries have to present material in numbered sections for each sense, but in real language use, and perhaps above all in literary use, one sense will shade into another, or more than one sense will be understood at the same time. Polysemy is the simultaneous existence of different senses, more than one of which may be operating in a particular instance. *Fond* itself presents examples of this.

The older sense of 'foolish', possibly with the strength of 'stupid', presides in these lines, when a servant tries to persuade his young master not to take up a challenge to a fight:

Why would you be so *fond* to overcome
The bonny prizer of the humorous Duke?   [*bonny prizer*: stout fighter]
(*As You Like It*, 2.3.7–8)

Just like *nice, fond* is transferred from denoting 'being foolish' to describing things which it is foolish to be concerned about: it means 'trivial, worthless'. This is how *fond* is being used here:

> Hark how I'll bribe you ...
> Not with *fond* shekels of the tested gold,
> Or stones, whose rate are either rich or poor
> As fancy values them ...
> (*Measure for Measure*, 2.2.150–5)

The newer sense of 'affectionate' establishes itself in Shakespeare alongside the old one. Perhaps affection is distrusted because it is so often a cause of foolish behaviour; or perhaps it is foolish because it seems so irrational. In the next lines, a fondness for a son is certainly affection, but the sense of being 'foolish' in a pleasant, self-deprecating manner may be there too:

> My brother,
> Are you so *fond* of your young prince as we
> Do seem to be of ours?
> (*The Winter's Tale*, 1.2.164–5)

More complex instances of polysemy occur where the two main meanings seem equally valid. Thus, Shakespeare's Lear could mean both 'foolish' and 'affectionate' (and foolishly affectionate) when he recognises his beloved daughter Cordelia, and says *I am a very foolish, fond old man* (*King Lear*, 4.6.53). The main sense is perhaps suggested by the word before it, as if that is doing a defining role. The same thing happens in Hamlet's vow to remember his murdered father: *Yea, from the table of my memory I'll wipe away all trivial fond records* (*Hamlet*, 1.5.98–9). The records of memory are indeed trivial next to the mighty news that his father has been murdered, but they would presumably also include things which Hamlet was affectionate about.

By some association of love and belief, the sense of 'foolishly credulous' emerges in the seventeenth century, as in this verse by Carew:

> *Celia, Bleeding, to the Surgeon*
> *Fond* man, that canst believe her blood
> Will from those purple channels flow,
> Or that the pure, untainted flood
> Can any foul distemper know ...
> (Thomas Carew, *Poems*, 1640)

Meanwhile, the core sense of 'foolish' survives. Here, it combines with ideas of excessive affection and hence unreasonable desire. Both senses are supported by other words in the verse, the first by *lunatic* and the second by *affection*; the intention of the whole is made a good deal clearer by the fact that the poem is a warning against sex before marriage:

> *Fond* lunatic, forbear! Why dost thou sue
> For thy affection's pay ere it is due?

> Love's fruits are legal use, and therefore may
> Be only taken on the marriage day.
>> (Henry King, 'Love's Harvest' (1657), 1–4)

'Foolishly credulous' alongside 'affectionate' emerge as the surviving senses. In these lines from Milton, Samson regrets his marriage to the treacherous Dalilah. There is an implication of 'vain' here, a sense which we might still attach to this phrase in modern English. Perhaps in the context of the subject of meeting and marrying a woman, we pick up the idea of misplaced affection as well:

> She proving false, the next I took to wife
> (O that I never had! *Fond* wish too late)
> Was in the vale of Sorec, Dalila . . .
>> (Milton, *Samson Agonistes* (1671), 227–9)

Polysemy is an important aspect of word meaning, and regularly occurs in literary texts. But the temptation to read all possible meanings of a word into one instance should be avoided: the likelihood of any particular sense being present needs to be evaluated by seeing how that sense fits the context.

Strengthening and weakening

Even when words retain their basic denotative sense, they can change in their intensity. Emotional words of praise, condemnation, horror, joy and so on are used a good deal and in time become worn out. As we have seen, *disease* used to mean simply a lack of comfort: with its specialised sense, its emotional connotations have strengthened. We have also seen that *fond* means foolish in earlier texts, but although we can register that fact on an intellectual level it is much harder for us to appreciate the strength of feeling which the word might have conveyed to its original audience. The word has undergone weakening. Another example of weakening is the word *amaze*. Until the early eighteenth century it retains a strong sense of utter bafflement: to be amazed is to be rendered crazy, perplexed, in a panic. This is the force of the word when Horatio tells Hamlet that the sight of his father's ghost *would have much amazed you* (1.2.235), and when Hamlet describes the effects of an actor's pretended passion:

> HAMLET   He would drown the stage with tears
> And cleave the general ear with horrid speech,
> Make mad the guilty and appal the free,
> Confound the ignorant and *amaze* indeed
> The very faculties of eyes and ears.
>> (2.2.550–5)

In the same lines, *appal* is another emotional word whose force has perhaps decreased through use. Polysemy may plausibly be detected here, as its two chief senses of 'to make pale' and 'to dismay' both work in context.

A further example of *amazed* in its stronger sense occurs in Milton. Here he describes the fate of the fallen angels:

Groveling and prostrate on yon Lake of Fire,
As we erewhile, astounded and *amaz'd*.
(Paradise Lost, I.280)

The phrase *astounded and amaz'd* carries the idea of being rendered physically and mentally helpless by the punishment: they are scarcely conscious and deprived of all sense.

Weakening is often accompanied by generalisation: for example, *astounded* passes from the specific and vivid 'put into a swoon' to the vaguer, and hence weaker, 'very surprised'.

Intensifiers

We can see examples of both strengthening and weakening in words used as intensifiers: ***very*** *good*, ***really*** *good*, ***dead*** *good* etc. These are among the most-used words and change very rapidly. Indeed, we might pass through several intensifiers in a lifetime. Here, the danger is not that we miss the older force of a word, but that we give it too much. With older intensifiers, the temptation is to take them in too strong a sense. When we encounter characters who are ***passing heavy*** (as we do on most pages in Malory) or ***sore*** *grievèd* the words may simply mean 'very' (*sore* is related to German *sehr*, which means 'very'). Hyperbole, or over-the-top speech, accounts for such words, as when we claim to be *awfully* tired or *absolutely* fascinated. This is still the case when the intensifier is itself intensified and we get phrases such as ***most*** *excellent*. A further consideration is grammatical: we tend to take literally the *most* in *most excellent*, or the *more* in Shakespearean phrases like *more worser*, and imagine a comparison is going on. But superlatives in Renaissance writing seem to be used often simply as a kind of intensifier, without any implied comparison. Again, today when we say something is *excellent* we are not usually conveying the idea that it excels over all others of its kind.

Word meanings – Exercises

1. Below is the beginning of a letter by Edmund Spenser to Sir Walter Raleigh, in which he explains the scheme of *The Fairy Queen*. Find out the meanings of the italicised words in Spenser's time, and describe the changes they have undergone since then.

    Sir knowing how *doubtfully* all Allegories may be *construed*, and this booke of mine, which I have entituled the Faery Queene, being a con-tinued Allegory, or *darke conceit*, I have thought good aswell for *avoyding* of *gealous opinions* and misconstructions, as also for your better light in reading therof, (being so by you commanded,) to *discover* unto you the general intention & meaning, which in the whole course therof I have fashioned, without expressing of any particular purposes or by *accidents* therein occasioned. The generall *end* therefore of all the booke is to fashion a gentleman or *noble* person in vertuous and *gentle discipline*: Which for that I *conceived* should be most *plausible* and pleasing, being *coloured* with an historicall fiction, the which the most part of men delight to read, rather for variety of matter, then for profite of the *ensample*: I chose the historye of king Arthure, as most fitte for the excellency of his person, being made famous by many mens former workes, and also furthest from the daunger of envy, and *suspition* of present time.

(Edmund Spenser (c.1552–99), 'A Letter of the Authors' (1590))

2. Find out the earlier meanings of these words of praise and critisism.
    Praise: *fantastic, marvellous, brilliant, superb, great, inspiring, fabulous.*
    Criticism: *terrible, ghastly, pathetic, dismal, dire.*

4.5   Words and tropes: transference of meaning

Transference of meaning occurs when words are used to denote something different from their usual sense. Rhetoric calls some of the devices for transference of meaning **tropes**, literally 'twists', as words are twisted from their standard literal meaning. **Metaphor**, **metonymy** and **synecdoche** are all rhetorical tropes, more commonly called figures of speech because they are ways of figuring, that is patterning, linguistic expression.

Metaphor

A word which usually means A is used to signify B, in the process bringing out the similarity between A and B. Sometimes metaphor is a surprising effect as we would not normally think of A and B together or even as being similar. Much of the time, though, metaphors have become so familiar that we use them without realising that is what they are: *a stroke of bad luck* and *thunderous applause* are examples of dead metaphors which have become idioms in the language. Indeed, the English language is full of dead metaphors (*dead metaphor* is one itself).

The standard distinction, 'simile is when something is *like* something else, metaphor is when it *is* something else' only really works for noun metaphors. But the figure applies to other parts of speech: *clouds **sailed*** (verb), *the **bald** moon* (adjective). In these, two ideas are brought together in an intense, compressed way.

The expression 'transference of meaning' implies that the literal meaning comes first, then at some point its metaphorical expression follows. This is not necessarily what happens. It may be that at an earlier stage of the language words did not have distinct literal and figurative senses, but carried deep metaphorical, symbolic resonances, connected to magic and religion. At a later stage, a 'pure' literal sense then developed. We understand metaphor as being a deviation from the literal, but literal meaning could be a 'deviation' from the essentially metaphorical nature of language.

Metonymy

In metonymy, one word substitutes another. This generally happens when two concepts are already closely associated. There are various types of metonymy which suggest something about the way our minds naturally make connections. *A **beer**, please* is metonymy for *A **glass of beer*** (content for container). *Give*

James a glass means *Give James a glass of wine* (or some other drink), where the container stands for its contents. A sharp *tongue* is metonymy substituting cause (*tongue* – instrument of speech) for effect (the words spoken). A well-known example is ***the pen*** *is mightier than* ***the sword***, coined by Edward Bulwer-Lytton (1803–73). A woman who *takes the veil* becomes a nun: the symbol (*veil*) is a metonym for what it stands for (the religious life). Metonymy might be regarded as a class of metaphor: the difference is that in practice metonymy tends to reinforce already existing associations, while metaphor – of the living variety – creates new ones.

Synecdoche

This is another substitute, not operating between separate concepts but between two elements of the same concept: in other words, we refer to a thing by naming a part of it, or a greater thing to which it belongs. The basic principle is one of scale: small stands for big, big for small. *Mortals* for *men* substitutes a large set for a smaller one: *two thousand souls* for *people* is little for big. A *vehicle* referring to a *car* is a synecdoche as there are other kinds of vehicles besides car; *silver* for *money* substitutes the substance for the thing made from it. In each case, there is a perceived shared identity between the two things.

Synecdoche is hard to distinguish from metonymy because conceptual distinctions themselves can be blurred. It is hard to decide sometimes whether we regard something as unified and indivisible or as the sum of smaller parts. In *All hands on deck, hands* and *deck* are small things standing for bigger things (bodies and the ship). But are they metonyms – separate things referring to something else – or synecdoche, parts of a thing referring to the whole thing? The answer depends on how we perceive these items ourselves. Because of this difficulty, metonymy is often taken to include both metonymy and synecdoche as we have defined them.

The following sonnet by Shakespeare illustrates the usefulness of these figures in literature:

> Not marble nor the gilded monuments
> Of princes shall outlive this powerful rhyme,
> But you shall shine more bright in these contents
> Than unswept stone, besmeared with sluttish time.   4
> When wasteful war shall statues overturn,
> And broils root out the work of masonry,
> Nor Mars his sword nor war's quick fire shall burn
> The living record of your memory.   8
> 'Gainst death and all-oblivious enmity
> Shall you pace forth; your praise shall still find room,
> Even in the eyes of all posterity
> That wears this world out to the ending doom.   12
> So, till the judgment that yourself arise,
> You live in this, and dwell in lovers' eyes.
>
> (Sonnet 55)

Commentary

Lines 1–4

In the first line, *marble* is a synecdoche for *statue* or *memorial*: the material stands for the object made out of it, a 'whole for part' substitution. This focuses our attention on one aspect of statues, their solid and durable substance. This duration is implicitly compared with human longevity in the metaphor *outlive*. These substitutions are part of a chain of other connections: *powerful rhyme* is not in itself a striking idea, but the proximity of *Princes*, and the alliteration linking this to *powerful*, cause us to read the words together, so the power of art becomes implicitly contrasted to the worldly power of princes. Another implicit relation is that between living people and non-living works of art, which seem to change places: the statues become like humans by *living*, so the person addressed becomes more like a statue in the metaphoric phrase *shine more bright* (3).

The *unswept stone* is synecdoche for the memorial stone on the floor of a church. The contemptuous adjective *sluttish* (4), means 'dirty, untidy' (it didn't necessarily mean sexually free at this time) and has the function of a metonym: time is described by what it causes, grime and decay.

Lines 5–8

Wasteful (5) has undergone weakening. Here it means 'causing devastation'. *Root out* is a stock metaphor for 'destroy', as is *living* (8) for 'enduring'. In *Mars his* [Mars's] *sword* (7), *sword* is a metonym for war (cause for effect). Like *Mars* (the god of war), it allows the poet to repeat the *idea* of war without repeating the *word*.

Lines 9–14

All oblivious enmity seems to refer to enmity that will bring oblivion to all; or it could be all enmity that brings oblivion. *Pace forth* against death and enmity is a metaphor for the survival of the beloved's memory: there may be a wordplay on the similar Elizabethan sounds of *pace* and *pass*, hinting that the beloved will 'pass' from the poem into the minds of future readers.

These minds are figured in the metonym of *eyes* (if we interpret *eyes* as the means or cause by which her image reaches the mind), a word which makes vivid the image of future readers. They 'see' a picture of the person addressed, presumably in their imagination, preserved in verse. This must be an image of pure shining beauty, since we are given no information at all about what this person does actually look like. The final line shifts *live* and *dwell* to a higher metaphorical plane: they no longer mean simply being mortal and occupying a space, but now signify being present until the end of time, inhabiting in pure non-bodily form the minds of future lovers. Through the figurative language, the survival of the person's memory has been portrayed as an ascent from the world of mortals to a plane of perfect spiritual existence.

Irony

Another way in which meaning is transferred is through verbal irony. When we perceive irony, we interpret a word as meaning the opposite of its usual meaning: to take an example with a sarcastic tone, *That was clever*, meaning *stupid*. We 'pick up' what is really meant, which lies 'beneath' the words as a subtext. For irony to work, we also have to 'pick up' the real meaning, and feel we have established a private understanding with the speaker. This understanding depends on our sharing a wider set of cultural and social values which come from experience.

Example

In this extract from *Gulliver's Travels* (1726) by Jonathan Swift, the traveller Gulliver describes to the inhabitants of another country the Parliament of Britain. He has just described the House of Lords, and now moves on the House of Commons:

> [I told him] That, the other Part of the Parliament consisted as an Assembly called the House of Commons; who were all principal Gentlemen, freely picked and culled out by the People themselves, for their great Abilities, and Love of their Country, to represent the Wisdom of the whole Nation. And, these two Bodies make up the most august Assembly in *Europe*; to whom, in conjunction with the Prince, the whole Legislature is committed.
>
> I then descended to the Courts of Justice, over which the Judges, those venerable Sages and Interpreters of the Law, presided, for determining the disputed Rights and Properties of Men, as well as for the Punishment of Vice, and Protection of Innocence. I mentioned the prudent Management of our Treasury ...
>
> (Brobdingnag, ch. 6)

The parliamentary and legal systems of England have never been as good as this, and they certainly were not in Swift's time, when corruption was rife. From this, we infer that the Members of Parliament are undemocratically chosen, incompetent and certainly not motivated by patriotism; and that the judges are unworthy of veneration and the Treasury is wasteful. A clue to irony in this passage is the hyperbole: *august, venerable.*

Synaesthesia

We talk of warm colours, clear sounds and sharp smells. All of these are examples of **synaesthesia**, whereby a word used to denote one sense impression is used to describe another. Synaesthesia is a part of the way we perceive the world, though some people have it in an unusually intense form. It arises in language partly because each kind of sensual impression has only a limited range of terms directly relating to it.

Concrete for abstract

We considered earlier the difference between abstract language, naming intangible ideas, and concrete, which describes things we can sense around us. Another kind of transference of meaning occurs when concrete words are used to describe abstract notions. This occurs, for example, when mental events are described in terms of physical ones: we can be *bowled over* by something, *stunned, gobsmacked* or *gutted*.

In time the abstract meaning can become the normal one, and we forget its concrete, physical source. *Horrid* in Shakespeare's time could mean much what it does today, but it still retained its physical sense of making your hair stand on end. To describe an act as *horrible* was to describe its physical effects as well as its emotional ones. Another example is *thrill*, which originally meant to pierce, penetrate. A less familiar example occurs in these lines, in which a gentleman traveller describes a lady he has just met:

> When we had got to the door of the Remise [coach], she withdrew her hand from across her forehead, and let me see the original – it was a face of about six and twenty – of a clear transparent brown, simply set off without rouge or powder – it was not critically handsome, but there was that in it, which in the frame of mind I was in, which attached me much more to it – it was interesting.
>
> (Laurence Sterne, *A Sentimental Journey* (1768), Remise Door I)

This is the first recorded example of *interesting* being used in its usual modern sense of 'arousing curiosity', a fact which helps to explain its climactic position at the end of the sentence. Previously the word referred to *material* interest or profit (as it still does when we talk of the interest charged by a bank). This is its basic sense in these lines from *Cymbeline*, when a lady, Imogen, is discovered next to a dead body and asked by a Roman captain *What's thy interest / In this sad wreck?* (*Cymbeline*, 4.2.367–9).

Sterne's use of *interesting* to refer to a mental experience takes us into the sentimental movement, in which writers like him looked for a language to describe the psychological experiences of characters in novel and convincing ways. The narrator in the passage above is enjoying the sentiments aroused by the woman's face, and, as ever in this book, he is fascinated by *the frame of mind I was in*. Several other words at this time were extended to encompass the abstract world of feelings: *affecting* in the sense of moving or touching (themselves examples of the phenomenon) is recorded from 1720; *pathetic* in its usual sense of arousing pity (later contempt) appears from the 1730s; *bore* in its usual modern sense is also first recorded in 1768; *embarrass*, which formerly meant to encumber by debt or by too many possessions, started to mean 'render awkward' in the early nineteenth century. Through the accumulation of such linguistic facts we see emerging a significant shift in the perception of human experience.

The act of understanding has a whole cluster of words around it, all illustrating our need to get at the mental world through the physical one: we can *seize, get hold of* or *pick up* an idea. Speakers of earlier ages could *conceive* one. Such differences in expression suggest underlying differences in the way different ages have regarded the operation of the mind.

Often, literary texts do not so much transfer a concrete word to the depiction of an abstract experience, but collapse the distinction between the two: internal experiences of soul and mind are felt as physical events, and a transcendent significance is found in the concrete, sensual world. This is the experience described by Wordsworth, who writes of how remembered images of nature are felt before they are analysed, causing *sensations sweet, / Felt in the blood, and felt along the heart.* This physical experience eventually transmutes into a transcendent one, in which *we are laid asleep / In body and become a living soul.*

Subjective and objective

In Shakespeare's *King John*, a character about to leap from a wall prays *Good ground, be pitifull* (4.3.2). Here, the subject – the ground – is, as it were, experiencing the pity. 'Feeling pity' is thus the *subjective* sense of the word.

By logical association, *pitiful* can also describe something that would excite feelings of pity: Tyndale describes people as *pale and pitifull* (*OED*, sense 3). Here he means they are objects of pity: we are providing the pity, not them. 'Inspiring pity' is the *objective* sense. In many cases, the objective sense has persisted while the subjective one has fallen into disuse. *Dreadful* and *awful* have undergone this process. The original spelling helps to underline how the words are formed:

> *Dreadful* of daunger that mote him betyde,
> She oft and oft adviz'd him to refraine
> From chase of greater beasts.
> (Spenser, *The Faerie Queene*, III.i.37)

> We are amazde, and thus long haue we stoode,
> To watch the *fearefull* bending of thy knee,
> Because we thought our selfe thy lawful King:
> And if wee be, how dare thy ioynts forget
> To pay their *awefull* duty to our presence?
> (*Richard II*, 3.3.76)

The words here have their subjective sense of being full of dread, fear or awe. As such words become objective, and mean 'inspiring awe' etc., they can slip away from the precise meaning they started out with – fear, awe – and become general emotive terms, whose function is more to exclaim and emphasise than to signify something particular: *that was an awful joke, this is a dreadful mess, what a pitiful sight.* This process is no doubt helped when another term like *awe-inspiring* is employed to take over the old meaning. We need to put this later usage to one side to appreciate lines like Donne's:

> Death be not proud, though some have called thee
> Mighty and *dreadful*, for thou art not so.

Dreadful is objective here, but in its strict sense: something that makes you full of dread. Where objective senses denote strong feelings, they are liable to weakening.

It is not only words with the *-ful* affix which can have objective as well as subjective meanings. *Marvellous* and *fabulous* have also largely lost their subjective sense of having the qualities of a marvel or a fable. Another example is *amiable*, a favourite word in Jane Austen, which can mean both friendly (subjective) and inspiring friendly feelings (objective):

> A week had not passed since Miss Hawkins's name was first mentioned in Highbury, before she was, by some means or other, discovered to have every recommendation of person and mind; to be handsome, elegant, highly accomplished, and perfectly amiable.

> (*Emma*, vol. 2, ch. 4)

Coming at the end of a list of personal attributes, *amiable* suggests its subjective sense of 'friendly' here, rather than 'likeable' – though it has the effect of making her likeable, of course. The loss of this sense is understandable, given that *friendly* and *amicable* are available.

A final example of subjective and objective sense is the word *fear*. Today this names an emotion, but up to the nineteenth century it could also refer to a cause of fear. The expression *no fear* does not mean 'have no fear', but is a relic of this earlier meaning: *There is no feare in him; let him not die* says a character in Shakespeare's *Julius Caesar* (2.1.197) meaning 'He is no cause for fear'.

Conversion

Conversion (also known as *functional shift* or by the rhetorical term *anthimeria*) is a grammatical substitution, in which a word in one part of speech does duty for another. Adjective to noun is most common, and not necessarily literary: *You're aiming for the **impossible***. Noun to verb is more striking: in Shakespeare we find many examples, among them *the thunder would not **peace** at my bidding* and *Lord Angelo **dukes** it well*. With frequent usage, a word can operate in more than one part of speech in the normal course of things, and the surprise which comes from transference is lost: *he **thundered**, they **quaked**, they all go into the **dark*** are conversions taking their place with thousands of other dead metaphors.

Other transferences of meaning

There are still other routes along which words can move from one sense to another, as they do whenever we avoid calling something by its name: slang, swearing, argot, fashionable jargon, euphemism and taboo are all powerful sources for the coining of new words and hence for the creation of new effects on literature. Another device which assigns a further sense to a word is the symbol: *rose* can signify *love*, if writer and reader are both familiar with the code.

4.6   Words in relation

In speech and writing, words have their meaning in the context of other words. It is not only the origin, history and dictionary definition of a word which tells us what it means: the other words around it also cast their own light, bringing out subtleties of sense and suggestion specific to a single text. These associations between words will be further enriched by allusion to other works, and by the wider cultural context of ideas which a piece of writing expresses. 'The Night' by Henry Vaughan (1621–95) starts like this:

> Through that pure *Virgin-shrine*,
> That sacred veil drawn o'er thy glorious noon
> That men might look and live as glow-worms shine,
> And face the moon:
> Wise *Nicodemus* saw such light
> As made him know his God by night.

The stanza, which is also a sentence, describes the night as a veil which protects men from the full brightness of the divine, allowing them to face the heavens. At night, Nicodemus had a mystical experience of God. If this argument is the melody of the stanza, then the harmonies are added by the ideas suggested through the rhythm, arrangement and choice of words. The noun phrase *pure Virgin-shrine* gathers a range of meanings: the *shrine* is the night, an enclosing or enshrining screen, and the *Virgin* is Christ's mother. *Pure* next to *Virgin* indicates sexual purity as well as moral excellence and the physical image of a serene night. (Theologically, the Virgin-shrine is also Christ's earthly body.) *Virgin*, in the context of night and the moon, also suggests the pagan goddess of hunting and chastity Diana, whose symbol was the moon. In the next line, the parallelism of *sacred veil* and *glorious noon* suggests a connection between the ideas of sacred and glorious. In turn, the force of *shine* is strengthened by the preceding *glorious*: the glow-worms' radiance, reflecting the moon, is not a feeble light but a recollection of divine glory (*glorious noon* itself alludes to the image of Christ as the Sun of Righteousness). The image of men and glow-worms in the same line also brings them together in the context of Christian thought: *But I am a worm, and no man* (Psalm xxii.6). Verbal pattern and allusion create a rich texture of harmonies, and the experience of reading resembles religious meditation.

Mutual influence between words, and allusion to other texts and ideas, are to some degree inevitable in real use of language: memory is part of our process of understanding, whether of books read a long time ago, or of words encountered a line earlier. Some writers seem to draw on a stream of association as one image summons up another: perhaps the pre-eminent example of this is Shakespeare. In the eighteenth century, much of the energy of literary invention comes from a desire to do the opposite – to use words in their pure and precise signification, without allowing them to contaminate each other.

Synonyms and antonyms

The precise relations at work between words have to be gauged in each piece of writing, and will escape any rigid linguistic classification. Some basic relations of meaning can, however, help us. The two basic types are: synonyms, words which mean the same; and antonyms, words with opposite senses. It is doubtful whether perfect synonyms exist: for this to be the case, either word would have to be as appropriate as the other in any situation – and thus be equal not only in denotation but in connotation as well. Antonyms can be absolute (such as *right* and *wrong*) or gradable, when we perceive a range of intermediate states between (*hot* and *cold*).

Synonyms and antonyms are both necessary when we are trying to convey an idea. A piece of writing can draw words into these relations, particularly by placing them in parallel grammatical structures. The more we accept an author's system of resemblances and oppositions, the more we are drawn into a particular way of perceiving and understanding:

> To begin, then, with Shakespeare. He was the man who of all Modern, and perhaps Ancient Poets, has the largest and most comprehensive soul. All the Images of Nature were still present to him, and he drew them, not laboriously, but luckily; when he describes anything you more than see it, you feel it too. Those who accuse him to have wanted learning give him the greater commendation: he was naturally learned; he needed not the spectacles of Books to read Nature; he looked inwards, and found her there. I cannot say he is everywhere alike; were he so, I should do him injury to compare him with the greatest of Mankind. He is many times flat, insipid; his Comick wit degenerating into clenches, his serious swelling into Bombast.
>
> (John Dryden (1631–1700), *Of Dramatick Poesie* (1668))

The gradable antonyms *Ancient* and *Modern* define two kinds of literature, that of the classical and the 'modern', perhaps post-medieval, world. This is a particular perspective on literature which tells us something about the presence of classics in Dryden's age. Two words are set up as antonyms to describe Shakespeare's creative process: *laboriously* and *luckily*. We have to understand one against the other. I take *luckily* to mean something like 'success coming by good fortune, without effort'. At a certain analytical distance we might think that even Shakespeare probably wrote his plays by a combination of effort and inspiration, but the set of antonyms does not allow for middle ground: we are drawn on by the rhythm, by the expectation of the syntax resolving at the end of the sentence, and, perhaps, by the attractiveness of the idea itself.

Other pairs in the passage include *see* and *feel*, as two kinds of response: *feel* is not used as an opposite to *see*, but seems to denote a stronger, more internalised emotional and even physical reaction to Shakespeare's writing. Then we have *accuse / give commendation*, and looking at books as a source of knowledge as contrasted with looking inwards; *Comick* is set against *serious* – not, as we might expect, *tragic*: Dryden is working with a notion of 'wit', or invention, that differs from ours. Each opposition brings into our mind a certain way of measuring things: the accumulative effect is to present a rational but civilised kind of analysis.

Just as interesting as the antonyms, though less immediately dramatic, are the words apparently employed as synonyms. We have already seen a common stylistic trait in English writing of doubling up epithets, often pairing an English with a classical term. It is not always easy to see where mere synonymity is intended: does the phrase 'largest and most comprehensive' convey the same idea twice, or two different ideas? *Largest* seems to bring out the idea of containment, of holding; in *comprehensive* (the sense in 'comprehensive school', in which all kinds and types are meant to gather) not only the scale but also the capaciousness of Shakespeare's understanding are being stressed.

Grades of importance

Still another kind of semantic relation between words is that of importance. Sometimes terms in a list imply a scale of size or significance: *sun and moon*, *bread and butter* go from greater to smaller; perhaps at certain times *town and country* was felt to do the same. The following lines are from Donne's sonnet about death, beginning *Death be not Proud*:

> From rest and sleep, which but thy pictures be,
> Much pleasure; then from thee much more must flow,
> And soonest our best men with thee do go,
> Rest of their bones, and soul's delivery.
> Thou art slave to fate, chance, kings and desperate men,
> And dost with poison, war and sickness dwell.

These lines present several lists. It is not necessarily the case that each represents a graded scale of significance: sometimes terms will simply be variations on the same idea, or a means of emphasising it. Questions of rhythm and sound pattern will also play a part. Nonetheless, ascents and descents seem to be a part of the drama of these lines. Are *rest* and *sleep* more or less the same thing, or do we take *sleep* to be a greater thing than *rest*, unconscious after semi-conscious? Following them, *thee* (Death) is clearly a stage further in perceived importance (a perception which Donne wishes to undermine). In *bones* and *soul* the immortal soul is surely more important than earthly remains. The next two lines contain lists of several terms. The first perhaps uses a descending scale: *fate* (destiny) is more important than accidental *chance*; both of these are stronger forces than *kings*, and the suicidal *desperate men* are at the bottom. *Poison, war* and *sickness* do not appear to have such an ordering – one might perhaps imagine a single murder through poison, many deaths through war (though not as many in Donne's time as in ours), and mass death through sickness or plague (the word has lost many of its darker connotations). But the associations of these words are far too varied for us to be sure that the poet had such an ordering in mind.

Semantics and context

Meaning does not only occur at the level of the word. Each aspect of language we have discussed relates to meaning: stress, rhythm and sound symbolism; word form, phrase and sentence structure and the surrounding environment of other words all play a part in the way we process and understand a piece of writing. The meaning of a text depends on non-linguistic elements, too: the way it is transmitted, through speech and through writing, where spelling, page layout, typography and even the physical makeup of a book will affect our response. Beyond this, what we know about the world which the book comes from will have a bearing on how we read it, as will the world we live in ourselves. The genre of a book – is it fiction or non-fiction, a 'literary' or popular work? – will be part of our consciousness and thus part of the sense-making activity we bring to what we see. Context is rather like the schoolboy Molesworth's address: Britain, Europe, the World, The Universe, Space. When we understand (or think we understand) a text it often feels fairly simple. When we try to analyse that act of understanding, it is infinitely complicated. As a first step, though, the close familiarity with a text and its meanings along the lines which this section has described is surely indispensable.

Words in relation – Exercise

Read the following passage, and find examples of: synonyms, or words with closely related meanings; antonyms; terms which suggest grades of importance. How do the grammatical structures of the text affect the way we interpret the words in relation to each other?

> *The discontent of Rasselas in the happy valley*
> Here the sons and daughters of Abissinia lived only to know the soft vicissitudes of pleasure and repose, attended by all that were skilful to delight, and gratified with whatever the senses can enjoy. They wandered in gardens of fragrance, and slept in the fortresses of security. Every art was practised to make them pleased with their own condition. The sages who instructed them, told them of nothing but the miseries of publick life, and described all beyond the mountains as regions of calamity, where discord was always raging, and where man preyed upon man.
>
> To heighten their opinion of their own felicity, they were daily entertained with songs, the subject of which was the *happy valley*. Their appetites were excited by frequent enumerations of different enjoyments, and revelry and merriment was the business of every hour from the dawn of morning to the close of even.
>
> These methods were generally successful; few of the Princes had ever wished to enlarge their bounds, but passed their lives in full conviction that they had all within their reach that art or nature could bestow, and pitied those whom fate had excluded from this seat of tranquility, as the sport of chance and the slaves of misery.
>
> (Samuel Johnson (1709–84), *Rasselas* (1759), start of Chapter 2)

Commentaries

Commentary 1

Our first piece is the opening of the Old English poem, *The Wanderer*. This really has to be approached as a foreign language. The accompanying translation is a literal rendering, keeping to a word-for-word version as far as possible. Give yourself time to go back and forth between translation and original a few times, working out as much of the original as possible.

The Wanderer, and other Old English verse, makes special demands on our understanding of sound, grammar and syntax. We not only have to learn the language, but consider the very different time when it was written. Despite its difficulty, The Wanderer is well worth spending time with for its great poetic qualities. I hope that the commentary gives an idea of the challenges of reading and interpreting the lexis of Old English, and of how this interpretation has to take account of the very different circumstances in which texts were composed and received.

In the text, I have preserved the Old English characters eth (ð) and thorn (þ). These are both pronounced as in modern *th*. The old character ash (æ) is pronounced like the first sound in *a*sh.

> *The Wanderer* (c.950)
> Oft him anhaga are gebideð
> Metudes miltse, þeah þe he modcearig
> geond lagulade longe sceolde
> hreran mid hondum hrimcealde sae,
> 5   wadan wraeclastas: wyrd bið ful aræd!
>   *Swa cwæð eardstapa, earfeþa gemyndig,*
>   *Wraþra wælsleahta winemæga hryre.*
>   Oft ic sceolde ana uhtna gehwylce
> mine ceare cwiþan – nis nu cwicra nán
> 10   þe ic him modsefan minne durre
> sweotule asecgan. Ic to soþe wat
> þæt biþ in eorle indryhten þeaw
> þæt he his ferðlocan fæste binde,
> healde his hordcofan, hycge swa he wille.
> 15   Ne mæg werig mod wyrde wiðstondan,
> ne se hreo hyge helpe gefremman:
> forðon domgeorne dreorigne oft
> in hyra breostcofan bindað fæste,
> swa ic modsefan minne sceolde
> 20   (oft earmcearig, eðle bidæled,
> freomagum feor) feterum sælan,
> siþþan geara iu goldwine minne
> hrusan heolstre biwrah, ond ic hean þonan
> wod wintercearig ofer waþema gebind,
> 25   sohte seledreorig sinces bryttan,
> hwær ic feor oþþe neah findan meahte
> þone þe in meoduhealle minne myne wisse,
> oþþe mec freondleasne frefran wolde,
> wenian mid wynnum.
>
> *Literal translation*
> Often the solitary one experiences mercy,
> the creator's mercy, though he, troubled in thought
> throughout the sea-ways long has had
> to stir with his hands the ice-cold sea,
> 5   to wade the paths of exile; man's lot is fully fixed!

So spoke the wanderer, mindful of hardships,
Of fierce battles with the deaths of kinsmen.
Often I have had, alone, each dawn
to lament my cares. There is now none living
10   to whom I my thoughts dare
openly relate. I know as a fact
that it is in a warrior a noble custom
that he should bind fast his breast,
hold fast his heart, think as he will [i.e. whatever he thinks].
15   Neither may a discouraged state of mind alter the course of events,
nor resentful thought provide help.
And so those who are anxious for renown their sadness often
in their breasts bind fast,
and so likewise I my heart have had
20   (often wretched and troubled, deprived of my native land,
far from my noble kinsmen) to bind in fetters,
since long ago my generous lord
earth covered in darkness, and I hence from there
went, desolate as winter over the frozen waves,
25   sought, sad at the loss of a hall, a giver of treasure,
wherever I far or near might find
one who in the mead-hall might know my thought,
or who me, friendless, would comfort,
entertain with delights.

Background

Before exploring the lexis of this poem, we shall consider some important features of its cultural and linguistic environment. About 30,000 lines of Old English poetry have survived. The earliest piece we have is *Caedmon's Hymn*, a glorification of God and His creation, composed about 657–80, though there must have been a tradition of oral and written composition before this. The latest poem generally regarded as in Old English is *Durham*, composed about 1104–9. Almost all Old English verse to be preserved appears in four great books, or codices, made roughly between 950 and 1050. *The Wanderer* appears in one of these, the Exeter Book (so-called because it was given to Exeter Cathedral by a former owner, Bishop Leofric.)

The Exeter Book is a collection of different sorts of writings, including religious pieces, riddles and the 'elegies' (to use a name given by modern literary historians) *The Wanderer* and *The Seafarer*. The handwriting has been dated to 970–90, but this is of course only the date at which the scribe copied it, not necessarily the date of composition. It has been suggested, but not proved, that the codex is itself a copy of an earlier book, made at the beginning of the tenth century.

Old English has various dialects, with West Saxon being the most represented in writing. This appears to have had the status of a standard, which could be adopted by scribes who themselves spoke a different form. The text of the Exeter Book is in this West Saxon dialect, which was that used by the scribe, but since that was a standard then the original poem could have come from anywhere in the country.

The Wanderer has been tentatively dated by some scholars to the early tenth century, when some of the chief sources the poem apparently draws on would have been more readily available. Beyond this, we know nothing about who wrote it, or why; nor can we tell how far its present form has been affected by transmission through both recitation and intermediate copies before the one surviving manuscript version.

Clearly *The Wanderer* is the work of an educated Christian author, probably a cleric, and reflects an aristocratic code of conduct. Beyond this, it is unlikely that the poem will tell us anything more about its author. It describes exile and loss in vivid and moving imagery, but this does not mean that the poet must have had a similar experience: there is a long tradition of writing on these themes, in both Latin and in Germanic writing, which would have provided the poet with literary sources. Nor should we assume that the emotions described are an act of self-expression by the writer: in a tradition of rhetoric which prevailed until the late eighteenth century, writers selected images and topics relevant to the subject, not as a means of communicating their own personal feelings. Moreover, we do not know for sure what genre of piece the poet thought he was writing: it has been called by various experts a consolation, an elegy and a lament, and undoubtedly has elements of all three. But whether, or how far, it is conforming to or deviating from expectations set up by a genre it is extremely hard to tell.

In the manuscript the poem has no title: *The Wanderer* is the rather romantic name it has acquired in modern editions, and this perhaps leads us to read it in a certain way, giving prominence to those parts of it most directly concerned with exile and personal grief. But it could equally well be called 'The Wise One' or 'Man's Lot', to use just two other suggestive phrases in the text. Indeed, titles are so important for us it is a challenge to imagine a conception of poetry in which they appear to be unnecessary. We can certainly be sure that the linguistic and literary environment in which this piece was composed was vastly different from today's: the poem was not 'published' in any sense we have of that word, simply copied one or more times. It seems likely that it was directed to a noble audience, since it discusses noble and pious virtues, but we do not know anything more about who heard it, or read it. We can however be sure that none of them were students or teachers of English Literature, or English language, since no such subjects existed as scholarly disciplines. Possibly the first readers regarded poetry more as a source of wisdom than as an object of analysis.

The great beauty and sophistication of Anglo-Saxon poetry, and the other arts, suggest a highly developed appreciation of artistic skill: perhaps the worst mistake we can make when reading Old English poetry is to regard it as primitive. Appreciation of the form might have been more tightly bound up with reflection on the message than we are used to today. The notion of 'literature' which we have is quite different from that of a medieval audience's, and collections like the Exeter Book are good evidence of this. *The Wanderer* is a poem, but it also incorporates theology and philosophy. Near the end (if it is the end), the poem changes to a series of pious declarations, which can be jarring for a modern reader, but this sense of moving across boundaries is ours, not the poet's.

Against this background of the linguistic environment, we can now attempt to describe the particular effects of some of the lexis.

Lexis

There are many words in Old English poetry which seem to belong to poetic diction – that is, they only appear in poetry and not prose. This suggests that the language of verse was traditional and specialised, and probably at several removes from ordinary speech.

The specialised nature of poetic diction means that many of the words in the surviving corpus are rare. Indeed, many words appear only once. These one-off words are called *hapax legomena*. In the passage under discussion from *The Wanderer*, the following words appear nowhere else in Old English: *eardstapa, hrimceald, modcearig, wintercearig, seledreorig. Gebind* (24) occurs only here in poetry, but is also found in prose; *earmcearig, lagulad* and *waðum* appear here and only once in other verse. No doubt if more poetry had survived, we would find other examples of these words, but then we would probably find more *hapax legomena* too: coining words for the occasion seems to be a common feature of Old English poetic composition. Because the *hapax legomena* listed above are compounds, formed from pre-existing words, their general meaning is not necessarily obscure. But the precise sense of a word where it appears can be hard to work out, and its connotations are even more a matter for discussion. Moreover, words which do appear elsewhere can have several possible meanings: in the first line alone, the words *anhaga, are* and *gebideð* are given several pages of learned discussion in the editions, and these discussions are themselves summaries of scholarly articles.

As mentioned above, compounding is an important aspect of Old English verse. A compound takes two words and joins them to create a new idea. The group of words used to describe the wanderer's sorrowful state illustrates some of the possibilities open to the poet: *cearig* means 'desolate, troubled, sorrowful'. The compound *earm + cearig* (20) joins together two adjectives to give a sense of 'wretched and troubled', fused together in a single term. In *mod + cearig* (2) the combination is noun + adjective, and the noun refers to what exactly is troubled: it means *mind-careworn*, or 'troubled in thought'. In *winter-cearig*, which is also noun + adjective, the relation between the two words is less clear. The noun could refer to the cause, 'troubled *because* of winter', or it could be a comparison, 'desolate *as* winter'. Both meanings are possible, and even if one is preferred the other sense could also be held in the mind. Still another noun + adjective relation is offered by *dom-georn*, 'anxious for renown' (or possibly 'anxious for judgment').

Compounding is a feature not just of Old English but of Germanic, as we can see in *hrim-ceald*. This compound, which is paralleled in modern English 'ice-cold', is one of the *hapax legomena*, though its meaning can easily be guessed. The same word exists in Old Norse, *hrimkaldr*: it could have been coined independently in English, or it might have come into English from the Vikings. Sometimes it is not certain whether the word in the text is a compound – two words made into one – or two separate words: in line 25, if *seledreorig* is taken as a compound, the meaning is 'I sought, sad [dreary] for a hall ...', which makes good sense. But if we take it as two words, *sele dreorig*, then the meaning changes: 'I sought, sad, the giver of a treasure and a hall', with *sele*, 'of a hall' separated from giver. Again, one may suspect that both meanings could exist in the mind of the audience, especially when listening, for then it would be impossible to tell whether the elements are single or compounded.

Like compounding, the device of variation is an important feature of the language of Old English poetry. Variation occurs when the same thing is referred to in more than one way. In modern English we can have two phrases in apposition: 'Ted, the village postman'. Both phrases – one giving his name, the other his occupation, refer to the same thing. In linguistic parlance, they have the same referent. In Old, but not modern, English, it is possible to say 'Ted arrived, the village postman'. Variations like this can work within and across lines.

Sometimes, one phrase can amplify another: thus *are* (grace, mercy) is 'explained' in the following phrase as *Metudes miltse*. *Lagulade* (the sea-ways) seems to refer to the *wraeclastas* (exile paths): each variation colours in a little further the main idea. Across the text, key ideas – the solitary man, the misery of exile, hope – are developed and enriched by this device. Part of the challenge for the reader is to ask whether phrases are related as synonyms through variation, or whether they are introducing a new idea.

Commentary 2

Our second example comes from English many centuries later. This soliloquy from Shakespeare's *Romeo and Juliet* (c.1595) is a marvellous example of how words in Shakespeare seem to suggest each other, and form associations across lines, offering all sorts of meanings and dramatic possibilities.

Juliet speaks these lines as she waits for Romeo to join her at night and consummate their marriage (the text given here is that of the First Folio (1623)):

> Gallop apace, you fiery footed steedes,
> Towards *Phoebus* lodging, such a Wagoner
> As *Phaeton* would whip you to the west
> And bring in Cloudie night immediately.
> Spred thy close Curtaine Loue-performing night,   5
> That run-awayes eyes may wincke, and *Romeo*
> Leape to these armes, vntalkt of and vnseene,
> Louers can see to do their Amorous rights,
> And by their own Beauties: or if Loue be blind,
> It best agrees with night: come, ciuill night,   10
> Thou sober suted Matron all in blacke
> And learne me how to loose a winning match,
> Plaid for a paire of stainlesse Maidenhoods,
> Hood my vnman'd blood bayting in my Cheekes,
> With thy Blacke mantle, till strange Loue grow bold,   15
> Thinke true Loue acted simple modestie:
> Come, night, come *Romeo*, come thou day in night,
> For thou wilt lie vpon the wings of night

Whiter than new Snow vpon a Rauens backe:
Come, gentle night, come louing, blackebrow'd night.   20
Giue me my *Romeo*, and when I shall die,
Take him and cut him out in little starres,
And he will make the Face of heaven so fine,
That all the world will be in Loue with night,
And pay no worship to the Garish sun.   25
O I have bought the Mansion of a Loue,
But not possest it, and though I am sold,
Not yet enioy'd, so tedious is this day,
As is the night before some Festiuall,
To an impatient child that hath new robes   30
And may not weare them, O here comes my Nurse:
                                    (3.2.1–31)

Some of the vocabulary here is typical of the high style: classical references (*Phaeton*, *Phoebus*), extravagant images and hyperbole (*Gallop apace, all the world will fall in love*) are appropriate both to the **epithalamium** (marriage hymn) genre of the soliloquy, and to the elevated language which is customarily given to aristocratic characters like Juliet in Renaissance verse drama. This language shows Juliet's imagination in an exalted state, transcending the narrow confines of normal thought. At the same time as marking Juliet's experience as elevated and special, the lexis works with the rest of the language to bring home the fact that she is still an uncertain young girl. Shakespeare's assurance with the verse is used to show the lack of assurance of the speaker. One way in which this happens is the way in which words link with each other across structural and syntactic boundaries. This soliloquy, for all its prayer-like arrangement, is only a step away from rambling, as one thought suggests another in an extraordinary chain of association, through which we follow the mercurial movement of Juliet's mind.

This association between lexical items starts in the first line. Juliet's first thought, at a basic level, is something like 'I wish the sun would set', which is duly 'dressed' in elevated rhetorical language. Here the thought ends, but *Phoebus* seems to call up memories (from the schoolroom?) of *Phaeton*, who was allowed to drive the chariot of the sun with disastrous results. So *Phaeton* is now mentioned, for no greater reason, it would seem, than that one idea has suggested another.

This sense of freedom and expansiveness around the original thoughts is continued. The phrase *Cloudie night* uses the adjective metaphorically for 'dark', but this literal *night* then triggers off the figured, personified *Love-performing night* of the next line. Equally, *vnseene* brings *Louers can see*, *Maidenhoods* suggests *Hood*, which starts the next line and clause, and *vnman'd* is echoed in *mantle*. The image of the falcon is transmuted later into a raven, and *vpon a Ravens backe* in turn brings to mind an image of horseriding, which is arguably buried beneath the pun of *Come, gentle night*. The language seems to be breeding on the page as metaphors spawn and merge. Even where the words do not match, we can find more subtle links. There seems no obvious connection between *Garish sun* (the first recorded use of this adjective for the sun in English) and the next little allegory of Romeo's body as *the Mansion of a Loue*. But *sun* suggests the zodiac, in which the sun passes through its various astrological houses or mansions. These kind of associations, which occur frequently in Shakespeare, convey the impression of extremely quick composition, as if images form into ideas almost as soon as they come into the poet's mind. In this case, they also transmit Juliet's excitement: beneath the stable structure of the prayer there is a flurry of thoughts and half-thoughts catching up with each other.

Juliet is both great orator and inexperienced girl. We become aware of the second way of seeing her partly through the way she misuses rhetorical language. This subverts the voice of the grand style to reveal something much more vulnerable. For, from quite early on, we notice that there is something about her eloquence which, in terms of decorum – the suitability of style to subject – misses the mark. The speech is too fast and too urgent to suit the solemn celebrations appropriate to an epithalamium, and its imagery is also slightly out of keeping with the genre. The night here is asked to do humdrum things like close the curtains; and the pictures which come through the metaphors are not of sublime celestial events but of everyday things which a young noble girl would have been familiar with, at least as a topic of conversation: horses being driven, a falcon being trained, games (of tennis?) and property purchases. There is an affecting bathos in the odd word choice: *Take him and **cut him out** in little starres* is redolent of innocent childhood games and undercuts the erotic charge established earlier.

In aiming for the high style and not quite getting there, Juliet reveals to us her real youth. She comes across as exposed and defenceless even as she is grandly invoking the magical powers of night. By such creative transformations of the stock of high-style rhetoric images, Shakespeare achieves a definite poignancy in the speech. (He also finds a way of depicting a woman's sexual yearning in terms which a boy actor could make convincing.) Everything is preparing us for the imminent moment at which Juliet is introduced to the world of adulthood in a horribly different way from that which she is excitedly expecting: for as the audience knows, she is about to learn that Romeo has been banished. A tragic dramatic irony has hovered over the whole speech. In this context, the fate of Phaeton and the repeated *night* take on in the audience's mind sinister suggestions of impending disaster. The presence of grand rhetoric itself has a kind of ironic status. Its figures and schemes take us back to ancient poetry and thus let us see the falling off from ancient to modern. It is a remnant of a golden age, reminding us of the protagonists' greatness of heart in a world overrun by meaner feelings, and paints a golden world which they can capture in their imagination but which is also tragically beyond their reach. The music which Juliet sings becomes more lovely and more human through her mistakes. But it is sadly out of key in the rancorous, mercantile world in which she finds herself. The more we notice the artifice, the more it draws us to a recognition of the feelings being presented: the truest poetry is the most feigning.

Commentary 3

Our final commentary is the start of chapter 2 of Jane Austen's *Persuasion* (1818). The story so far: Sir Walter Elliot, a vain baronet, is in financial difficulties. Here various characters consider how to help him: Mr Shepherd, his agent; Lady Russell, his neighbour; and Anne, his second daughter. Elizabeth is the eldest daughter of Sir Walter.

Mr Shepherd, a civil, cautious lawyer, who, whatever might be his hold or his views on Sir Walter, would rather have the *disagreeable* prompted by anybody else, excused himself from offering the slightest hint, and only begged leave to recommend an implicit deference to the excellent judgment
5 of Lady Russell, from whose known good sense he fully expected to have just such resolute measures advised, as he meant to see finally adopted.

Lady Russell was most anxiously zealous on the subject, and gave it much serious consideration. She was a woman rather of sound than of quick abilities, whose difficulties in coming to any decision in this instance were
10 great, from the opposition of two leading principles. She was of strict integrity herself, with a delicate sense of honour; but she was as desirous of saving Sir Walter's feelings, as solicitous for the credit of the family, as aristocratic in her ideas of what was due to them, as any body of sense and honesty could well be. She was a benevolent, charitable, good woman, and
15 capable of strong attachments; most correct in her conduct, strict in her notions of decorum, and with manners that were held a standard of good-breeding. She had a cultivated mind, and was, generally speaking, rational and consistent – but she had prejudices on the side of ancestry; she had a value for rank and consequence, which blinded her a little to the faults of
20 those who possessed them. Herself, the widow of only a knight, she gave the dignity of a baronet all its due; and Sir Walter, independent of his claims as an old acquaintance, an attentive neighbour, an obliging landlord, the husband of her very dear friend, the father of Anne and her sisters, was, as being Sir Walter, in her apprehension entitled to a great deal of compassion
25 and consideration under his present difficulties.

They must retrench; that did not admit of a doubt. But she was very anxious to have it done with the least possible pain to him and Elizabeth. She drew up plans of economy, she made exact calculations, and she did, what nobody else thought of doing, she consulted Anne, who never seemed
30 considered by the others as having any interest in the question. She consulted, and in a degree was influenced by her, in marking out the scheme of retrenchment, which was at last submitted to Sir Walter. Every emendation of Anne's had been on the side of honesty against importance. She wanted more vigorous measures, a more complete reformation, a
35 quicker release from debt, a much higher tone of indifference for every thing but justice and equity.

The passage is largely taken up with a description of the characters, particularly Lady Russell. This involves many evaluative terms: *cautious, civil, good sense* and several others. We see that universal, ideal qualities are a chief object of interest, and an abstract language is needed to define them.

The evaluative terms used by Austen illustrate how connotations and the general force of a word can change, even while its basic denotative meaning remains largely the same. Thus the *excellent judgment* and *good sense* which Mr Shepherd praises in Lady Russell mean much what they do today, and describe her capacity to decide on the basis of common sense. The difference is that these were stronger terms in a society which especially prized those particular qualities. Later we learn that Lady Russell is *benevolent* (kindly), *rational* and *consistent*. These are all still positive terms for us, but we may have difficulties feeling the strength they had for Austen's first readers. This is particularly the case with *rational*. There are not many contexts in which this would be a high term of praise today; indeed it could even be used critically to imply a lack of feeling or imagination. In Austen's time, though, it had a wider range of senses embracing 'civilised' and 'cultivated'. It also signifies a commendable control over indulgent emotion. In the sentence in which it occurs here, we are being told that Lady Russell has most of the necessary qualities needed to make a good judgment on this issue. An affection for rank is her only weakness. These words, then, might be hard to intuit with their original force even if we understand their basic meaning – and that meaning has in many cases specialised, as in the case of *rational*. To get an idea of their original power, we could imagine the terms we might use to praise someone highly today: *original*, *perceptive* and *brilliant*, say. In Austen's time, *rational* and *consistent* may have carried something like the emotional power that these words have for us today.

No definition can make up for the general loss of force in these words; nor can it encompass the subtle shades of meaning in context that each usage would have had at the time. It would not be easy for us to explain exactly what *brilliant* or *cool* mean for us, so ingrained are they in our way of seeing the world. A 'felt' understanding of key words, though ultimately impossible, can best be approached by reading novels and other texts as a whole. With repeated use, they grow in significance. For example, we are told in this passage that Mr Shepherd is *cautious*, which would seem a good quality in a lawyer. But elsewhere in Austen's writings, the word often has a distinctly negative connotation: in *Emma*, Jane Fairfax is criticised for being *reserved*, which is similar in sense to the modern 'secretive', and this word is often associated with *cold* and *cautious*. In these lines from *Persuasion*, it may denote not simply careful thought, but a lack of openness with Sir Walter, something which we are not meant to commend. *Benevolent* has weakened: today it conveys a gentle kind of well-wishing, but in Austen's novels the word implies a much stronger virtue. It is high praise indeed to call Lady Russell *benevolent, charitable* and *good*: these describe a kindly, unmalicious disposition, genuinely wishing the good of others. These qualities, which make up a particular type of attitude to others, are higher even than friendship. In *Emma* we read that *General benevolence, not general friendship, made a man what he ought to be*.

Some words have changed in meaning or use in ways we can work out as we go along. In the phrase *the **credit** of the family*, the word has the sense of 'the quality or reputation of being worthy of belief or trust' (*OED*, sense 1) – an etymological sense which explains why we have credit cards. Where Austen writes *she had a value for rank* we would say 'she placed a value on rank'. Anne is not considered to have any *interest* in the question. Here the word retains some of its older sense, which we considered earlier. It suggests not only that she had no curiosity in the plight of her father and the family estate, but that she had no *material* interest in its fate – presumably as an unmarried and unloved daughter she was not thought an important factor in the decision. She is certainly unlikely to inherit either the house and grounds – or, for that matter, the debts. In preferring *honesty* to *importance*, Anne places an acceptance of the true state of things before the self-importance of 'personal consequence, consideration or dignity' (*OED*, 1b).

Finally we may note two words which suggest aspects of the world in which Austen lived. *Cultivated* is here applied to a person; but possibly, in a largely agrarian society such as Jane Austen lived in, its literal sense of working the earth was never far away and lent the primary sense of 'accomplished' an aura of worthy exertion. Finally we find the word *influence*, which derives from the power of the stars 'flowing in' to people on earth, applied to persons, as it is today. The original astrological sense is clearly falling away, giving us another dead metaphor in which an older world-view is fossilised. Set in a society still based on land, but settling into modern habits of mind, Austen's lexis seems to join an older world with our own.

Suggestions for Further Reading

Dictionaries

Dictionaries and glossaries are of course the main resources for learning the meanings of words in literary texts. Chief among them is the great *Oxford English Dictionary* (*OED*), which describes and illustrates the meanings of words over the centuries. Help on using it, and on its history, is provided by Donna Lee Berg, *A Guide to The Oxford English Dictionary* (Oxford: OUP, 1993). The *OED* is also available online (by subscription) and on CD-ROM. Electronic formats make possible types of searches which book form does not, for example searches for an individual author's contributions to vocabulary, or loan words by country and period.

Beyond this, there are numerous specialist dictionaries dealing with etymology, slang, names and other topics. Then there are the dictionaries of English produced over the centuries, from Elizabethan times onwards. While it is important to use the *OED* and other modern works, it is also instructive to remember that most English authors did not have it, or anything comparable, to refer to. Other dictionaries I have found useful are:

David Crystal and Ben Crystal, *Shakespeare's Words: A Glossary and Language Companion* (London: Penguin, 2002). Besides entries on individual words, this also has treatments of numerous aspects of Shakespeare's language.
Norman Davis and others, *A Chaucer Glossary* (Oxford: OUP, 1979).

Eric Partridge, *Origins: A Short Etymological Dictionary of Modern English*, 4th edition (London: Routledge, 1966).

A very useful (free) online resource is http://www.concordance.com, which will give examples of word use in a wide range of texts.

To cultivate an interest in words beyond looking them up in dictionaries, a good first step might be to browse through works which have readable short essay-like entries on individual words, such as the following:

Linda and Roger Flavell, *Dictionary of Word Origins* (London: Kyle Cathie Ltd, 1995).

Linda and Roger Flavell, *The Chronology of Words and Phrases: A Thousand Years in the History of English* (Enderby: Silverdale Books, 1999). A history of the lexis since 1066, arranged chronologically to show when words, and the things for which they stand, entered the culture.

Jeffrey Kacirk, *Altered English* (Rohnert Park, California: Pomegranate Communications Inc., 2002). Informative and light-hearted.

Adrian Room, *Dunces, Gourmands and Petticoats* (Chicago: NTC Publishing, 1997).

Raymond Williams, *Keywords: A Vocabulary of Culture and Society* (London: Fontana, 1976).

After this, I would recommend the witty and learned essays collected in the following volumes:

Ernest Weekley, *The Romance of Words* (London: John Murray, 1912); *Words Ancient and Modern* (London: John Murray, 1926); *Adjectives and Other Words* (London: John Murray, 1930).

For Romance lexis in particular, see:

Donald M. Ayers, *English Words From Latin and Greek Elements* (Tucson, Arizona: University of Arizona Press, 1965; many later editions). An invaluable coursebook, with exercises.

For fuller academic treatments, see:

Geoffrey Hughes, *A History of English Words* (Oxford: Blackwell, 2000). Also has a full bibliography.

Joseph M. Williams, *Origins of the English Language: A Social and Linguistic History* (New York: The Free Press (Macmillan), 1975). Includes an extensive section on semantic change.

Lexis and criticism

The following all focus on words and their meanings, and so bring language study and literary criticism together:

Owen Barfield, *History in English Words*, 2nd edition (London: Faber, 1954; originally published 1926). Traces the relationship between vocabulary change and the climate of ideas of different ages.

Owen Barfield, *Poetic Diction* (London: Faber and Gwyer, 1928).

Donald Davie, *Purity of Diction in English Verse* (London: Routledge, 1952).

Hilda Hulme, *Explorations in Shakespeare's Language* (London: Longman, 1962), especially the chapter on Latin reference in Shakespeare.

C.S. Lewis, *Studies in Words* (Cambridge: CUP, 1960).

M.M. Mahood, *Shakespeare's Wordplay* (London: Methuen, 1957; reprinted London: Routledge, 1988).

Logan Pearsall Smith, *The English Language* (London: Williams and Norgate, 1912). This concentrates mainly on vocabulary, and has three chapters on the connection between the lexis and cultural change, a topic pursued by Barfield in *History*, above.

Ian Robinson, *The Survival of English: Essays in Criticism of Language* (Cambridge: CUP, 1973). Essays on the use and misuse of language in various modern media.

ⓥ 5 Conclusion

It is time to draw some of the strands of this book together. Confronted by a text, how should we start to describe its language? There are many possible answers to this question, and there are numerous techniques of language analysis which fall outside the topics we have covered here – from ancient rhetoric to nineteenth-century philology to modern linguistics. (Some suggestions for further reading on these are given at the end of this chapter.) All have something to offer the student of literature.

We have to start somewhere, though, and I hope that the key areas which we have covered in this book will provide a foundation for any further work on literary language. Quite apart from its use as a foundation for learning other methods, the close study of sound, grammar and lexis is also a valuable approach to critical appreciation in its own right. As a way of consolidating the work we have done so far, here is a poem by Marvell, followed by some questions. This step-by-step approach will, I hope, illuminate some aspects of this poem, and suggest some lines of inquiry which you can apply to other texts.

Andrew Marvell
'The Mower to the Glow-worms'

I
Ye living Lamps, by whose dear light
The Nightingale does sit so late,
And studying all the Summer-night,
Her matchless Songs does meditate;   4

II
Ye Country Comets, that portend
No War, nor Princes funeral,
Shining unto no higher end
Then to presage the Grasses fall;   8

III
Ye Glo-Worms, whose officious Flame
To wandring Mowers shows the way,
That in the Night have lost their aim,
And after foolish Fires do stray;   12

IV
Your courteous Lights in vain you wast,
Since Juliana here is come,
For She my Mind hath so displac'd
That I shall never find my home.   16

Background

- When was this poem published? When might it have been written? What is the significance of these dates to the appreciation of the language of the text?

Sound

- Describe the stanza form and rhyme scheme which the poet employs. Why might this form be suitable for the content of the poem?
- Describe the metre being used. Is the regular metre disrupted at any point, and, if so, what is the effect of this?
- How does the poet use rhyme to clarify or accentuate ideas? How far do rhyme sounds correspond to pauses? By what means, if any, does the poet create a pause or focus away from the rhyme word?
- To what extent does the word order of lines seem to be dictated by the rhyme scheme? Discuss possible reactions to this practice.
- Do any rhyme words have a semantic relation to each other, for example by having meanings which are similar (*bright, light*) or contrasting (*breath, death*)? If so, how does this affect your reading of the poem?
- How varied are the different rhyme sounds? Are there any sounds which different rhymes have in common, and if so what is the effect of this?
- Besides rhyme, what other patterns of repeated sound can you find? What is the effect of these?
- What is the general pace of the poem? Are there places where it seems markedly to slow down or speed up? What kind of voice do you hear?
- Read the poem aloud. Where does it seem suitable to rise and fall in volume or pitch?
- In Marvell's time *war* would have rhymed with *star*. How does this affect your reading of the second stanza? Which other sounds do you think may have changed between the poet's time and ours?

Grammar

- How many sentences are there in the poem?
- Grammatically, what do the first three stanzas have in common?
- What is the relation between verse form and syntax? How far do the divisions between clauses correspond to divisions between lines and stanzas? Comment on the effect of this relation.
- What is the effect of the syntax of the poem as a whole on the way we read it?
- Look at the noun phrases of the poem. Can you find any repeated structures?
- Comment on the poet's use of verbs and modifiers.
- What is the function of the word *does / do* in this poem? Has there been a change in taste since Marvell's time?
- What tenses does the poet use? In particular, how do you interpret *is come* in the last stanza?
- What does *Since* mean in line 14?
- How far, if at all, is word order used to emphasise a meaning or feeling?

Lexis

- Find out as much as you can about the connotations of the following words in Marvell's time: *Mower, glow-worms, grass, comets, princes, wandering*. Consult the *OED*. You should also find a critical edition of the poems helpful.
- What is the meaning of these adjectives: ***Dear** light* (line 1), ***higher** end* (7)?
- Using the *OED*, define the sense in this poem of: *studying, officious, courteous, wast(e), displac'd*. What kinds of semantic change have these words undergone?
- What are the *foolish Fires* referred to in line 12?
- Find out what you can about the name *Juliana*. Why do you think the poet chose this name, in this form?
- Who is represented by the Nightingale and the Mowers?
- What do you think the poet means by his *home* (line 16)?
- Given everything you have observed and learned, what kind of audience do you think this poem is aimed at? What are the main challenges faced by a modern reader who wants to understand and appreciate this poem?

Of course, these are not the only questions which we could ask about this poem. You may feel I have concentrated on minor aspects and missed things which are important. There is no questionnaire which will fit all texts, and different features of the same text will strike different readers as interesting. There is always a subjective element in choosing which aspects of a work to concentrate on, and in exploring their significance.

If you would like to pursue linguistic analysis further, some Suggestions for Further Reading follow, though needless to say the most valuable reading you can do is of English literature itself. I hope that this book has made you feel that the analysis of what Wordsworth called the minutiae of texts is a worthwhile and fruitful exercise. Linguistic analysis is not the whole of literary criticism, nor even perhaps the most important part of it. But it does take us into the raw material of literature – the sounds, shapes and endlessly shifting meanings of words, and the historical changes they undergo. And the more we know about this material, the better we can appreciate the skill with which authors fashion it into rich and complex works of art, and the more vividly we can hear them speaking to us, in words, through texts, across time.

Suggestions for Further Reading

Textbooks on the language of texts

The following textbooks cover similar ground to this one:

Ronald Carter and Michael N. Long, *The Web of Words: Exploring Literature through Language (for Upper-Intermediate and Advanced Students)* (Cambridge: CUP, 1987).

Ronald Carter and others, *Working with Texts: A Core Book for Language Analysis*, Intertext series (London: Routledge, 1997).

Dennis Freeborn, *Style: Text Analysis and Linguistic Criticism*, Studies in English Language (Basingstoke: Palgrave Macmillan, 1996).

Style manuals

Manuals on writing are another useful source for insights into literary style. See, for example:

Francis-Noël Thomas and Mark Turner, *Clear and Simple as the Truth: Writing Classic Prose* (Princeton, New Jersey: Princeton University Press, 1994).

G.H. Vallins, *The Best English*, The Language Library (London: André Deutsch, 1960). Follows the same author's *Good English* (1952) and *Better English* (1955).

Joseph M. Williams, *Style: Toward Clarity and Grace* (Chicago: University of Chicago Press, 1990). The same material is presented in a textbook format in *Style: Ten Lessons in Clarity and Grace*, 5th edition (New York: Addison Wesley Longman, 1997).

From here, there are perhaps two main directions one can take. One is to learn more about the development of English and changes in style over time. The other is to explore Stylistics, the application of linguistics to literary analysis. The two approaches are not, of course, mutually exclusive.

The history of English and literary language

See the suggested works by Freeborn, Smith, Hogg, and Smith and Horobin in the Suggestions for Further Reading at the end of Chapter 3. In addition, the following are useful:

W.F. Bolton, *A Short History of Literary English*, 2nd edition (London: Edward Arnold, 1972). An older work which covers much ground in a short space.

Robert McCrum and others, *The Story of English*, BBC Publications (London: Faber, 1986). A very readable one-volume account of the development of the language, concentrating on external history (the effect of invasions, printing, the empire etc.).

Thomas Pyles and John Algeo, *The Origins and Development of the English Language*, 3rd edition (New York: Harcourt Brace Jovanovich, 1982). An older history which goes further into the internal development of the language than McCrum, with many illuminating examples.

George Watson, ed., *Literary English Since Shakespeare* (Oxford: OUP, 1970). A collection of essays representing various approaches to the subject.

There are some series of monographs specialising in the language of particular authors and related topics. These are especially helpful for research:

Language and Style (General Editor Stephen Ullmann, published by Blackwell). This includes some titles on English authors, together with works on continental European writers and linguistic theory.

The Language Library (General Editor Eric Partridge, published by André Deutsch). The oldest of the three series. Generally employs traditional grammatical terms.

The Language of Literature (General Editor N.F. Blake, published by Palgrave Macmillan). A series of monographs on individual authors and periods; the tools of modern grammar and linguistics are employed, and the focus is more on literary analysis than that of the *The Language Library*.

The Cambridge History of the English Language (General Editor Richard Hogg, Cambridge University Press) represents the most recent work in language study, and the level is very advanced. The chapters in each volume on the literary language are approachable and full of insight.

Stylistics

To get an idea of what stylistics is about, browse through Katie Wales, *A Dictionary of Stylistics*, 2nd edition (Harlow: Pearson, 2001). The following is a selection of textbooks and other introductory works:

Richard Bradford, *Stylistics*, The New Critical Idiom (London: Routledge, 1997).
Urszula Clark, *An Introduction to Stylistics*, Investigating English Language (London: Nelson Thornes, 1996).
Nigel Fabb, *Linguistics and Literature*, Blackwell Textbooks in Linguistics (Oxford: Blackwell, 1997).
Nigel Fabb, *Language and Literary Structure: The Linguistic Analysis of Form in Verse and Narrative* (Cambridge: CUP, 2002).
Roger Fowler, *Linguistic Criticism* (Oxford: OUP, 1996).
Roman Jakobson, *Language in Literature*, ed. Krystyna Pomorska and Stephen Rudy (Cambridge, Mass.: Belknap Press of Harvard University Press, 1987).
Geoffrey N. Leech, *A Linguistic Guide to English Poetry*, English Language Series, 4 (London: Longmans, 1969).
David Lodge, *Language of Fiction* (London: Routledge, 1966).
Mick Short, *Exploring the Language of Poems, Plays and Prose*, Learning About Language (London: Longmans, 1996).
Paul Simpson, *Language through Literature: An Introduction*, Interface (London: Routledge, 1996).
Michael Toolan, *Language in Literature: An Introduction to Stylistics* (London: Edward Arnold, 1998).
Laura Wright and Jonathan Hope, *Stylistics: A Practical Coursebook* (London: Routledge, 1995).

Teaching Stylistics

For the teacher, the works by Widdowson are thought-provoking:

H.G. Widdowson, *Stylistics and the Teaching of Literature*, Applied Linguistics and Language Study (London: Longman, 1975).
H.G. Widdowson, *Practical Stylistics* (Oxford: OUP, 1992).

The following series of publications specialise in stylistic analysis:

Interface (General Editor Ronald Carter, published by Routledge) includes numerous interesting titles on linguistic criticism.

Intertext (General Editors Ronald Carter and Angela Goddard, published by Routledge) is a series which applies the techniques of text analysis to the language of various types of discourse. The result is a collection of useful introductory guides: there are titles on *The Language of Fiction* (by Keith Sanger, 1998), *The Language of Drama* (Keith Sanger, 2000) and *The Language of Poetry* (John McRae, 1998).

Linguistic Approaches to Literature (General Editors Mick Short and Elena Semino, publisher John Benjamins Publishing Company) and *Textual Explorations Series* (Longman) make use of further linguistic techniques such as cognitive science in literary analysis.

Journals

The academic journals *Style* and *Language and Literature* specialise in publishing the latest research into the linguistic analysis of literature.

▼ Glossary

This glossary covers the key terms of the text. For fuller treatment of these and other linguistic topics, see any of the following:

Kim Ballard, *The Frameworks of English: Introducing Language Structures* (Basingstoke: Palgrave Macmillan, 1997).

David Crystal, *The Cambridge Encyclopedia of Language*, 2nd edition (Cambridge: CUP, 1997).

Victoria Fromkin and Robert Rodman, *An Introduction to Language*, 6th edition (Fort Worth: Harcourt Brace College Publishers, 1998).

Sara Thorne, *Mastering Advanced English Language* (Basingstoke: Palgrave Macmillan, 1997).

Abstract	Abstract nouns refer to intangible things which cannot be seen: *courage, practice, argument*. Contrast to **concrete** nouns.
Accent	In the study of speech sound, another term for **stress**.
Adjective	Traditionally a 'describing' word. Can act as a **modifier** in a **noun phrase**, denoting the attribute of a noun: *the **new** car, my **broken** umbrella*.
Adjunct	Adverbial clause element that modifies the verb / predicator (*They shouted **loudly***) or the sentence (*They pay me **on the last day of each month***). Some grammarians also class **conjuncts** as a species of adjunct, since they fall outside the essential elements of a **clause**.
Adverb	Adverbs have many functions. Broadly, they can modify anything which is not modified by an adjective, i.e. adjectives, verbs and other adverbs: *they talked **rapidly**, he was **very** frightened*. The same can be done by adverbial phrases: *They talked **in a loud whisper*** etc.
Affricate	A sound which starts with a plosive and ends with a fricative: *he**dge** and scra**tch** are the affricate sounds in English.
Alexandrine	A line of twelve syllables: *That, like a wounded snake, drags its slow length along* (Pope).
Alliteration	The repetition of consonants (usually in initial position): *In pious times, ere priestcraft did begin, / Before polygamy was made a sin; / When man on many multiplied his kind, / Ere one to one was cursedly confined* (Dryden).
Amelioration	A type of *semantic change*, in which a word takes on a positive sense, or loses its negative one: in the seventeenth century *prestige* meant 'illusion, imposture, deception', normally referring to conjuring tricks. Its modern positive sense dates from the nineteenth century. Amelioration is rather rarer than its opposite, **pejoration**.
Analytic	An analytic language indicates grammatical relations between words by means of **grammatical words** like **prepositions**. English has gone from being a heavily **synthetic** language in the Old English period to an analytic one today.

Anapaest	A metrical foot of two unstressed syllables and one stressed (xx/): *When a mán / hath no frée / dom to fíght / for at hóme* (Byron).
Antecedent	The noun referred to by a **relative pronoun**: *This is the car which I want.*
Antonym	A word opposite in meaning to another: *good, bad*. **Gradable antonyms** allow for possibilities lying between two extremes: *cold, tepid, warm, hot.*
Apostrophe	In rhetoric, a calling out, often addressing some abstract and/or supernatural body: *O fickle Fortune!* etc.
Apposition	Two or more noun phrases next to each other, both referring to the same thing: *He seyde, '**Apollo, god and governour / Of every plaunte** ...'* (Chaucer).
Approximant	Approximants, or semi-vowels, seem to be midway between vowel and consonant, and involving less contact between parts of the mouth than other consonants: *Will you remember me when I am dead?*
Archaism	A word or usage which has fallen out of ordinary use and become obsolete (though it may continue in non-standard dialect). Sometimes used deliberately for poetic effect, e.g. to satisfy metre or to convey associations of former ages.
Article	One kind of **determiner**, divided into **definite** (*the*) and **indefinite** (*a, an*).
Aspirate	A sound produced with an exhalation of breath: *have you heard?* In *spot the pot* only the second *p* is aspirated; in *kill the king*, the first *k* is aspirated.
Assonance	The repetition of vowel sounds: *Where the remote Bermudas ride / In the ocean's bosom unespied, / From a small boat that rowed along ...* (Marvell) mixes assonance and full internal rhyme.
Auxiliary	A verb which 'helps' the main verb to denote number and tense. The primary ones are *be, have, do*: *I **am** running, I **have** bought, I **do** eat*. These can be combined: *I **have been** bullied*. They can also stand as main verbs themselves. *Do* is sometimes referred to as the dummy auxiliary or expletive. See **modals**.
Cadence	Literally 'falling'. In the study of rhythm, the arrangement of stressed and unstressed syllables bringing a phrase or sentence to a close. See **cursus**.
Caesura	A pause in a line of verse which is not part of the metre. It may be indicated by a punctuation mark, as in *Oh for a muse of fire, that would ascend / the brightest heaven of invention* (Shakespeare), or it may be a pause which comes naturally because of the shape of phrases: *Shall I compare thee . to a summer's day? / Thou art more lovely . and more temperate* (Shakespeare) where I have indicated likely pause marks with a stop. While keeping to a regular metre, poets can vary pace and rhythm through the placing of caesuras.
Case	In a **synthetic** or **inflected** language, the case of a word describes its relation to other words. For example, in Latin, a noun functioning as subject would be inflected for the nominative case, and as object would be in the accusative case.
Class	The grammatical class of a word is the **part of speech** it functions as – **noun**, **verb** etc.
Clause	A finite clause consists of a **subject** and **predicate** and can stand as a single sentence: *Mary weeded the garden*. A **sentence**

can consist of more than one clause. To the main clause above, we could add dependent or **subordinate** clauses to make a **complex sentence**: *Mary, **who was nearly sixty**, weeded the garden* (**relative clause**); *Mary weeded the garden **although it was raining*** (**subordinate clause**); *Mary weeded the garden, **starting with the roses, to give herself a sense of achievement*** (two dependent **non-finite** clauses). Non-finite clauses do not necessarily have subject and predicate.

Cleft sentence
A sentence 'cleaved' to bring information to the topic position at the front and so highlight it. For example, *The King sent the messenger to the castle* has cleft variations of (i) *It was the King who sent the messenger to the castle*, (ii) *It was the messenger whom the King sent to the castle* and (iii) *It was to the castle that the King sent the messenger*. In each case, the initial information is emphasised.

Coherence
A discourse is coherent if, for example, it follows a discernible logical direction, and refers consistently to a world we recognise.

Cohesion
The formal links, lexical and grammatical, between statements in a discourse, marking it as cohesive.

Cola
The members of a **period** marked out by the punctuation marks of semicolons and colons. A rhetorical *colon* (a statement closed by a semicolon or colon punctuation mark) may be a whole clause or sentence in its own right, but the punctuation marks it as belonging to a larger whole. The following period has its original sixteenth-century punctuation *per cola et commata*. This system aids the speaker in pausing and breathing, and brings out the essential unity of the utterance:

> O Lorde oure heauenly father, almighty and euerliuying God, whiche haste safelye brought us to the beginning of this day: defend us in the same with thy mighty power; and graunt that this daye wee fall into no synne, neyther runne into any kinde of daunger, but that al our doings may be ordered by thy gouernaunce, to do always that is righteous in thy sight: through Jesus Christe our lorde. Amen.
> (Third Collect at Matins, First Prayer-book of Edward VI,
> 1549)

Collocation
The coexistence of lexical items, often adjective and noun, which can become predictable and commonplace. Typical set collocations are idioms like *spick and span, green with envy* or *purple passages*. Words frequently go to the same partners: thus *auspicious* often collocates with *occasion*, *plain* with *simple*, and *cream* tends to be *sour* rather than *bitter*. The collocations writers use make up a key feature of their style. Ideas not normally associated are brought together in phrases like *my particular grief / Is of **so flood-gate and o'erbearing nature*** (Shakespeare, *Othello*), making the image striking and memorable.

Commata
The members of a **period** marked by commas. The following example of Elizabethan punctuation shows how a period marked by commata suggests the rhythms of the speaking voice and moves more quickly than modern punctuation would allow:

> I must not discover what ungodlie dealing we had with the blacke iackes, or how oft I was crowned King of the

drunkardes with a Court cuppe, let mee quietly descend to the waining of my youthfull daies, and tell a little of the sweating sickness, that made me in a cold sweate take my heeles and run out of England.

(Thomas Nashe, *The Unfortunate Traveller* (1594))

To start a new sentence with *let mee*, as modern conventions dictate, would take away from the sense that the period, here composed of four commata, is a rhythmic whole, following one complete passage of thought.

Complement
A clause element which tells us more about the subject (*This dinner is **delicious**, He's becoming **impatient***) or the object (*They pronounced the dinner **delicious**, You're making me **impatient***). The term is also used in another sense in **SPCA** analysis.

Complex sentence
A sentence consisting of a main clause with one or more dependent / **subordinate** clauses: *I left home because I was unhappy, although I was unready for the world* (the subordinate clauses are introduced by the subordinators *because* and *although*).

Compound sentence
A sentence composed of two or more clauses linked by **co-ordinating conjunctions**: *She went to town and I stayed at home.*

Concrete
Concrete nouns name things which can be seen: *pigeon, lorry, palace.*

Conjunctions
Words which tie clauses or parts of clauses together: the **co-ordinating conjunctions** are *and, or, but*. There are numerous **subordinating conjunctions** or **subordinators** which introduce a **subordinate clause**: *as, so, although, unless* etc.

Conjuncts
Adverbials which link larger units such as clauses, sentences and paragraphs: *meanwhile, however, nevertheless* etc.

Connotations
The associations carried by a word or phrase. Thus *home* for many might have connotations of warmth and security. Literary writing often exploits the connotations of words.

Consonance
The repetition of consonant sounds, usually after a vowel, with the vowel being changed: *slip slop*; *take the bike.*

Consonant
A speech sound formed by the partial obstruction of the breath (*b, c, t, f* etc.). A consonant needs a vowel to form a syllable.

Continuous
Continuous verbal forms describe a continuing action: *I am writing, they were writing*. Continuous constructions like this are more common in present-day English than in the medieval and Early Modern periods. Also referred to as the *progressive aspect* of verbs.

Conversion
In grammar, the use of a word which is normally confined to one part of speech in another part of speech. The most common is turning a noun into a verb: *The thunder would not **peace** at my bidding, **Knee** thy way into his mercy* (Shakespeare). *I want to do the **impossible*** makes an adjective into a noun. This process is called *anthimeria* in Renaissance rhetoric.

Cursus
The Latin term for the pattern of syllables which brings phrases and sentences to a close. There are three classical types: **cursus planus** (/xx /x) *lóvely to sée you*; **cursus tardus** (/xx /xx) *párt of the fámily*; and **cursus velox** (/xx xx/x) *Háppily ever áfter*. English writers have used these forms, and

	also varied them by adding extra syllables, to suit the natural rhythms of English.
Dactyl	A metrical foot of one stressed syllable and two unstressed (/xx): *Thís is the / fórest pri / méval* ... (Longfellow, 'Evangeline'). (Note how in hearing this example we create an extra beat in the last foot to make it a dactyl.)
Decasyllabic	A line of ten syllables, *but not necessarily rhythmical.*
Deixis	Literally 'pointing'. Deixis occurs when a word or language feature like tense points to something in the space, time and material or personal context of a situation: *you, now, here, then, those* are typical deictic items, pointing to a non-linguistic reality.
Demonstrative	A word which distinguishes something from another of the same class, typically according to how near or far it is: *this* book, *that* book, *these* books, *those* books.
Denotation	The **denotative** sense of a word is its dictionary definition, that which it denotes: *Jewel* denotes 'a precious stone'. Compare **connotation**.
Determiner	A pre-head element in a noun phrase: *the* gardener, *my* cat.
Diction	The choice of words one uses. **Poetic diction** is the idea that poetry properly requires a special language, removed from everyday speech, to express exalted feeling: *Ye distant spires, ye antique towers / That crown the watery glade* etc. (Gray). This idea was particularly influential in the eighteenth century.
Diphthong	A vowel sound in which one vowel glides into another: *Thy voice is on the rolling air; / I hear thee where the waters run* (Tennyson).
Doublet	In grammatical discussion, pairs of words, a common characteristic of English writing, particularly in the Renaissance: *There are certaine frivolous and vaine inventions, or as some call them, subtilties of wit, by meanes of which, some men doe often endevour to get credit and reputation* (Montaigne (1533–92), 'Of Vaine Subtilties', translated by John Florio (?1553–1625), trans. published 1603).
End-focus	Making the end of a clause or sentence strong, by putting the important information there. The end can also be strengthened by making it resolve the syntax of the sentence, and by rhythmic means.
End-stopping	A line of verse is said to be end-stopped when punctuation at the end of a line enforces a pause. Sometimes we may pause even when no punctuation is present.
Enjambment	Also spelled *enjambement*. Where a verse line ends but the syntax continues into the next line: *Who says that fictions only and false hair / Become a verse?* (Herbert). Sometimes we may still pause at an enjambment, even where there is no punctuation. Also referred to as **run-on**.
Epithalamium	A marriage hymn. Originally a genre in ancient Greek, it has been adapted by several English writers, notably Spenser.
Ethic dative	A construction in which a pronoun is added which is not necessary to the grammar of the sentence but shows that someone has an interest in the action: *Knock me the door*. A feature of Latin and Early Modern English, not now in use.
Etymology	The study of the origins of words, and of the history of their forms and meanings. The **etymological fallacy** is the notion that the original (i.e. earliest recorded) meaning of a word is its 'true' meaning.

Euphemism	An accepted expression used as a substitute for one considered harsh, unpleasant or offensive. *Pass away* is a euphemism for *die*.
Extension	(1) In a verb phrase, a preposition completing the sense of a **prepositional verb**: *Then he hung **up***; or an **adverb** particle completing a **phrasal verb**: *He turned **aside***. (2) Extension is also the name of a type of **semantic change**, whereby a word goes from a specific meaning to a more general one: *dismal* was once a noun meaning 'unlucky or evil time' (from the Latin *dies mali*, meaning *evil days*). From the sixteenth century it was used as an adjective and acquired the wider sense of 'sinister, wretched, dreary, dreadful, disastrous' etc. which it has today. Also called **generalisation**.
Falling ending	A phrase or sentence ending which falls from a stressed to an unstressed syllable: *Happily ever áfter.*
Finite	Finite forms of the verb are marked for number, tense, person and mood: *He **laughs**, they **laughed**, long **live** the King* etc. Contrast to **non-finite**.
Foot	A pattern of stressed and unstressed syllables, creating the **metre** and **rhythm** of a line of verse.
Fricative	A sound made by forcing air through a narrow space, causing friction: *Deep in the **sh**ady **s**adnes **of** a vale, Far sunken **f**rom the **h**ealthy breath **of** morn* (Keats).
Gender	A grouping of words into types, traditionally referred to as masculine, feminine, neuter. Old English has grammatical gender, but this has since been lost.
Genitive	The one surviving case in English (besides the non-inflected common case), denoting possession: *the child's bicycle.*
Grammatical words	Words which have a grammatical function, relating other words but not indicating something in the world. Typically conjunctions, prepositions, determiners etc. These are called closed class words, since it is rare for new ones to be added.
Great vowel shift	A complex process, which occurred over several centuries, particularly the fifteenth and sixteenth. In it, the vowel structure of English was radically altered: for example, *life* would have sounded something like *leef* for Chaucer and *lafe* for Shakespeare before reaching its present pronunciation. Long vowels are still unstable, and may be heard pronounced in different ways by different speakers. When analysing the sounds of earlier writers such as Shakespeare, it is worth remembering that the vowels (especially the long vowels) may have sounded very differently in his time.
Head	In a noun phrase, the only compulsory element, to which other elements are dependent: *The little **house** on the prairie. Bob* is a *noun phrase* consisting of a head alone. In a verb phrase, the head is the main verb: *I have **read**.*
Hendecasyllabic	A line of eleven syllables: *Flood-tide below me! I see you face to face* (Whitman).
Historical phonology	The study of how English sounds have changed over time.
Homophones	Two words which sound the same: *tear, tare; for, four.*
Iamb	A foot of one unstressed followed by one stressed syllable (x/): *I sáw / the vír / tues sí / tting hánd / in hánd* (Herbert). The iamb is the most common foot in English verse.
Imperative	The verbal mood in which orders (directives) are expressed: *Come here, Sit down.* The **subjunctive** can be used to express

	an order less directly: *Let them speak now, or forever hold their peace.*
Indicative	The usual verbal mood, generally used for stating something held to be real and factual: *It is freezing, I hope so.*
Infinitive	The base form of the verb, which is **non-finite**, and occurs with and without *to*: *I must **go**, I want **to go**.*
Inflection	A suffix, added to the end of a word to indicate grammatical meanings (*We watch**ed**, he run**s**, thou ha**st**, he give**th**, the King'**s** man*). English has gone from being a heavily inflected language in the Old English period to a largely non-inflected one today.
Intensifier	A word or phrase adding force or emphasis: ***very** pleased, **extremely** concerned*. Intensifiers are heavily used and change rapidly: compare the feel of ***awfully** good, **really** good, **dead** good*. In earlier English, intensifiers may seem stronger to us than they did at the time: *sore amazed, excellent good* etc. Intensifiers can themselves be intensified: *most excellent.*
Intonation	In phonetics, the pitch contours as the voice rises and falls when speaking.
Inversion	The reversal of the usual order of elements: *crown imperial* (noun–adjective), *The castle of Macduff I will surprise* (object before subject). An important characteristic of poetic language.
Irony	A word or phrase used in an opposite sense to what it usually means. Often, but not always, implying a sarcastic tone: *So you've overspent on the credit card again – well done!* Irony binds reader and writer together as we see, or think we see, what the writer really means.
Isochrony	The even spacing of stressed syllables, speeding up and adding pauses if necessary.
Lateral	Lateral and **liquid** are two words for the *l* sound. Lateral because the air comes down the sides of the mouth. Often associated with a sensual idea: *Lolita, light of my life, fire of my loins. My sin, my soul. Lo-lee-ta: the tip of the tongue taking a trip of three steps down the palate to tap, at three, on the teeth. Lo.Lee.Ta* (Nabokov).
Lexical words	Words with lexical meaning, typically **nouns**, **verbs** and **adjectives**. These refer to objects and experiences, and are also called open class words since new ones can easily be added to the **lexis**.
Lexis	Or **lexicon**. The vocabulary of a language.
Liquid	See **lateral**.
Manner of articulation	How a sound is produced in the mouth: for example, the *labiodental* sounds *v, f* are produced by the upper teeth meeting the lower lip.
Metaphor	A figure of speech or **trope** in which a word is used in a sense different from its usual one, in order to stand for another idea. Used to form striking comparisons between two unlike things to bring out something they have in common: *That man is a **pig**, The breeze **caressed** the trees, The **brutal** day*. The metaphorical words are used figuratively, i.e. not in their literal sense (the man is not really a pig, but has porcine characteristics). Metaphor occurs naturally, and the language is full of dead metaphors. These do not convey any surprise, but they do suggest ways in which we perceive experience: *a storm of applause, a stunning idea.*

Metonymy	One thing is named, to suggest another related thing: *the top brass, he lives by his pen*. Only distinguished from **synecdoche** if we perceive the two things (e.g. pen and writing) as separate.
Metre	From Greek meaning 'measure'. The metre of a verse line is the sequence of feet it contains. The study of metre is called both **metrics** and **prosody**.
Modals	A class of auxiliaries which express an attitude towards events: *I **must** go, I **might** go* etc. Modals can change in force and meaning. In medieval and Early Modern English the modal auxiliaries *shall* and *will* often carry much more meaning than they do today. Broadly, *shall* frequently implies a fixed inevitability (Lear: *this **shall** not be revoked*, when he has banished Kent) while *will* implies volition (Macbeth: *We **will** proceed no further in this business*, meaning he does not want to proceed with the plan of killing King Duncan).
Modifier	A pre-head element in a noun phrase, describing some attribute of the head: *the **oldest** building*. There can be several modifiers in a noun phrase: *the **eccentric rich reclusive** writer*.
Mood	The mood of a verb is **indicative** (stating a matter: *He is here*), **subjunctive** (describing an imagined situation: *I wish he were here*) or **imperative** (giving an order: *Come here!*).
Morphology	In grammar, the study of the form of words – chiefly, how prefixes and suffixes are added to base forms.
Narrowing	A common kind of **semantic change**, whereby a word goes from a general sense to a more specific one: at various times in the past, *deer* meant any animal, *starve* meant die, *hound* meant any dog, not only hunting dogs, and *meat* meant any food. All have specialised to their modern sense. Also called **narrowing**.
Nasal	A sound made with the front of the mouth blocked, so that most of the air is released through the nose: *Alas, you **might** have dragged **me** on / Another day, a single one!* (Wordsworth).
Neologism	A new word or phrase introduced into the language. It might be entirely new, a new formation from existing elements, or an old word given a new meaning. Also called **coinage**.
Nominal	The adjective corresponding to **noun**. The noun phrase is sometimes referred to as the nominal group.
Nominative	In an inflected language, the case for the **subject**.
Non-finite	Verb forms which do not express tense, number, person and mood. These are the **participles** and the **infinitive**. A non-finite form can introduce a non-finite clause: *He started **to count** them, **beginning** with the eldest*.
Noun	Traditionally, a naming word like *table* or *courage*, a definition which fits most nouns. Another way of identifying nouns is not by their meaning but by their function. For example, in *The yellow jobblies are coming*, we can tell that *jobblies* is a noun because (a) it is in the position of **head** word in a **noun phrase**, and (b) it takes plural *-s*. We do not need to know what it means to know it is a noun.
Noun phrase	A phrase consisting of a **head**, sometimes accompanied by other elements: *The (**determiner**) old (**modifier**) man (**head**) of the sea (**qualifier** / **post-modifier**)*. There can also be a **pre-determiner**: ***All** the old men of the sea*. In earlier English we meet some noun phrases with structures that are no longer possible: *that whiter skin of hers than snow, the King's son of Prussia*. The phrase structure head–modifier is a common

kind of poetic **inversion** which places more emphasis on the modifier: *Much castigation, **exercise devout*** (Shakespeare).

Number In English, whether something is singular or plural: *She is, they are* indicate number in both pronoun and verb.

Object The object usually follows the **subject** and **verb**, if the verb takes an object at all. A direct object 'suffers' the action of a verb, which is said to be used transitively: *The dog found **the bone**, I love **you***. An indirect object is usually the recipient of an action: *I gave **you** the letter / I gave the letter **to you*** has, as is usual, a direct object (*the letter*) as well as an indirect one. Several pronouns retain object forms: *I, me; he, him* etc. In older English we also find the pairs *thou, thee; you, ye* – the second in each case is the object form.

Objective See **subjective**.

Objective genitive A construction which we find in English of the time of Shakespeare but which is no longer in use: *I am joyful of your sight* means *I am joyful at the sight of you*.

Octosyllabic A line of eight syllables: *She walks in beauty, like the night* (Byron).

Parallelism Where a structure is repeated. There could be a repeated pattern of sound: *Round the cape of a sudden came the sea* (Browning); or there may be a repeated structure: *the mighty prince, the everlasting father* – where the **noun phrases** have the same order of elements. When we see phrases or clauses in parallel, we often intuit a similarity of meaning as well as structure.

Parataxis Where clauses stand alongside each other either with no **conjunction** (*I stayed. She left*) or linked by *and* (*I stayed and she left*). The opposite of **hypotaxis**, where clauses are linked by multiple subordination (*I stayed although she had left, because I wanted to see the end*). Parataxis is an important stylistic feature of texts as various as Malory, the Bible and Hemingway. Other terms for parataxis and hypotaxis are *asyndeton* and *polysyndeton*. **Paratactic ambiguity** occurs where we interpret a missing conjunction as expressing a logical link: in *It started to rain. I went inside* we might intuit an implied *so* in the gap.

Participle Participles are **non-finite** forms of the verb: despite their conventional names, they do not express tense. There is a present participle (*hating, eating*) and a past participle (*hated, eaten*).

Passive In the passive voice, the **subject** suffers the action of the verb: *the boy was punished, I am being questioned*. The opposite to the active voice.

Pejoration A type of **semantic change** in which a word acquires a negative sense: *crafty* once meant 'strong' and then 'clever, skilful' though today it is often used disparagingly; *counterfeit* formerly had the sense of any represenatation, such as a painting, before its modern denotation of 'fake' – Shakespeare uses the word in both senses. King James II is said to have called St Paul's Cathedral *amusing, awful* and *artificial* – meaning pleasing to look at, awe-inspiring and skilful – at least the last two of these words have undergone pejoration.

Pentameter A line of verse which has five feet: *When I / do count / the clock / that tells / the time* is an iambic pentameter because it consists of an iamb repeated five times.

Perfect	Also called present perfect. The past form of a verb with auxiliary *have*, describing a past action in a time period which is still continuing: *He **has written** ten books* implies 'in the period of his life' which is still continuing. **Preterite** *He wrote ten books* implies that the time period of his life is closed, i.e. that he is dead, unless the time period is otherwise specified, as in *He wrote ten books before he retired*. An interesting construction in Early Modern English is the similar *The King is come* on the model of French *est venu*, stressing the present significance of the action.
Period	A term of ancient rhetoric, describing a bundle of statements, which may be **phrases**, **clauses** or **sentences**, that make up a larger unified whole and end in a full stop. Divided not into modern grammatical categories like phrase and clause but into **cola** and **commata**. The punctuation of periods in original texts often follows speech patterns as much as, or more than, grammatical logic.
Personification	The device of giving something that is inanimate personal attributes: *Cruel Fortune!*
Phrasal verb	A verb completed by an adverb: *go astray, sit down*.
Pitch	The wave frequency of the voice, that is whether it is high or low like a musical note. **Stress** commonly involves a rise in pitch.
Place of articulation	The place in the mouth where a sound is produced.
Plosive	A sound made when the passage of air is stopped and then suddenly released: *b, p, k, d* are examples of plosives. Another word for plosives is stops.
Pluperfect	The expression of a past time before another past time, as in *When I arrived they **had left***. Also called past perfect.
Polysemy	Literally 'many meanings' (Greek), e.g. *plain* can mean both dull and simple. Literary writings often exploit multiple senses. *Paradise Lost* begins *Of man's first disobedience, and the fruit / Of that forbidden tree, whose mortal taste …*: here, *fruit* may be understood both in its literal sense (the fruit of the tree) and its figurative sense of 'result, consequence' at the same time; similarly, in the same lines *mortal* could mean both 'by mortals' (Adam and Eve ate the fruit) and 'deadly' as in 'mortal wound'. Polysemy is also an important source of wordplay – and indeed Milton's line is an example of highly serious punning.
Predicate	Everything that comes after the subject in a clause and which tells us something (i.e. predicates) of the subject: *The messenger **brought the terrible news***.
Predicator	In **SPCA** analysis, the predicator is the verb or verbal group. A discontinuous predicator is one that is broken up: ***Have** you **seen** him? I **have** hardly **seen** him*.
Prefix	An affix that can be added to the root of a word, to make a new word: ***post**-natal, **de**-salinate, **dis**-continue, **semi**-precious*. Prefixes can have poetic connotations: *Let all the tears that should **bedew** my hearse* (Shakespeare). The meanings of some earlier prefixes have been forgotten: in *withstand, with* means *against*; and in *midwife, mid* is of Germanic origin and means *with* (i.e. a midwife is one who is 'with the woman').
Preposition	A grammatical word which indicates relationships between other words or sentence elements: *I went **to** the shops, They sat **in** the bus stop* etc. Prepositions in Early Modern English often

have a different sense, and a wider range of meaning, when compared to the language today: *Say, you chose him / More **after** our commandment* (according to: Shakespeare, *Henry IV, Part Two*); *What **in** your own part can you say to this* (on, for: *Othello*).

Prepositional verb A verb completed by one or more prepositions: *come in, meet up with, go for*. As with prepositions, so the sense of prepositional verbs can change over time: Lady Macbeth calls to *the spirits that **tend on** mortal thoughts* where we would say *attend **to***.

Preterite The simple past tense form of a **verb**, usually in UK English describing a completed action within a finished time period: *I **arrived**, you **told** me*.

Pronoun A type of noun which stands for (*pro*) another noun: *I, it, we, they, this*. The **relative pronouns** *which, who, whose, that* refer to an **antecedent noun** and start a **relative clause**. Sometimes there is a zero relative and the pronoun is understood: *the house* [which] *I told you about*. In earlier English, an important pronoun distinction is between intimate *thou* and formal *you*.

Qualifier In a **noun phrase**, the qualifier follows the **head** and gives more information about it: *the man **of my dreams***. It can itself contain one or more subordinate clauses with other noun phrases: *the dream **I had last night***. Also referred to as a postmodifier.

Quatrain A stanza of four lines. Frequent rhyme schemes are: *abab / abba / aabb*.

Received pronunciation Commonly abbreviated to RP. A standardised English accent, not regional and associated with a high social status.

Register The variety of language appropriate to a given situation: thus, the register of a business meeting will involve a more formal vocabulary than the register of a party. Legal, religious and scientific occasions are all examples of social events that affect register. Certain words and syntactical customs may be held in certain periods to be suited to a poetic register: *rose*, for example, may feel more appropriate to poetry than *word processor*.

Relative clause A subordinate clause introduced by a relative pronoun: *The subject **that I have been studying***. In this example, as is usual, the relative clause is a qualifier in the noun phrase. Sometimes the relative is not said or written, but understood. This is the zero relative: *The subject **I have been studying***. Can contain an embedded non-finite clause: *The subject **I wanted to discuss with you***.

Rhotic An accent in which the *r* is sounded in words such as *formal* and *water*: standard American and West Country English are examples of rhotic accents. English in the time of Chaucer and Shakespeare was more rhotic than standard English is today.

Rhyme **Pure rhyme** is the repetition of the vowel and final consonant sounds (if any) of a stressed syllable, together with any unstressed syllables which may follow: *And Christabel awoke and spied / the same who lay down by her **side*** (Coleridge). Rhyme can occur, as here, at the end of a line, or within a line as **internal rhyme**.

Rhythm The repetition of a metrical arrangement, forming a regular pattern. Rhythm can occur in prose as well as verse.

Rising ending A phrase or sentence ending, rising from an unstressed to a stressed syllable: *until the day he died*.

Run-on	See **enjambment**.
Schwa	The unstressed vowel sound we hear in *pitter patter*, *half a gallon*.
Semantic change	The process by which words change their meaning over time. For example, *buxom* has changed from meaning 'yielding, compliant' in medieval English to 'bright, lively, spirited' in the sixteenth century, and thence to 'healthy, vigorous' and so to 'plump, comely'. Only the last of these, attested from the nineteenth century, applies chiefly to women. Common types of semantic change are **extension**, **narrowing**, **pejoration** and **amelioration**.
Sentence	The largest unit covered by traditional grammar. Sentence types are **simple**, **compound** and **complex**.
Sermo	Latin for 'speech'. In rhetoric, writing in the *sermo* style imitates speech.
Sibilant	A hissing **fricative** sound: *s*, *sh*.
Simple sentence	A sentence consisting of a single **clause**: *I went to town yesterday*.
Simple verb	Simple verb forms are the opposite of the **continuous** or progressive: *I write, they wrote*.
Slant rhyme	Together with half-rhyme and pararhyme, a term for a near-rhyme, usually using **consonance** or **assonance**: *Happy are men who yet before they are **killed** / Can let their veins run **cold*** (Wilfred Owen, 'Insensibility').
SPCA	A system for analysing clauses which defines elements as **subject**, **predicator** (verb or verbal group), **complement** (anything completing the verb, such as object or extension) and **adjunct** (anything left over, commonly adverbial). Thus *Macbeth killed the King in the night* analyses as *Macbeth* (Subject) + *killed* (Predicator) + *the King* (Complement) + *in the night* (Adjunct). This is a simple kind of clause analysis, which is useful for discerning the structure of clauses without analysing every lexical item individually. Note that in SPCA analysis *complement* has a special sense.
Strengthening	With regard to lexis, where words in time take on powerful connotations. Often a result of semantic change: *disease* has a range of meanings in Shakespeare under the general idea of 'lack of ease'. As it has undergone **specialisation** to mean medical illness, so it has strengthened in its emotional **connotations**. Similarly, *sick*, which used to mean 'ill' (and still does in US English) in UK English now has stronger moral resonances of 'evil, disturbed'. See **weakening**.
Stress	The syllable in a word or phrase which carries most weight. Stressed syllables are pronounced with greater volume, and are often lengthened and go up in pitch: *Did you see the news today?* We can distinguish both **primary** and **secondary** stress: *tradítionàlly* – the acute accent marks the primary and the grave accent the secondary stress. By describing speech in terms of **graded stress** – for example from 1 (weak) to 4 (strong) – we can identify still more levels that naturally occur in speech.
Subject	A subject typically precedes the **verb** in a statement and agrees with it in number: *Fred walks*, *The family discuss*. In a question, it follows the first verb: *Are you happy?* A subject can be a **noun phrase** (*The old man* says), a string of noun phrases (*The staff, the head teacher and governors* agree), a **pronoun**

	(*I accept*) or a **subordinate clause**, which may have its own embedded clauses (***Who she says she is*** *isn't important*). A subject is typically the agent of the verb (***He*** *hit me*), or the **topic** that the verb is about (***My aunt*** *is tired*). Verb–subject is a common kind of **inversion** in poetry (*So spake **the angel***).
Subjective	With regard to lexis, a certain kind of sense: in *He would sometimes catch her large, worshipful eyes* (Hardy, *Tess of the d'Urbervilles* (1891)), *worshipful* has a subjective sense as we could say that here the eyes worship, i.e. the eyes are the subject. The **objective** sense of this word occurs when something is the object of worship: *Will he give us the remains of his worshipful and economical housekeeping* (Scott, *Woodstock*, 1826), where we might say we worship the housekeeping, making housekeeping the object. Sometimes one kind of sense is lost: a Renaissance King could be *pitiful* in the subjective sense of giving pity as well as the modern objective sense of deserving it.
Subjunctive	A verbal mood referring to an action that is not real but imagined, for example because it is wished for, wondered about or feared: *Would he **were** here! If you **be** he ..., Let him **come** forward, if the King should **hear** of this.* Subjunctives are more common in Early Modern English than in modern English, which is why such expressions as the examples just given may seem old-fashioned, though we might still say something like *I demanded he **confess*** or use stock expressions like *if I **were** you*.
Subordinate	A subordinate **clause** is a dependent clause linked to the main clause by a subordinating **conjunction** / subordinator. It does not necessarily follow the main clause: ***Although he was getting on**, he did not want to retire, **because he felt he was still strong**.* Here we have a main clause flanked by subordinate clauses. The second of these (*because he felt*) has its own embedded subordinate clause (*he was still strong*), for which the subordinator *that* is not stated but understood. Multiple subordination is referred to as **hypotaxis**.
Suspended syntax	A characteristic of Latinate style in which we feel a suspense as we read on, waiting for the grammar to resolve: *The corruption of the schools of high art, so far as this particular quality is concerned, consists in the sacrifice of truth to beauty* (Ruskin). Here there is suspense as we wait for the verb *consists*, which is some way from the subject, and which leads us to the powerful final idea. Or the most important idea is kept until the final phrase or clause: *I know that, since the Revolution, along with many dangerous, **many useful powers of Government have been weakened*** (Burke). Suspended syntax is an effective way of creating **end-focus**.
Synaesthesia	A term from psychology rather than linguistics, but one which describes a certain kind of **metaphor**. A word or phrase relating to one kind of sense impression is used to describe another: *a warm sound, a cold colour*.
Synecdoche	A part of something is named to stand for the whole: *a village of three hundred souls* (*soul* for whole person, i.e. soul and body); *many hands make light work* (*hands* for people). Only distinct from **metonymy** if we perceive the two related things (e.g. hands and bodies) as part of a unified concept. The term metonymy is sometimes used to describe both tropes.

Synonym	A word of similar meaning to another in a certain context: *cold, chilly*; *mount, ascend, climb*.
Syntax	From the Greek meaning 'tied together'. The study of how words are joined together to make sentences.
Synthetic	In a synthetic language, grammatical relations between words are indicated by inflections. The opposite of an **analytic** language.
Tense	The time at which an action takes place, indicated by the form of the **verb**, either through an affix, an auxiliary or a change in the spelling and sound of the root: *I watch, he watched, they were watching; I swim, I swam*.
Tetrameter	A verse line with four stressed syllables: *Téll me / nót, in / móurnful / númbers* is trochaic tetrameter. *We sát / within / the fárm-/ house óld* is iambic tetrameter. (Both lines are by Longfellow.)
Topic	The subject about which something is said, usually corresponding to the grammatical subject: ***The old man** is ill*. The **topic position** is customarily at the front of the sentence, and so non-subject elements can be turned into the topic through reordering: *though yet **of Hamlet our dear brother's death** / The memory be green* topicalises the post-modifying part of the noun phrase so that *of Hamlet* ... appears as the topic rather than *the memory* ... ; compare ***For your voices** I have fought* (*Coriolanus*) and ***Somewhat** we shall do* which carry a different emphasis from *I have fought for your voices* and *We shall do somewhat*.
Trochee	A metrical foot consisting of one stressed and one unstressed syllable (/x): *Sómewhere / ín the / búrning / désert*.
Trope	Literally, 'twisting'. In rhetoric, a term for the artful deviation of words from their usual sense: common tropes in literature are **metaphor**, **metonymy** and **synecdoche**.
Unvoiced	Unvoiced or voiceless consonants are made without vibrating the vocal cords: *Can you tell me, politely?*
Verb	A word which can have **tense** (past, present), aspect (whether the action is regarded as finished or continuing), voice (active and passive) and **mood** (indicative, imperative, subjunctive), and which generally denotes an action, state or sensation: *He **runs**, I **understand**, I **love** you*.
Verb phrase	A phrase which functions as a **verb**: in *has been running* the **auxiliaries** *has been* precede the **head** *running*. In **phrasal and prepositional verbs** the head takes an **extension**: *has been running **out***. Also known as a verbal group.
Voiced	Voiced consonant sounds are made by vibrating the vocal cords: *Did he go there?*
Vowel	Vowel sounds are made when the air flows freely through the mouth: *Twelve year since, Miranda* ... (Shakespeare). The sounds in bold are pure vowels, unmixed by other sounds. The final sounds of *Power* and *Miranda* are examples of **schwa**. Vowels can be short (*ship*) or long (*sheep*).
Weakening	In **lexis**, where a word loses some of its original **connotations**, and becomes milder in effect: *discomfort* in Shakespeare has an earlier, stronger sense of 'sorrow, distress, grief', but it has since weakened to signify any physical inconvenience (another word which has weakened).

▼ Bibliography of Primary Texts

Ancrene Wisse: Parts Six and Seven, ed. Geoffrey Shepherd, revised edition, Exeter Medieval English Texts (Exeter: University of Exeter Press, 1985). Translation: *Ancrene Riwle*, trans. M.B. Salu, Exeter Medieval English Texts and Studies (first published, 1955; reprinted Exeter: Exeter University Press, 1990).

Apuleius, *The Golden Ass*, trans. William Adlington, Wordsworth Classics of World Literature (Ware: Wordsworth, 1996).

Roger Ascham, *Toxophilus*, ed. E. Arber (London: Constable, 1902).

Jane Austen, *Northanger Abbey and Persuasion*, ed. R.W. Chapman (Oxford: OUP, 1933), reproduced with slight emendations by the Folio Society (London, 1960). Other Austen references are also to Chapman's text.

Sir Francis Bacon, *Advancement of Learning*, in *The New Oxford Book of English Prose*, ed. John Gross (Oxford: OUP, 1998), 53 (extract).

The Essays, ed. John Pitcher (London: Penguin, 1985).

Samuel Beckett, *Trilogy: Molloy, Malone Dies, the Unnamable* (London: Calder, 1959).

The Book of Common Prayer: The First and Second Prayer Books of King Edward VI, Everyman's Library, 448 (London: J M Dent, 1910). *The Book of Common Prayer, 1662 version*, Everyman's Library, 241 (London: Everyman, 1999).

Sir Thomas Browne, *Selected Writings*, ed. Sir Geoffrey Keynes (London: Faber, 1968).

Sir Thomas Carew, Selected poems, in *The Later Renaissance in England: Nondramatic Verse and Prose, 1600–1660*, ed. Herschel Baker (Boston: Houghton Mifflin, 1975), 220–32.

Chaucer: Unless otherwise stated, references are to *The Riverside Chaucer*, ed. Larry D. Benson, 3rd edition (Boston: Houghton Mifflin, 1987).

The Prioress's Prologue and Tale, ed. Beverly Boyd, *A Variorum Edition of the Works of Geoffrey Chaucer* vol. II, Part 20 (Norman and London: University of Oklahoma Press, 1987).

The Prioress's Prologue and Tale, ed. J.A. Burrow and Thorlac Turville-Petre, in *A Book of Middle English*, 2nd edition (Oxford, Blackwell, 1996), 306–15. Edition of the tale with helpful notes on the language and Glossary.

The Ellesmere Manuscript of Chaucer's Canterbury Tales: A Working Facsimile (Woodbridge: D.S. Brewer, 1989) [reproduction of facsimile published by Manchester University Press, 1911].

Clarendon, *Selections from the History of the Rebellion*, ed. G. Huehns, with introduction by Hugh Trevor-Roper (Oxford: OUP, 1978).

Stephen Crane, *The Open Boat*, in *'The Red Badge of Courage' and Other Stories*, ed. Fiona Robertson and Anthony Mellors, World's Classics (Oxford: OUP, 1998).

Sir Ranulph Crewe, 'Oxford peerage case' in *The New Oxford Book of English Prose*, ed. John Gross (Oxford: OUP, 1998), 51 (extract).

Daniel Defoe, *Robinson Crusoe*, ed. M. Shinagel (New York: W W Norton, 1975).

Denham, Sir John, translation of Aeneid II, from *Virgil in English*, ed. K.W. Gransden (London: Penguin, 1996), 79.

Thomas De Quincey, 'On Murder Considered as One of the Fine Arts' (first published, *Blackwood's Magazine*, 1827): *Works of Thomas de Quincey*, vol. 5, ed. David Groves and Grevel Lindop (London: Pickering and Chatto, 2000).

Charles Dickens, *The Old Curiosity Shop*, ed. N. Page (London: Penguin, 2000).

John Donne, *Holy Sonnets*, in *The Divine Poems*, ed. Helen Gardner (Oxford: OUP, 1952), 1–16.

The Complete English Poems, ed. C.A. Patrides, Everyman's Library, 5 (London: Everyman, 1985).

John Dryden, *A Discourse Concerning the Original and Progress of Satire*, in *Essays of John Dryden*, selected and edited by W.P. Ker, 2 vols (Oxford: OUP, 1900), vol. 2, 15–114.

'Epilogue to the Second Part of Granada', in *The Poems*, vol. 1, ed. James Kinsley (Oxford: OUP, 1958), 134–5.

Essay of Dramatic Poesy, in *Essays of John Dryden*, selected and edited by W.P. Ker, 2 vols (Oxford: OUP, 1900), vol. 1, 21–133.

James Ellroy, *The Cold Six Thousand* (London: Century, 2001).

Sir Thomas Elyot, *The Book Named the Governor*, ed. S.E. Lehmberg, Everyman's Library, 227 (London: J M Dent, 1962).

Ralph Waldo Emerson, *Experience*, in *The Norton Anthology of American Literature*, 4th edition, vol. 1, ed. Nina Baym and others (New York: W W Norton, 1994), 1088–103.

William Faulkner, *Absolom, Absolom!* (London: Chatto & Windus, 1937; reprinted London: Vintage, 1995).

Oliver Goldsmith, *The Deserted Village* (1770), facsimile edition (London: Noel Douglas, 1927). See also *The Poems of Gray, Collies and Goldsmith*, ed. Roger Lonsdale, Annotated English Poets (London: Longman, 1969).

Sir Edmund Gosse, *Portraits and Sketches: The New Oxford Book of English Prose*, ed. John Gross (Oxford: OUP, 1998), 592 (extract).

Thomas Gray, *Poems*, see Goldsmith above.

Thomas Hardy, *Selected Shorter Poems*, chosen and introduced by John Wain (London: Palgrave Macmillan, 1966).

Nicholas Harpsfield: Roper and Harpsfield, *Lives of Saint Thomas More*, ed. E.E. Reynolds, Everyman's Library, 19 (London: J M Dent, 1963).

George Herbert, *The Temple* (1633), facsimile edition (London: Scolar Press, 1968).

Howard, Henry: see Surrey.

Samuel Johnson, *The History of Rasselas, Prince of Abissinia*, ed. J.P. Hardy, (Oxford: OUP, 1968; revised Word's Classics edition, 1988).

Ben Jonson, *The Alchemist*, in *The Oxford Jonson*, vol. 5, ed. C.H. Herford and Percy Simpson (Oxford: OUP, 1937).

'Epitaph on Elizabeth, L.H.', in *The Norton Anthology of Poetry*, 4th edition, ed. Margaret Ferguson and others (New York: W W Norton, 1996), 296.

John Keats, *Selected Poems*, ed. J. Barnard (London: Penguin, 1988).

Henry King, Selected poems, in *The Later Renaissance in England: Nondramatic Verse and Prose, 1600–1660*, ed. Herschel Baker (Boston: Houghton Mifflin, 1975), 188–93.

Charles Lamb, *Elia and The Last Essays of Elia*, ed. Jonathan Bate, World's Classics (Oxford: OUP, 1987).

William Langland, *Piers Plowman: the C-text*, ed. Derek Pearsall, Exeter Medieval English Texts and Studies (Exeter: University of Exeter Press, 1994).

D.H. Lawrence, *The Rainbow*, ed. Mark Kinkead-Weekes (London: Penguin, 1995).

The New Oxford Book of English Prose, ed. John Gross (Oxford: OUP, 1998), 748 (extract).

Ross Macdonald, *The Drowning Pool*, Canongate Crime Classics (Edinburgh: Canongate Books, 2001).

Malory, *Le Morte Darthur: The Winchester Manuscript*, ed. Helen Cooper, Oxford World Classics (Oxford: OUP, 1998).

The Works of Sir Thomas Malory, ed. Eugène Vinaver, 3 vols., 3rd edition, revised by P.J.C. Field (Oxford: OUP, 1990).

The Winchester Malory: a Facsimile, with introduction by N.R. Ker, Early English Text Society, Supplementary Series 4 (Oxford: 1976).

Christopher Marlowe, *Hero and Leander*, in *The New Oxford Book of Sixteenth Century Verse*, ed. Emrys Jones (Oxford: OUP, 1991), 488–506.

Andrew Marvell, texts from Michael Craze, *The Life and Lyrics of Andrew Marvell* (London: Palgrave Macmillan, 1979).

Montaigne, *The Essayes*, trans. John Florio (London: Gibbings, 1906).

John Milton, *Poetical Works*, ed. H. Darbishire, 2 vols (Oxford: OUP, 1952).

St. Thomas More, *A Dialogue of Comfort against Tribulation*, ed. Frank Manley (New Haven and London: Yale University Press, 1977).

Thomas Nashe, *The Unfortunate Traveller*, ed. H.F.B. Brett-Smith, The Percy Reprints, 1 (Oxford: Blackwell, 1920).

Wilfred Owen, *Poems*, ed. E. Blunden (1920; London: Chatto & Windus, 1972).

The Parlement of the Three Ages, in *Alliterative Poems of the Later Middle Ages*, ed. Thorlac Turville-Petre (London: Routledge, 1989), 67–100.

Pope, *The Rape of the Lock*, ed. Elizabeth Gurr, Oxford Student Texts (Oxford: OUP, 1990).

Samuel Richardson, *Clarissa*, ed. Angus Ross (London: Penguin, 1985).

The Ruin, in Bruce Mitchell and Fred C. Robinson, *A Guide to Old English*, 4th edition revised (Oxford: Blackwell, 1990), 237–9.

John Ruskin, *Selected Writings*, ed. Philip Davis (London: J M Dent, 1995).

Sir Walter Scott, *Lay of the Last Minstrel (1805)*. Facsimile edition, Revolution and Romanticism series (Banbury: Woodstock Books, 1992). See also *Poetical Works*, vol. 1 (Edinburgh: Robert Cadell, 1843), 3–212, which has notes by the author.

William Shakespeare. Unless otherwise stated, references are to the *Complete Works*, ed. Stanley Wells and Gary Taylor (Oxford: OUP, 1986).

1623 Folio text: *Mr William Shakespeares Comedies, Histories & Tragedies*, facsimile edition prepared by Helge Kökeritz, with introduction by C.T. Prouty (London: OUP, 1955).

Shelley, *Poetry and Prose*, ed. Donald H. Reiman and Sharon B. Powers (New York: W W Norton, 1977). *A Defence of Poetry* is on pp. 478–508.

Sir Philip Sidney, *An Apology for Poetry*, ed. Geoffrey Shepherd, Old and Middle English Texts (Manchester: Manchester University Press, 1973).

Sir Gawain and the Green Knight, ed. J.R.R. Tolkien and E.V. Gordon, 2nd edition, ed. Norman Davis (Oxford: OUP, 1967).

Robert Southey, *Life of Nelson: The New Oxford Book of English Prose*, ed. John Gross (Oxford: OUP, 1998), 323 (extract).

Edmund Spenser, *Amoretti*, in *Minor Poems*, ed. Ernest de Sélincourt (Oxford: OUP, 1910), 372–419.

The Faerie Queene, ed. A.C. Hamilton, Longman Annotated English Poets (London: Longman, 1977). 'A Letter of the Authors to Sir Walter Raleigh' is on pp. 737–8.

Laurence Sterne, *A Sentimental Journey*, ed. Gardner D. Stout (Berkeley: University of California Press, 1967).

The Life and Opinions of Tristram Shandy, ed. Melvyn New and Joan New (London: Penguin, 1997).

Surrey: Henry Howard, Earl of Surrey, translation of *Aeneid* II, from *Virgil in English*, ed. K.W. Gransden (London: Penguin, 1996), 9.

Jonathan Swift, *Gulliver's Travels*, ed. A.B. Gough (Oxford: OUP, 1915).

The Selected Poems, ed. A. Norman Jeffares (London: Kyle Cathie, 1992).

Jeremy Taylor, Holy Dying: from *The Later Renaissance in England: Nondramatic Verse and Prose, 1600–1660*, ed. Herschel Baker (Boston: Houghton Mifflin, 1975), 645–51 (extract).

'Sermon preached at the Funeral of the Lord Primate', in *The Oxford Book of English Prose*, ed. Sir Arthur Quiller-Couch (Oxford: OUP, 1925), 164 (extract).

Alfred Tennyson, *In Memoriam, Maud and other Poems*, ed. John D. Jump (London: J M Dent, 1974).

Edward Thomas, *Collected Poems* (London: Faber, 1979).

The Towneley Plays, ed. G. England and A.W. Pollard, Early English Text Society, Extra Series, 71 (London: EETS, for OUP, 1897).

Henry Vaughan, *The Complete Poems*, ed. Alan Rudrum, revised edition (Harmondsworth: Penguin, 1983).

The Wanderer:

Richard Hamer, *A Choice of Anglo-Saxon Verse* (London: Faber, 1970, many later impressions). Text, with facing verse translation.

The Wanderer, ed. Roy F. Leslie, revised edition, Exeter Medieval Texts and Studies (Exeter: University of Exeter Press, 1985).

The Wanderer, ed. T.P. Dunning and A.J. Bliss, Methuen's Old English Library (London: Methuen, 1969).

Mary Wollstonecraft, *A Vindication of the Rights of Woman*, ed. Miriam Brody (London: Penguin, 1992). Extract from *The Norton Anthology of English Literature*, 6th edition, vol. 1, General Editor M.H. Abrams (New York: W W Norton, 1993), 101–26.

■ ⌄ Index